WHERE
Shadows
LINGER

The Untold Story of the RCMP's
Olson Murders Investigation

W. Leslie Holmes with Bruce L. Northorp

Heritage House

Canadian Cataloguing in Publication Data

Holmes, W. Leslie (William Leslie), 1936-
    Where shadows linger

    Includes index.
    ISBN 1-895811-92-9

1. Olson, Clifford Robert, 1940-
2. Murder—British Columbia.
3. Evidence, Criminal—Political aspects—British Columbia.
4. Trials (Murder)—British Columbia.
I. Northorp, Bruce L., 1927-
II. Title.
HV6535.C32 B75 2000   364.15'23'09711   C00-910119-5

First edition 2000

Heritage House wishes to acknowledge the financial support of the Government of Canada and Heritage Canada through the Book Publishing Industry Development Program, and of the British Columbia Arts Council.

Edited by Rodger Touchie

HERITAGE HOUSE PUBLISHING COMPANY LTD.
Unit #108 - 17655 66 A Ave., Surrey, BC V3S 2A7

Printed in Canada

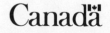

The Child Sees

In my secret garden
roses grow
the scent of blossoms
earth's sweet breath
surrounds me
keeps me warm
I ask my child
what do you want
she slowly turns to me
I see her face is lined
with the tracks of many tears
tears for all the children
who have no place to be
tears for all the children
who lay dead among the leaves

Kelly Holmes '95

Acknowledgments

The author wishes to thank his daughter, Kelly Holmes, for assuming the enormous task of editing and organizing the massive manuscript of a couple of novice writers in preparation for the publisher's editing process. He also thanks his wife, Violet, for her encouragement, input, and proofreading.

Bruce Northorp would like to acknowledge his wife, Louisa, for her full support not only during the summer of 1981, but also during the past two years of reliving that era by assisting him in organizing and reviewing his many references dealing with the murders.

He would also like to thank the many unnamed officers and civilian employees for their great efforts and voluntary overtime during the trying months of July to September 1981. It would be impossible to name them all, but their efforts did not go unnoticed.

Contents

Foreword

It has been almost two decades since Clifford Olson ended his horrific murder spree in British Columbia. In the same way that serial killers in other countries have shocked the general public, this tragedy affected Canada from coast to coast and also had an impact in much of the United States. Olson proved once again that evil knows no boundaries.

In August 1981, only weeks after a seasoned RCMP officer was appointed to head the investigation into a series of murders of children, Clifford Olson led his captors to the graves of his victims and brought a tragic certainty. While the speed and efficiency with which this killer was confined impressed many observers, for others there remained no sense of closure.

Many aspects of the Olson case remain unique, and there has never been a complete public record of how the case developed and how the police investigation proceeded. The B.C. Coroner's report was based on limited information, and the standard RCMP post-case analysis is not a public document. Regardless, at least one man who should know believes that the RCMP report must be incomplete. He was the man in charge of the Olson investigation and he was never interviewed.

Superintendent Bruce Northorp found himself at the eye of the hurricane in July 1981 when the Olson murders were a fast-breaking story. Anxious reporters, head-office Mounties in Ottawa, and a frightened public all wanted answers. After 32 years of police work, one of Canada's most respected police officers found himself in a situation like no other he had ever encountered.

Northorp was less than six months from retirement when he took on the murder investigation in Vancouver, B.C., and after confessions were garnered from a pathological murderer, Bruce Northorp quickly returned to a full agenda of other police matters. Out of respect for the many families who continued to live with the tragedy, Bruce refrained from commenting publicly on the murders and their investigation. Even when two books were published about the Olson case, Bruce Northorp declined to be involved.

Two other Mounties, both with lower profiles than Northorp, but both with deep scars left over from the Olson case, also shied away from the public forum in the early 1980s. In a sense, they too were victims of Clifford Olson. Events surrounding the investigation forever changed the lives of Corporal Les Forsythe and Corporal Darryll Kettles.

Ironically, to this day Northorp, Forsythe, and Kettles have never met together though Northorp has met Forsythe and Kettles separately.

As officer in charge of the General Investigation Section (OIC-GIS), I was also close to the investigation in 1981. Although I had no direct responsibility in the case—I was transferred to a new assignment outside Vancouver headquarters in mid-July, at the height of the internal tensions—I was always within hearing distance of the scuttlebutt. At the time I knew and had great respect for Northorp; I also knew Forsythe and Kettles and considered them both to be good, capable cops.

This account may prove surprising on some levels to all those with an established interest in the case. I had a few surprises myself as I pursued my research. My original goal was to put to rest some misunderstandings, baseless rumours, and innuendo that had lingered like shadows without substance long after Olson went to prison.

No one can really understand the workings of the case without some knowledge of the internal dynamics of the RCMP's "E" Division, B.C. Headquarters, in 1981. The structure and some of the personalities assigned to specific tasks strongly affected how the investigation unfolded.

There are some policemen, both active and retired, who may prefer that this book not be written. However, there are members and ex-members of the Force who hold the opposite opinion and who still believe that introspection and self-criticism are in the best interests of a police force we have served proudly. When all factors are considered, meaningful conclusions can be drawn. The public may be able to make more informed judgments based on the facts. Police professionals and prosecutors may better comprehend the magnitude of the investigation and the logistics problems encountered. This story may help future investigators who find themselves in similar situations.

★ ★ ★

I was first encouraged to develop this story by Bill McCheyne, now president of the Dominion RCMP Veterans' Association. At first the aim was to simply prepare an article for the B.C. RCMP veterans' publication, *Scarlet and Gold*. I soon realized that the scope of the story demanded a book, and I subsequently discussed my intentions with Bruce Northorp. Still in possession of his legendary notepads (Bruce was known widely in RCMP circles for his meticulous attention to detail and his personal record keeping), this happily retired and much-decorated ex-cop slowly warmed to the idea. In his heart he too knew there was an untold story. It is fair to say that this book would not have materialized without Bruce's co-operation. However, I have retained an autonomy that allows me to say some things about Bruce that he would never agree to as co-author.

In 1999, while researching the book independent of Bruce Northorp, I uncovered and verified the startling information about Darryll Kettles and his May 1981 encounter with Clifford Olson. I also heard the colourful recollections of former criminology teacher and ex-RCMP detective, Jim Steenson, who had spent a good portion of his career handcuffing Clifford Olson. Jim sent Olson to the B.C. Penitentiary three times.

Gaining the trust of people connected to the Olson case has not been easy, particularly in the case of Randy Cook, or Randy Ludlow as he is now known. Long suspected as an Olson pal and thus tarred with guilt by association, Randy, it appears, was just another Olson victim. His story sheds light from a unique perspective.

Four young people portrayed in the story had dark encounters with Clifford Olson, and I have given them aliases to protect their identity. The aliases of these characters in order of appearance are Kathy Sallow, Sandra Docker, Rose Smythe, and Ivan Jones.

One aspect of the Olson investigation will not be dealt with here—I will not make any unnecessary reference to Olson's young victims or describe the crime scenes. Both Bruce Northorp and I agreed early that our respect for the families of victims would preclude any graphic detail of these murder sites. Also, I have opted not to seek out family members as a part of this research. The loss of a child at any time is a parent's nightmare. The circumstances surrounding these losses were extreme and the least we could do was continue to respect their privacy.

Possibly the most controversial aspect of the Olson case was the payment for bodies that was made after Olson's arrest. By the time this unfolded, I was ensconced in my new position with the Co-ordinated Law Enforcement Unit (CLEU) in Vancouver. Still, I participated in meetings where it was ultimately decided to advance money to Joan Olson if her husband agreed to lead the police to his victims' bodies. The local police decision to support the government strategy in this matter did not come easily. Such conciliation was repugnant in the extreme. I am not sure that complete background on these sessions has ever been provided. Both Bruce Northorp and I were there, and we can shed light on the discussions that were held.

Not everyone comes out of this story unscathed. As a 38-year veteran I know that a police officer's judgment is constantly being tested, and it is impossible to always get it right. At the core of the Olson investigation, some players made mistakes, some made questionable strategic calls, and others possibly overstepped their authority. That doesn't make them bad cops—just human.

By the end of my work, one final reason for writing this book became paramount. Worthy men like Kettles, Forsythe, and Northorp simply deserved to be recognized. Possibly Darryll Kettles' late father said it best upon hearing stories from another day of police work.

"Good for you, son."

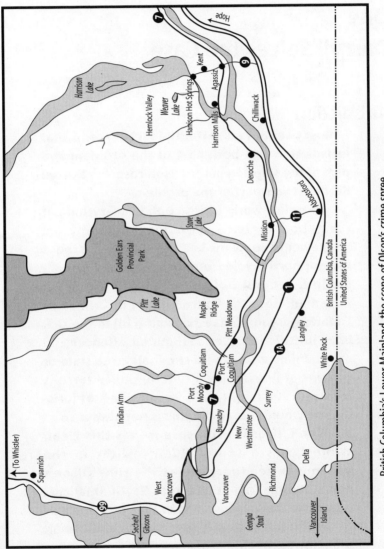

British Columbia's Lower Mainland, the scene of Olson's crime spree.

One
Darryll Solves the Case

Jurisdiction

Almost twenty years after the fact, it seems that jurisdiction was both part of the problem and part of the solution in the Olson case. For Darryll Kettles it was part of the problem.

In police work, jurisdiction is everything. It covers both the territorial range of authority and the power to apply the law. It distinguishes those in a supportive role from those with the responsibility. Federal police forces like the Royal Canadian Mounted Police (RCMP) in Canada or Federal Bureau of Investigation (FBI) in the U.S. have jurisdiction over designated offences and assume it in cases where criminals cross state or provincial lines. Once a federal police force is involved, you might think the problem of jurisdiction would disappear. This is not always so.

The Clifford Olson case makes this clear. While I was a senior RCMP officer in the Vancouver headquarters at the time Olson's name became infamous across North America, I was never directly involved in the case. One way or another, just about every other policeman mentioned in this story was. At times some assumed wrongly where the jurisdiction lay. Others seemed to claim it, and the power that came with it, when they should not have.

**In the Olson case, did ill-defined jurisdiction
lead to unnecessary deaths? For some involved,
it certainly led to years of nightmares.**

May 1981

It was early in May 1981, and Corporal Darryll Kettles of the RCMP detachment in Agassiz, B.C., was relaxing aboard a ferry bound for Horseshoe Bay. "Things had been so busy at work," he says today, "I really needed to get away for a couple of days." Darryll was returning after an idyllic weekend spent with friends from a previous posting at Sechelt on the Sunshine Coast.

Darryll sat alone reading a Vancouver newspaper when one article piqued his interest. The nude body of a young murder victim, Daryn Todd Johnsrude, had been discovered near Mission, a neighbouring community to Agassiz, situated about halfway up the Fraser Valley. Johnsrude was from Saskatoon, Darryll's hometown. He had recently been reported missing from a Smith Avenue residence in Coquitlam, another city familiar to him. "That was my old zone when I was posted there," thought Darryll. "I can visualize the street in my mind."

Darryll read further. He had noted the similarities in their first names and the fact that they were both "prairie boys." The actual crime site was east of Mission, in a small hamlet right next door to his present detachment. "So many coincidences," he said to himself, subconsciously filing the facts away.

On his return to Agassiz, his workload ensured that Darryll had no time to think about Daryn Johnsrude's fate.

May 26, 1981

Three weeks later, May 26, 1981, promised to be a very busy day. As the number two man at Agassiz Detachment, Corporal Kettles had more than enough to do and never enough hours in the day to get it done. Agassiz had a designated staff of thirteen, but for a number of reasons it was labouring with only nine.

"I have a trial at Kamloops and I'll be gone three days." Sergeant Dwight Gash dropped by Darryll's desk to give him more unwelcome news. "You'll be in charge of the detachment." Gash started to leave but looked back. "And by the way, Staff Sergeant George Allen will be here soon to do a quality review. I should be here for most of it, but I have to leave about four. I'm driving."

Kettles' face gave his thoughts away. "I know it's not a good time to go," added Gash, "but I don't have a choice. It will be tough covering the shifts with eight members. Do the best you can."

The inspection added to Darryll's already busy schedule, but there was nothing he could do. They were sacred to the brass and had always been a necessary evil in the life of a Mountie.

★ ★ ★

Blonde, petite, fifteen-year-old Kathy Sallow did not expect May 26 to be any different from most days in her restless adolescent life.

It was past noon and she was standing in front of Mac's Milk at North Road and Cottonwood Avenue in Coquitlam, unaware that this was only a block from where Daryn Johnsrude was last seen alive.

Sallow had recently quit school and was passively looking for work. Almost as an answer to prayer, a friendly, talkative man in work clothes approached her.

"Why aren't you in school?" he asked.

"I quit four months ago," Sallow replied.

The man gave a name she could not later recall. "I'm in the construction business," he confided. "I own a complex near here and I'm looking for a good worker."

"Doing what?"

"Doing odd jobs, cleaning carpets and windows. It's not hard work but the pay is good. I pay ten dollars and some an hour."

"This just might be my lucky break," thought Kathy, well aware that she possessed little work experience and had no special skills.

"Yeah, I guess I could do that," she replied.

"Good, you can start right away," her new boss told her. "I'm on my way to a job site right now. Hop in."

Sallow opened the door and settled into the front passenger seat of the stranger's brown Cougar station wagon. He drove off immediately.

"The job site for today is in Langley," he said.

They proceeded into New Westminster and crossed the Pattullo Bridge to Whalley, where the driver stopped at the Turf Hotel. "I'll just be a minute," he said. "I have to pick something up." Sallow was unconcerned when he returned carrying a case of Extra Old Stock beer, which he put behind her seat.

When they were once again underway, her new employer reached back, grabbed two bottles, and opened them with a flourish. He placed one in her left hand. "Let's drink to your new job."

Sallow was not much of a drinker, but she had no desire to irritate someone who was going to pay her ten bucks an hour. She looked straight ahead and sipped her beer.

They drove east on Fraser Highway to Langley. Sallow later remembered a sign saying "Tall Timbers." Her employer stopped at a house under construction. "Wait here while I see what's going on," he said as he left the vehicle. "Then we'll get you to work."

Sallow watched the driver approach a worker, then start talking, waving his arms, and gesturing. He soon trudged back in her direction. "They're not ready for us yet," he said. "I'm building other places. Let's take a look at them."

The fifteen-year-old had not eaten lunch and she breathed deeply, fighting the effects of the beer. Noticing this, the driver reached into his jacket pocket and brought out four tiny green tablets. "These will keep you from getting drunk, and people won't be able to smell beer on your breath," he said. "Be sure and take them all."

Sallow was beginning to feel uneasy about this man. Things were not adding up. They had visited one job site but there seemed to be no real effort to get her started on her job. Nervously, Sallow eyed the pills. "Should I do this?" she wondered. "Will these pills really keep me from getting drunk?" She swallowed three of the pills, jamming the other into her jeans pocket.

"Did you take them all?" asked the driver.

"Yes," she replied, hoping he had not seen her deception.

Sallow studied the unfamiliar landscape as they continued east on the Fraser Highway through Abbotsford. During their travels he gave her a five-dollar bill. When she finished a second beer, the driver dismissed her protests, immediately uncapped another, and placed it firmly in her hand. He pressed a fresh bottle to his own lips. "Drink up," he said.

The man was drinking beer constantly. She later estimated that he consumed at least six bottles. She finished four.

Becoming more apprehensive, Sallow wondered how much farther east they would travel. She breathed a sigh of relief when the driver turned around at Chilliwack and headed back west. It troubled her that they had not visited any other construction sites and there had been no further talk of her starting work.

She felt peculiar. "Maybe it's just the beer," she thought as her hands started to tingle and feel numb. The man seemed agitated. "Is he angry at me?" she wondered. "What have I done to make him mad at me?" Sallow did not like what was happening to her. Her mind seemed fairly clear, but other sensations began to alarm her. She was unable to control her arms and hands. Speech was difficult. Was she drunk? Were those pills doing something to her?

"He's speaking to me," she thought, watching his mouth move. Kathy could not respond. "What is he saying? Try to concentrate," she told herself. "Now he is feeling my face and my hair. How did I get myself into this? He is turning around again."

A sign said they were on Highway 7. The driver reached over and again ran his fingers down her cheek and through her hair. She barely noticed.

At that moment the inebriated driver lost control of the station wagon.

There was a loud crash and the teenager was violently thrown from side to side. Finally she was left hanging upside down, groping for some sense of balance. The impact had jarred her senses and it took a moment before she realized that the vehicle had flipped on its roof. The driver had lost control and ploughed into the ditch, where the vehicle rolled over. That was all she could remember.

★ ★ ★

Spud Dyer and his crew were returning from a job site at Hemlock Valley. He was driving a pickup followed by two five-ton Highways

Department trucks. Spud pulled to the side of the road when he saw the overturned car in the ditch.

The driver extricated himself from the station wagon. Spud watched as the passenger was disentangled from the vehicle. As the two staggered toward him, Spud studied their faces.

"I need a wrecker," declared the wild-eyed man as he grasped the traumatized girl's wrist in an iron grip. "No police."

Dyer radioed to his base station. "A car just flipped over at the east end of Mount Woodside. We need a wrecker. Phone Gord at Modern Tire," he instructed. "We'll take the occupants there."

"We can give you a ride into Agassiz," Spud told the driver of the Cougar station wagon. "Modern Tire has a wrecker. They'll look after you there."

Dyer did not tell the driver that he knew when the radio operator called Gord Sciotti at Modern Tire, Sciotti would automatically call the police. Sciotti would not turn a wheel without notifying them. Spud worked with them this way all the time. He believed that when you really need help, the police are your best friends.

"The guy didn't say much," observed Dyer later. "I didn't like the look of him. The girl was in bad shape. We thought she had been hurt in the accident. I told him the girl could ride with me and he could ride in one of the five-tons. I don't remember who was driving it. When we got to Modern Tire I walked over to the five-ton and said,'Don't forget to report the accident to the RCMP.'"

In fact, Constable Bill Hudyma of the Agassiz RCMP had already been dispatched to investigate, alerted by the Department of Highways dispatcher who reported the overturned vehicle. He passed Modern Tire on his way to the accident scene.

"The guy was standing outside Modern Tire," Dyer recalled. "He was asking for a taxi. The girl was sitting near the gas pumps. For some reason the guy got back in the five-ton. Just then an RCMP car went by. When he saw the police car he leaped out of the five-ton, grabbed the girl, and headed across the grass towards the high school. We told the police he had hightailed it behind the school.

"The girl was only a bit of a thing," he said. "She was between thirteen and sixteen. Not bad looking, but she wouldn't weigh a hundred pounds. She had fair hair and she was gone. She was completely out of it. At the accident scene we thought she was injured. It was only after we got back to the shed and we talked it over we decided she wasn't hurt at all but high on booze and drugs."

★ ★ ★

Desperate to get away, the driver dragged Sallow into the Agassiz High School office. "Get me a taxi," he shouted.

The startled office staff stared in trepidation at the strange duo. Their hearts went out to the scrawny, almost comatose, blonde teenager being bullied by the belligerent intruder. To get rid of him, they complied with his wishes and phoned for a cab.

They also summoned Vice-Principal Mike Chunys. "We have a very suspicious-looking man here. Please come as soon as you can."

Not content to stay in the main office, the madman entered the school library with Sallow still in tow. Library staff were alarmed by his outlandish behaviour. Bravely, the librarian challenged the intruder. "You can't come in here unless you fill out this card." The male glared menacingly at her and she was overjoyed to see Mike Chunys arrive.

Chunys knew immediately something was amiss with this strange twosome. The young teenager's eyes were not focussing. The surly male refused to answer questions.

"It's none of your business," he snarled. Eventually, he gave Chunys several different names. "I wrecked my car on Mount Woodside," he finally admitted. "Don't worry, the police are investigating it."

"He never took his hand off the young girl's arm," Chunys observed. "She didn't resist him or try to get away."

The pair abruptly left the school. He was extremely rough with the girl, forcefully pulling her along. "Come on, come on, keep moving," he commanded.

"Cancel the taxi," Chunys instructed the office staff. Picking up the telephone, he dialled the RCMP and implored, "We need you to check out a pair of spaced-out people."

Corporal Darryll Kettles was dispatched. His life was about to be changed forever.

As Darryll approached, the suspicious male saw the police cruiser and dragged Sallow behind a school building. Not seeing this subterfuge, Kettles circled the block. The fugitives doubled back the way they had come. The intruder berated Chunys, who was watching this drama, for calling the police.

Darryll appeared again a moment later. "He's through there," Chunys said, pointing between two nearby buildings. "You just missed him."

Darryll drove around the block.

"You just missed him again," Chunys informed Darryll when he next saw him. "He's gone back the same way. He dumped the girl. She's too stoned to walk." Chunys pointed to where he had last seen the elusive pair.

Heeding Chunys's advice, Darryll found his quarry standing near the Agassiz Taxi stand. He cautiously approached the suspect, who was wearing a blood-splattered yellow T-shirt. Darryll described his first take on this man. "He looked like someone standing in line waiting for the beer parlour to open. He was scruffily dressed, but he didn't look drunk."

Darryll Kettles was younger, over six feet tall, and weighed 188 pounds. He felt he could handle the five foot seven, 175-pound suspect.

He gestured towards the skinny blonde teenager sitting on a nearby retaining wall. "Is she with you?" Darryll asked.

"No," the suspect answered. "I've never seen her before."

"Let's see some identification," Darryll ordered. The man produced a British Columbia driver's licence in the name of Clifford Robert Olson. The original address was on King George Highway in Surrey. His amended address was shown as Suite 111, 675 Whitting (should have been spelled Whiting) Way, Coquitlam. Darryll knew the location. Olson also produced a British Columbia birth certificate declaring he was born in Vancouver on January 1, 1940.

"Were you involved in that accident?" Darryll inquired. "We've had some calls."

"No," Olson replied. "What accident?"

"Where did you get the blood on your shirt?" asked Darryll.

"From cuts at work," Olson claimed. "I work in construction."

People rarely take off when you have their identification, so Darryll felt more at ease once he held Olson's documents. As he radioed for a criminal record check, he glanced in his rearview mirror. Olson was fleeing the scene. Darryll caught a glimpse of him as Olson darted behind Burgess Feeds, leaving the corporal holding his identification and a severely intoxicated young female.

Acting quickly, Kettles scooped up the limp teenager and deposited her into the back seat. A surprise awaited him as he sped to the rear of Burgess Feeds.

"I couldn't believe my eyes," he recalled. Olson was nowhere in sight.

"Did you see a guy wearing a yellow T-shirt run by here?" Darryll asked two nearby workers."

"Yeah," they replied. "But we didn't see where he went."

Darryll wasn't particularly worried about Olson's escape. "After all," he thought, "where could he go in Agassiz?"

"Agassiz, 16A4," Darryll radioed. "Subject: Clifford Robert Olson; born Nineteen Forty, January, zero one; five foot seven inches, 175 pounds, brown hair, brown eyes; wearing yellow, blood-spattered T-shirt. Took off, last seen running behind Burgess Feeds westbound. Wanted for questioning regarding Contribute Juvenile Delinquency, possible Impaired Driving. I have intoxicated female here. Call a matron. I'll be coming in. 16A4 over."

Sallow was almost comatose. She could not speak or control her body as she sprawled across the cruiser's rear seat. Kettles elected to take her into custody for her own safety.

The matron opened the doors as Darryll carried the inert teenager right through the lobby into the cells.

Darryll summoned the paramedics. "We have a young girl here who appears drunk," he said. "She is not lucid and we can't rouse her."

The ambulance attendants arrived and examined Sallow. "As best we can determine, she's just drunk," they said. "Let her sleep it off. She'll be all right in the morning."

★ ★ ★

Meanwhile, Olson's incredible luck held as he continued to elude his pursuers. An intense search of the area by all available Agassiz RCMP members failed to locate him.

Puffing from exertion, Olson had flagged down the first car he encountered. Six kilometres later he exited the vehicle at Harrison Hot Springs. Olson barged through the door of the Harrison Hot Springs Hotel gift shop and shouted in a loud voice, "Where are your T-shirts? I need a new T-shirt." He quickly purchased a new shirt and departed.

In his travels, Olson disposed of his blood-stained shirt. It was never located.

Aware that Olson had already tried to summon a taxi, the RCMP kept a close watch out for occupied cabs.

Shortly after 4 p.m., Sergeant Dwight Gash, driving an unmarked police vehicle, broadcast, "Agassiz 16A2, stopping westbound Agassiz Taxi, Highway Seven." Inside, Gash found Olson clad in his newly purchased yellow T-shirt. It was inscribed "Sasquatch—Harrison Hotel—British Columbia—Canada."

Olson was arrested and returned to the Agassiz RCMP office where Gash handed the suspect over to Kettles. Gash looked at his watch and said, "He's all yours. I'm off to Kamloops."

Constable Hudyma had by this time established that Olson was the driver of the overturned station wagon. The vehicle was registered to his wife's former name, Joan Berryman.

Darryll was puzzled. "Why would someone take off for something so mundane as a motor vehicle accident and possible impaired driving?"

Hudyma was administering a breathalyzer test to Olson when Darryll entered the room. He noticed Hudyma had written Olson's address as #508 - 521 Foster Avenue, Coquitlam (which meant the current address on the man's ID was also out of date). Darryll was instantly troubled and studied Olson with renewed interest. His mind flashed back to the three-week-old news article. He remembered Daryn Johnsrude was last seen alive at Burquitlam Plaza, only two blocks from Olson's residence.

While processing impaired driving suspects, police routinely fill out a lengthy questionnaire titled "The Investigator's Guide for

Impaired Persons." Hudyma dutifully noted Olson's demeanour and recorded his responses while Darryll, sitting across from Olson, listened. Olson admitted to drinking two beers earlier in the day. When asked if he had taken any medication, he nodded and said, "Fifteen hundred milligrams of chloral hydrate at five this morning, to help me sleep."

Asked about the wrecked vehicle, the cocky Olson retorted, "I'm not saying anything until I speak with my lawyer, Robert Shantz." Without pausing for breath, he continued to talk.

"We couldn't shut him up," Hudyma said later. Both he and Darryll listened intently.

"Yeah, I was the driver of the station wagon," said Olson. "I was turning around and going back to Mission. No, I didn't have anything else to drink after the accident. No, I was alone. No one was with me," he claimed. "I got married May 15."

"I had a good friend, Gary Marcoux," Olson added. "We were in Mountain Prison together. He raped and murdered a nine-year-old girl at Mission seven years ago. I gave Crown evidence at the trial."

Darryll sensed something was very wrong. "As an investigator, you know what it's like when you have a guilty suspect and he gives off bad vibes," he said later. "That's what it was like. Olson was giving off bad vibes big time." His notes recorded the suspect's rambling conversation.

"Today I was going to visit a friend at Mountain Prison," said Olson. "I didn't get there because I was run off the road by a black Trans Am."

"A taxi driver picked me up at Harrison Hot Springs," he said later. "I was on the way to pick up my wife, Joan, at Mission. Then I was coming back to Agassiz to report the accident."

Asked about Sallow, Olson admitted, "The girl was with me. She was going to work for me at a construction [he pronounced it conception] site on 152 Street in Surrey. I was heading home to Coquitlam."

Later, he again said, "I was going to Mountain Prison."

Darryll attempted to obtain a written statement from Olson, cautioning, "You are not obliged to say anything but anything you say may be given in evidence. Do you understand the above warning?"

"Yes," Olson replied.

Both Olson and Darryll signed the document. Darryll then asked a series of questions, writing down Olson's answers.

To each question Olson replied, "I don't want to say nothing" or "I don't want to say anything on the advice of my lawyer Robert Shantz" or "I don't want to say anything until Shantz the lawyer talks to me."

Again, Olson signed the transcript "Cliff R. Olson." After the usual processing, Olson was lodged in the cells and advised he would be charged with impaired driving. Removed from his possession for safekeeping were a wallet containing 35 dollars and 34 cents, an address book, and a sheathed buck knife.

★ ★ ★

Kathy Sallow was still sleeping it off in the female cells. Darryll described his initial impression of her. "She didn't look like a hooker. She looked like a timid young girl, like anybody's daughter. She was not a street person. I felt she needed protection."

Kettles was having difficulty determining her identity. It appeared, as best he could discern, that she had been using two surnames. Documents indicated she probably lived in Coquitlam within two blocks of Olson's apartment.

His mind was inextricably drawn back to Daryn Johnsrude. "This is weird," he thought. "Is fate intervening? Could Olson be Johnsrude's killer? He certainly deserves a second look."

Darryll's instincts told him that Olson was dangerous. He sensed evil beneath the facade. "He gave me this really bad feeling," Darryll recalled. "It's hard to explain." He was shaken by his brief encounter with Olson. "There is more to this case than meets the eye," he told Hudyma. "Why would Olson run on a simple impaired driving charge? Sure, there is a possibility enough evidence can be obtained to charge him with contributing to juvenile delinquency, but would that cause him to run? I think not."

More troubling was Olson's bragging about being good friends with Gary Francis Marcoux, a known rapist and murderer. "Why would anyone brag about such a thing?" Darryll wondered. "Am I on to something here?

"And the addresses," he reasoned. "They all live within a block or two of where Johnsrude went missing. Just coincidences? I don't think so."

Darryll knew Olson was trying to ease any suspicions he might have by elaborating on how he had helped police convict Marcoux of murder. His comments had the opposite effect. Darryll became even more suspicious. "Holy Jeez," he thought. "This just doesn't make sense. There's a lot more to this than I know right now."

Darryll contemplated Olson's comments in the breathalyzer room. "I was on my way to pick up my wife, Joan, at Mission." Johnsrude's body had been found near the community of Deroche in the Mission Detachment's area.

"Is that why he crashed his car?" wondered Darryll. "Was he checking to see if the girl was lucid and, finding her defenceless, was he in the process of turning around? Was he going to take her to the area where Johnsrude was found? It all seems to fit."

★ ★ ★

Sallow regained consciousness as the evening progressed. She appeared groggy and confused. "Do you know where you are?" Darryll asked.

"White Rock?" Sallow answered hesitantly.

Once her identity was established, Darryll contacted her mother by telephone. He assured the anxious woman that her daughter seemed to be recovering from her ordeal. "She was really choked that Kathy had taken a ride with somebody," he recalled. He suggested Kathy could be released into her custody, but Sallow's mother was unable to travel to Agassiz to retrieve her daughter.

"I need to interview Kathy to find out what happened," Darryll explained. "I can't do that unless you, or someone designated by you, is present for her protection."

Mrs. Sallow authorized Darryll to speak with her daughter in the presence of a family friend who lived in Sardis. She also permitted Darryll to release Kathy into her friend's custody.

Sallow described her afternoon with Olson as best she could remember, from the time he picked her up until the accident. "He told me he owned a complex around where I live and said he wanted me to work for him." Sallow was still woozy. "I didn't want to drink beer," she declared. "He kept putting the bottles in my hand. He didn't listen even when I said no. "A preliminary statement was taken from her. She agreed to provide a more detailed statement when she was feeling better.

Darryll had been working several hours past the end of his day shift. His experience convinced him he was dealing with a very dangerous individual. He wondered if he had Daryn Johnsrude's killer within his grasp. He remembered reading a newspaper article that stated Johnsrude wanted to stay in British Columbia and was looking for work. "Is there a pattern here?" he asked himself. "He offered Sallow a job."

Kettles needed more information. Anxiously he dialled CIS. The Vancouver RCMP Crime Index Section is the central repository for criminal records in B.C. In response to Darryll's phone call, the clerk read page after page of Olson's criminal history.

"Has he any convictions for sexual assaults against either males or females?" Darryll could not help interjecting.

"Here, on the last page," was the response. "In January this year at Squamish. There are outstanding charges of rape, Section 144 Criminal Code; buggery, Section 155 CC; gross indecency, Section 157 CC; and possession of a weapon, Section 85 CC.

"Thanks," Darryll responded. "That's just what I've been looking for. Would you put a copy in the mail for me please?"

A picture was starting to emerge. Now more alarmed than ever, Corporal Kettles phoned the Squamish RCMP. He was fortunate to speak directly with Constable Jim Hunter, who investigated the Squamish incident.

"I have Clifford Robert Olson in custody here," Kettles told Hunter. "Right now we are holding him for impaired driving and contributing to juvenile delinquency. Help me out," he said. "If I don't get more soon I'll have to release him on a promise to appear. You charged him in January, tell me about that."

"He picked up a teenage girl in Whalley," Hunter explained. "He offered her a job at ten dollars an hour cleaning carpets at some condos he said he owned at Whistler. This was at night and he was driving a brown Mercury station wagon. She accepted the job and they drove to Squamish, drinking beer along the way. He became involved in an argument with several locals and ended up pulling a gun and threatening them. He violently sexually assaulted the girl in a Squamish motel room and again on a sideroad on the way back to Vancouver. She got away from him at a service station when she went into the washroom and didn't come out until he was gone."

"What happened to the charges?" Darryll asked.

"We had him charged with rape, buggery, gross indecency, and two charges of possession of a weapon," Hunter replied. "One of the weapons charges was from New Westminster. He was remanded into custody and we managed to keep him in jail for three months. Then our District Crown Counsel decided the girl wouldn't make a good witness and opted to stay the sex charges. I thought he was wrong," Hunter added. "So did Staff Sergeant Zaharia. We got permission from the Criminal Investigation Branch to meet with the Regional Crown Counsel, but it didn't do any good. Our charges, except for the weapons offences, were stayed in April."

"He's still at it," declared Darryll. "I'm sure that's the least that would have happened to the teenager he was with today. This guy worries me. He has a record as long as your arm. I'm convinced he's dangerous. I think he may be good for the murder of Daryn Johnsrude near here," Darryll added. "Johnsrude, Olson, and the girl live within a stone's throw of each other. We have him sexually assaulting females, I wonder if he likes boys as well?"

"You had better talk with Richmond," Hunter exclaimed. "Bill McBratney had him charged with buggery and indecent assault on a fourteen-year-old male. He beat those charges too. There was some problem with identification and Crown Counsel was concerned about the credibility of the identification."

Hunter's comments were like a light in the window to Darryll. "Everything I was looking for, Hunter gave me." Darryll was alarmed when he put Hunter's information together with his own observations about the geography, where they all lived, and Olson's familiarity with the area where Johnsrude's body was located. Olson's big mouth, bragging about Marcoux and his nine-year-old murder victim, had made him even more concerned. Now Hunter confirmed all his suspicions. Darryll was sure that Olson had killed Daryn Johnsrude.

Kettles called Sergeant Jack Randle of the Vancouver RCMP Serious Crime Section, who lived at the nearby community of Rosedale. It was convenient for Randle to assist detachments in the Central Fraser Valley, and Darryll knew him well.

"Fred Maile knows about the Johnsrude case," Randle informed the corporal. "You should call him."

It was now 10:30, more than five hours since Darryll was scheduled to go off shift. "I can't abandon this case without some answers," he thought as he dialled Maile's number.

"I have Clifford Robert Olson in the cells here," Darryll announced when Maile answered. "He picked up a fifteen-year-old girl at Coquitlam, got her drunk, and drove her out here, where he rolled the station wagon he was driving. The girl was picked up near the location Daryn Johnsrude was last seen alive. Olson lives a block away from there. He got her in the car by promising her a job at ten dollars and some an hour cleaning carpets. He used the same approach on a teenage girl he sexually assaulted at Squamish. We know Daryn Johnsrude was looking for work. We also know Olson is a switch hitter because he sexually assaulted a teenage boy at Richmond last year. He did time at Mountain Prison, so he is familiar with the area where Johnsrude was found. I think he killed Johnsrude, and he would have raped and maybe killed this girl here today, except he had too much to drink and rolled his car."

"If you think you've solved the Johnsrude murder, call Mission Detachment," said Maile as he hung up the telephone.

Surprised but not deterred by Maile's reaction, the corporal doggedly pressed on. Mission investigators Corporal Bob MacIntosh and Constable Mike Lysyk gave Darryll a more cordial reception. They were interested in what he had to say.

Unknown to Kettles, Maile called MacIntosh at Mission and suggested he go to Agassiz with an identification technician from Chilliwack to get particulars and examine Olson's vehicle for evidence. He told MacIntosh he and another Serious Crime

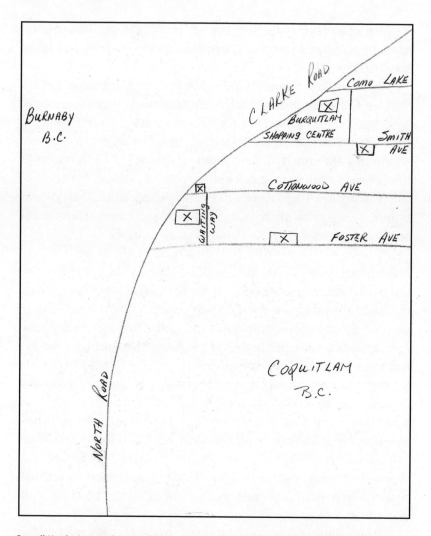

Darryll Kettles' original map, which he gave to Mission investigators in May 1981.

investigator would help out at Mission the following day. Maile then called Corporal Brian Tuckey and asked Tuckey to accompany him to Mission in the morning. Maile's primary interest in Olson at this time was as a suspect in the 1980 murder of Sechelt teenager Marnie Jamieson. Tuckey had been assisting on the Jamieson case.

MacIntosh and Lysyk soon arrived at Aggasiz with Bob Podwarny, an identification specialist. Kettles fully briefed them on his suspicions and why he deduced Olson was Johnsrude's killer.

"Johnsrude didn't really want to return to Saskatoon," MacIntosh and Lysyk agreed. "He was looking for a job so he could stay here."

This confirmation only reinforced Darryll's suspicions. "It's obvious Olson is luring these teenagers into vulnerable positions with a promise of employment," Darryll said. "He lulls them into a false sense of security by feeding them alcohol, then attacks them when they are unable to defend themselves."

"It looks that way," MacIntosh agreed. "He looks like a good suspect, but we have a more promising lead we are working on right now. It concerns the driver of a Saskatchewan pickup truck seen near where Daryn Johnsrude was found. If that lead fizzles, Olson will then be our number one suspect."

Darryll had already searched the Cougar station wagon, but they decided a more thorough search was advisable. Gord Sciotti, owner of Modern Tire, unlocked the bay at the garage. A hammer was seized from the vehicle. Despite Sciotti's claim that the hammer appeared bloodstained, analysis by the RCMP Crime Detection Laboratory failed to disclose any blood.

Kettles had photocopied all the documents in Olson's possession, including his address book, and now turned all the copies over to MacIntosh, but no hard evidence was found to allow Darryll to keep Olson in custody.

"We all agreed," Darryll said. "We had insufficient material to question Olson about the Johnsrude murder. He was released on a promise to appear on charges of impaired driving and contributing to juvenile delinquency."

Wearily Darryll wrote up the night's activities and prepared to go off duty. He had been working since 9 a.m. It was now 1:30 a.m., May 27. He went home confident others would see Olson for what he was: Daryn Johnsrude's murderer. He was happy with himself. He had just solved a homicide.

May 27, 1981

Darryll was back on the job later the same morning, at nine, preparing a more extensive report on Olson. A few hours later, Sallow's mother called with a chilling development.

"My telephone number is unlisted," she said. "I just received a telephone call from the man who caused all the trouble yesterday. He called to ask how Kathy is doing. He says she still has a job if she wants it. What really bothers me is he offered to pick her up and bring her home. I can't believe the nerve of him," she added. "I don't want him anywhere near Kathy. Will you be charging him for what he did? It worries me that he has our unlisted phone number."

Kettles told her that Olson would be charged with impaired driving and probably contributing to juvenile delinquency. Coquitlam's Constable Peter Blais was subsequently assigned to help the Sallow family through this crisis.

Throughout the day, Darryll worked on the Olson file whenever time allowed. Mike Lysyk from Mission and Rick Boyarski of the Serious Crime Section conducted follow-up interviews of potential witnesses, including the taxi driver who picked up Olson at Harrison Hot Springs. Their search for Olson's missing T-shirt yielded nothing.

Kettles did not know that Tuckey and Maile, while assisting Mission Detachment, interviewed Kathy Sallow at the Sardis home of the family friend. She had recovered from her ordeal with Olson and they obtained further information from her. Sallow did not consider Olson a threat, and she was not overly concerned about the events in Agassiz. Almost as an afterthought she gave Maile the little green pill she had hidden from Olson. They also examined and recorded particulars of a five-dollar bill Olson had given her.

Later, at Mission, Maile casually tossed the tablet on Lysyk's desk, suggesting, "You may want to get this checked out at the lab."

After another busy day, Darryll went off duty at 12:30 on the morning of May 28. The Olson case had captured his interest and he was logging long hours.

Kettles subscribed to the theory that a criminal usually operates in his own backyard, a locale familiar to him. Olson certainly bore this out when he picked up Kathy Sallow within a stone's throw of his residence. He then transported her to Agassiz, another area familiar to him from his time spent at Mountain Prison.

The same theory held true for Johnsrude, who was last seen near Olson's residence. His body was located near Deroche, just outside the Agassiz Detachment area. Jim Steenson, a retired RCMP staff sergeant who knew Olson well, later verified that "Olson had relatives on his mother's side who lived at Deroche. He was most certainly familiar with the Deroche/Agassiz area."

Darryll was so sure that Olson was responsible for the Johnsrude murder, the next time he phoned his father in Saskatoon he declared, "Guess what, Dad? I just solved the murder of Daryn Johnsrude, a teenager from Saskatoon."

"Good for you son," his father replied.

Within hours of his first encounter with Clifford Olson, veteran Mountie Darryll Kettles was sure he was in the presence of a child killer.

June and July 1981

Darryll was no rookie. A Mountie for fourteen years, the son of Saskatoon's former chief of police was an experienced, well-rounded investigator who had served in both uniform and plainclothes units. Darryll knew the RCMP's Vancouver headquarters from the inside, having worked there in the National Crime Intelligence Section. An intensely dedicated policeman, he had demonstrated he could carry a heavy workload and handle major investigations.

Once a tenacious sleuth like Darryll gets the taste of a major case, his instinct is to carry it through to its solution. There was only one problem. The Johnsrude murder was the responsibility of the Mission Detachment, assisted by the RCMP Serious Crime Section in Vancouver. Policy and procedures limited Darryll's further involvement. The rest was up to the other units having the prime responsibility for the murder investigation.

It was hard for Darryll to stand back and let go. He monitored the progress of the case through contact with the Mission investigators and was assured the Serious Crime Section was completing a profile on Olson.

As time went on, however, Darryll became alarmed at the lack of progress in the Johnsrude homicide.

He suggested Mission detectives urge the Serious Crime Section into a more assertive mode against Olson. "Do yourself a favour," he told MacIntosh and Lysyk. "Take a drive in and see where Johnsrude, Olson, and Sallow live, then go to where Sallow was picked up and where Johnsrude was last seen. You will see what I mean."

The Mission plainclothes officers said they were going in to the Vancouver headquarters to view the profile being prepared by Maile, but Darryll later was told Maile was on a day off when they arrived. Meanwhile, Kettles told everyone who would listen, "Olson is Johnsrude's killer."

May turned into June, and June into July, with no positive developments as far as Darryll could see. "I knew Mission eliminated the driver of the Saskatchewan pickup containing the clothing within two weeks of May 26. I couldn't understand why they weren't taking a more proactive approach towards Olson as a suspect. I urged them to set up surveillance on him to at least develop some intelligence on his habits and movements."

Lysyk took the little green pill he received from Maile to the RCMP Crime Detection Laboratory on June 3. The ensuing lab report dated June 26 read—

> *Exhibit 32 was found to contain chloral hydrate. Chloral hydrate is a sedative-hypnotic agent. Used with alcohol it has been referred to as "knock-out drops." The sedative and hypnotic doses are 250 mg and 500 mg respectively. After a hypnotic dose, drowsiness will occur in 10–15 minutes followed by sleep after 30 minutes. The sleep will generally last 5–8 hours.*

The lab report clinched it for Darryll. It was apparent to him that Olson was rendering his victims helpless by means of alcohol and chloral hydrate. Surely those who doubted his theory would now be convinced that Olson was Johnsrude's murderer.

Members of the Serious Crime Section and the Mission investigators were more cautious. They were not prepared to

Daryn Johnsrude's murder was uppermost in Corporal Kettles' mind the day he first investigated Olson. Two months after Kettles fingered Olson as the killer, another victim, Judy Kozma, was found in Agassiz, eight miles north of Highway 7 near a Weaver Lake campsite.

concentrate solely on Olson without some corroborating evidence to link him to Johnsrude's demise. Even Darryll's immediate superior, Sergeant Dwight Gash, thought Darryll was premature in branding Olson a killer at this stage of the case.

Undaunted, Darryll turned to Staff Sergeant George Allen, the Chilliwack Sub-Division NCO Supervisor, chiding the Serious Crime Unit for lack of progress on the promised Olson profile. He also expressed his dissatisfaction to Superintendent Cy Thomas, the officer in charge of Chilliwack Sub-Division. "I didn't just drop the case," Darryll commented. "I did my best to keep it moving."

Kettles learned there was to be a meeting at the Burnaby RCMP Office on July 14 (later changed to July 15) to discuss Olson in relation to some missing children.

"I want to go to that meeting," he told Sergeant Gash immediately.

"I really can't afford to let you go," Gash responded. "We're too short-handed, and it's not our case anyway. It's Mission's responsibility."

Not satisfied, Darryll pleaded with Superintendent Thomas for permission to attend.

"Sorry," Thomas sympathized. "Everyone is short of people. Johnsrude is a Mission case and I can't even afford to let them go. Your interests will be looked after by the Serious Crime Section."

Darryll was skeptical. "I knew the Serious Crime investigators were only treating Olson as a person of interest," he lamented. "They were not at all convinced Olson was Johnsrude's killer." His only comfort lay in knowing others were at least looking seriously at Olson as a murder suspect.

July 25, 1981

On Saturday July 25, Darryll's worst nightmare came true.

While he was on days off, the remains of a young female were discovered in the Agassiz Detachment area near Weaver Lake. Sergeant Dwight Gash and Corporal Larry Pelz secured the scene and conducted the preliminary inquiries in an attempt to identify the body with assistance from the plainclothes detectives from the Vancouver headquarters.

Darryll was convinced Olson had been at it again, and he once more expressed his concerns about the man. Until they found out who the victim was, however, police were limited in what they could do. When she was identified as fourteen-year-old Judy Kozma, who had gone missing from New Westminster on July 9, the investigation shifted into high gear.

"Kozma is another of his victims," Darryll told anyone even remotely involved in the Kozma investigation. "Kozma and Johnsrude were killed by Clifford Olson. I know I don't have any concrete evidence, but I know as sure as I'm standing here: Olson killed Johnsrude and Kozma."

"You should obtain the services of the Special "O" Surveillance Unit and concentrate on Olson," he suggested to several different Serious Crime investigators. "You will find he is responsible."

But the Serious Crime members were reluctant to narrow their focus and concentrate all their resources on Olson alone.

Darryll was in agony. He had no jurisdiction. He knew Olson was a rapist and multiple murderer run amok. He was filled with dread and apprehension that another child might meet a violent fate at the hands of Olson.

"What prevented others from seeing what to me was as plain as the nose on my face?" Darryll still wonders. "I knew Olson was a frighteningly dangerous killer."

Two
Les Solves the Case

Communication

Communication is a process that depends upon the effective exchange of information. The sound of a single voice falling on a deafened ear does not qualify. In the RCMP hierarchy, channels of communication often rely on intermediaries to receive and relay messages to appropriate authorities. In a case where a subordinate needs the approval of a commanding officer (CO) to act, the subordinate relies on the chain of command to acknowledge, absorb, filter, and respond based upon the facts provided.

That process did not work for Darryll Kettles in May 1981. He felt his concerns and suspicions were unheard. The process also did not work for Les Forsythe of the RCMP's Burnaby Detachment two months later. Corporal Forsythe's involvement in the Olson case was more direct. And because he respected good communication, Les Forsythe was hellbent on getting everybody on the same page early in the game.

For that reason, Forsythe's frustration with the powers-that-be and the way things unfolded may have been even more unbearable than was Kettles'. The entire Olson affair severely affected his career.

June 20, 1981

During the summer of 1981, things were going well for Les Forsythe. This dark, powerfully built young man was already a corporal with ten years' service. As the non-commissioned officer (NCO) in charge of the Burnaby RCMP Detachment Sex Crimes Unit, his future seemed bright. He was intelligent, energetic, and well respected within the police community.

Ada Court, a popular thirteen-year-old Burnaby elementary school student, was also enjoying life. Her parents were divorced and she lived with her mother and older sister, Darlene. Darlene was almost a mother to Ada, as Mrs. Court was in failing health. Ada was doing well in school and had the steady and loving support of her family, who considered her a perfect daughter. "Ada was always helping out," her teacher Betty Wells commented. "To know Ada was to love her."

On Saturday, June 20, 1981, Ada went to her brother's residence in Coquitlam to baby-sit. She looked after her two nieces, aged one and two, every Saturday night. The next morning, Ada hurried to catch a bus. Her destination was Boundary Road and Lougheed Highway in Burnaby, where she had arranged to meet her boyfriend.

He waited with growing anxiety for Ada, who never arrived. Confused and concerned, he alerted the Court family. "I have been waiting for Ada at Boundary and Lougheed since just after noon," he said. "She hasn't arrived. Have you heard from her?"

As the day progressed and Ada failed to appear, her family became more and more worried. This was not like Ada. Finally her father called the Burnaby RCMP.

"My thirteen-year-old daughter has not been seen since just before noon," he reported. "This is not like her. She is not one to run away from home. We are very worried something has happened to her. Ada would only go missing if, for some reason, she were unable to return home."

Police went to the Court residence, took particulars, and submitted a report. Staff Sergeant Alfie Erickson reviewed the file and agreed with the Courts' assessment.

"GIS [General Investigation Section] should take a look at this," he told his immediate supervisor, Inspector Dave Mortimer.

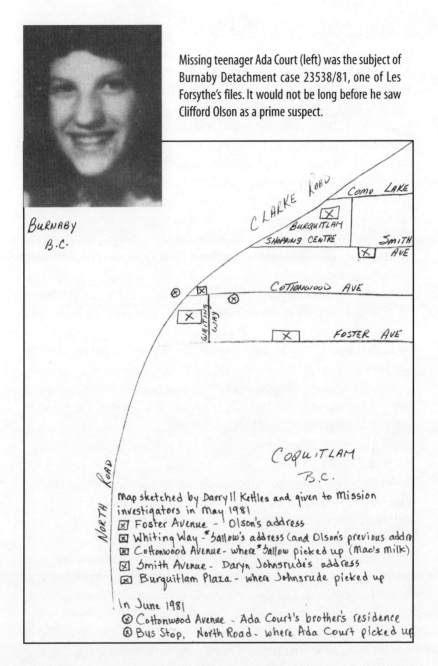

Missing teenager Ada Court (left) was the subject of Burnaby Detachment case 23538/81, one of Les Forsythe's files. It would not be long before he saw Clifford Olson as a prime suspect.

BURNABY
B.C.

CLARKE ROAD

Como LAKE

BURQUITLAM SHOPPING CENTRE

SMITH AVE

COTTONWOOD AVE

WHITING WAY

FOSTER AVE

COQUITLAM
B.C.

NORTH ROAD

Map sketched by Darryll Kettles and given to Mission investigators in May 1981
☒ Foster Avenue - Olson's address
☒ Whiting Way - *Sallow's address (and Olson's previous addr.
☒ Cottonwood Avenue - where *Sallow picked up (Mac's milk)
☒ Smith Avenue - Daryn Johnsrude's address
☒ Burquitlam Plaza - where Johnsrude picked up

In June 1981
⊗ Cottonwood Avenue - Ada Court's brother's residence
⊗ Bus Stop, North Road - where Ada Court picked up

Darryll Kettles' map with additional data relevant to the Court, Johnsrude, and Sallow cases.

"Everything points to foul play on this case. She certainly doesn't appear to be a runaway."

Mortimer assigned the missing person file to the plainclothes unit, where it was given to Corporal Les Forsythe for further investigation.

Les went through the usual missing persons inquiries. Very quickly, he too concluded that Ada Court was no runaway. "If Ada was physically able to get there, she would be at home," he said. As days passed, Les came to know and greatly respect the Court family. He still marvels at the strength and character displayed by Ada's sister, her mother, and her grandmother during their terrible ordeal.

Despite a thorough and intensive investigation over the next ten days, the case was going nowhere. Ada Court seemed to have vanished without a trace.

Les was busy and carried numerous files. Burnaby had countless sex offences to pursue. Nevertheless, Ada Court was constantly on his mind. He worked the case whenever possible, hoping for the break that would give him the key to a perplexing puzzle and bring Ada home.

Forsythe knew from his inquiries that Daryn Johnsrude had gone missing from the same general area as Ada, but on the surface, nothing seemed to connect the two cases.

July 3, 1981

On Friday July 3, 1981, sixteen-year-old Sandra Docker and her friend Rose Smythe were shopping at the Lougheed Mall at North Road and Lougheed Highway in Burnaby. They were approached by a man outside Lectro Fun, a games arcade.

"Are you looking for work?" he asked. "I'm in construction and I'm looking for good workers to clean carpets, wash windows, and do general cleanup. The pay is good. Ten dollars an hour."

"We might be interested," Docker replied. "Where do we have to go?"

"It's an apartment complex right near here," the man said. "Jump in and I'll show you. It will only take a minute."

They got into the silver Ford Pinto and drove a short distance to Cameron Street and Erickson Avenue where an apartment building was under construction. "This is the spot," he said. "If you are interested, you can start Monday. I'll pick you up at Lectro Fun at 7:30 Monday morning." Docker and Smythe agreed to start work Monday.

"We should have a beer on that," their new boss declared, and he handed them each an opened bottle. They finished their beer and returned to Lougheed Mall. "Don't forget," he reminded them. "I'll see you here Monday at 7:30."

July 6, 1981

Excited about their new jobs, both Docker and Smythe kept the appointment. Their employer picked them up in the silver Pinto he had been driving Friday. "I need a coffee to get me going," he said. "Hop in."

They drove to Nuffy's Doughnuts in the Sapperton area of New Westminster, where he bought coffee. The next stop was the familiar apartment complex under construction at Cameron and Erickson. "They aren't ready for you yet today," the man observed. Next they drove to a house in Coquitlam that was under construction. "I was going to get you to clean tiles here," he said. "But they're not ready for that either."

They returned to Lectro Fun without doing any work. "The way things stand, I only have enough work for one of you today," he declared. "I won't need you right now," he said, pointing at Smythe. "Maybe tomorrow."

Disappointed for Rosie but unconcerned, Docker departed with her employer. They drove to an apartment in Coquitlam. "I'll just be a minute," he said as he parked the car. He returned carrying a paper bag containing beer, promptly opened a bottle, and handed it to her. "We may as well start the day off right," he said. He then opened one for himself.

They drove to a downtown Vancouver photo shop and then to a Surrey liquor store where he purchased a bottle of whisky. Then he exchanged the Pinto at a Surrey car lot for a green Ford Granada.

Docker, who had been drinking beer and whisky, noticed a marked change in her boss's demeanour. He had become surly and was forcing her to drink, using threats and intimidation. Docker began to feel uneasy. "I don't want anything else to drink," she protested. He disregarded her comment and plied her with more alcohol. As time progressed she became sick to her stomach.

The driver eventually stopped at a secluded location near Guilford in Surrey. "This is my newest job site," he said. Olson's idea of a job was suddenly becoming clearer. He forced Docker into the back seat and started to rape her. Resisting as best she could, the teenager sobbed with each advance.

"You're fired!" he finally snarled at her. He drove her back to Lectro Fun and ordered, "Get out."

After exiting the Granada, Docker flagged down an approaching RCMP vehicle. "The driver of that green car just tried to rape me," she told Constable Smith. Docker sat in the police vehicle while Smith broadcast, "Burnaby, all cars, green Ford Grenada, B.C. licence JBH 616, departing Lougheed Mall. Proceeding east on Cameron. One male occupant, Caucasian, 40 years, brown hair. Wanted [for] sexual assault. It just happened."

Within moments, both Smith and Docker heard Constable Ewart respond to the alert. "Burnaby, stopping JBH 616, green Granada, North Road and Cameron. One male occupant, need backup. Out of car."

As Docker gave Smith details of the sexual assault, the driver of the Granada identified himself to Ewart as Cliff Olson. Because he showed signs of inebriation, he was arrested and transported to the Burnaby RCMP lockup. As the sexual assault had occurred in Surrey, the Surrey RCMP Detachment was notified and an investigator was dispatched.

In Burnaby, Les Forsythe was on duty. Constable Smith beckoned to him in the hallway. "We just arrested a guy for sexual assault and impaired driving," Smith told the corporal from the Sex Crimes Unit. "He's still in the cells. You might be interested in him. I wouldn't doubt he is good for some of our sexual assaults. This guy is weird. Surrey is sending an investigator to talk to him and the victim."

As Les learned more about Docker's sexual assault, he became more intrigued. Lectro Fun was only a short distance from where Ada Court had gone missing. Daryn Johnsrude was last seen in the same general area. Were these events connected? Forsythe proceeded to the cellblock to speak with Olson.

"I helped you guys by testifying against Gary Marcoux," Olson said, opening the conversation. "He raped and killed a nine-year-old girl at Mission."

Les immediately became wary. "Why would someone begin a conversation that way?" he wondered. The more Olson rambled, the more suspicious Les became. "This guy is talking too much," he thought. "There is something about him I don't like."

The real kicker came when Les realized Ada Court's brother resided across the lane from Olson's apartment. Ada had been baby-sitting for him immediately before she disappeared, The bus stop where she was to catch the bus bound for Burnaby was less than a block from her brother's residence.

As he continued to talk with Olson, Forsythe became convinced he was in the presence of a severely deranged and dangerous man. Les sensed that he was staring into the cold, cruel eyes of Ada Court's killer. "It's hard to describe what I felt," he says now. "The sensation was overwhelming. I could almost see the evil oozing from his pores."

When Les reflects at all on this case—something he prefers not to do—he identifies July 6 as the key date in the Ada Court investigation. It was then the pieces of the puzzle started to fit together.

The Surrey investigator was not at all enthused about the Docker file. There were questions about her credibility. She had been consuming alcohol, and he thought she would make a poor witness. Therefore, for now, no charges were to be laid for the sexual assault.

Les did his best to detain Olson as long as possible. He was charged at Burnaby for impaired driving, but he could not be held in custody on that charge. Ultimately, Olson was released on a promise to appear.

Sergeant Sid Slater of the Burnaby plainclothes unit listened as Les enlisted his help. "I think we just got our first big break in the Ada Court disappearance. General Duty just picked up an ex-con, Clifford Olson, for sexual assault and impaired driving. Surrey thinks the victim would make a poor witness so they cut him loose. Olson lives right near where Ada Court was baby-sitting for her brother. That's also where Daryn Johnsrude, a murdered teenager from Coquitlam, was last seen. The victim today was picked up near there, at the Lougheed Mall.

"This guy gives me the creeps," Les added. "He starts off the conversation by telling me he gave evidence against a guy he was in jail with who killed a young girl at Mission. The more I listened to him, the more I was convinced he killed Ada Court and Daryn Johnsrude. We'll probably find Ada's body near where they found Johnsrude. I want to do more checking on Olson," Les told Slater. "You would really be helping me out if you could get the helicopter to take us to Mission to see if we can spot any fresh graves. You only have to talk to this guy to know he's dangerous."

Darryll Kettles would have agreed.

July 8, 1981

The police helicopter was unavailable until July 8. On that date, Forsythe and Slater flew to the Deroche area, where they conducted an unsuccessful air-and-ground search for possible gravesites. To conclude the day they visited Mission Detachment to converse with the Johnsrude case investigators, whom they had not met.

MacIntosh and Lysyk met the Burnaby sleuths as they disembarked from the RCMP helicopter. Over coffee, Forsythe described events surrounding his encounter with Olson and conveyed his thoughts about Olson's involvement in Ada Court's disappearance.

"We know about Olson," Mike Lysyk countered. "He's a suspect in the Johnsrude case." Les listened intently as he heard for the first time about Kathy Sallow. "In May he picked up a girl in Coquitlam, fed her booze and some pills. We just got word from the lab that the pill the girl kept was chloral hydrate, commonly known as knock-out drops or a Mickey Finn. Before he got her to where he was taking her, he flipped his car at Agassiz. We searched his car but didn't find anything incriminating. Serious Crime has been promising us a profile on him, but so far we haven't seen it. He's a strong suspect in the Johnsrude murder, but so far we don't have anything concrete." Darryll Kettles' strong beliefs were not mentioned to Forsythe.

Hearing about the Agassiz incident only strengthened Forsythe's certainty. His gut feeling about Olson had been right. The corporal felt an urgent need for action, but before he could make an arrest, he had to know more about the ex-con. He would start immediately by garnering as much information as he could on Olson. Les was now impatient. "I have some things I want to check out, but we have to talk further. What do you say we meet at Burnaby on July 14? We'll share any new information we uncover."

Forsythe knew in his heart that Olson was his man. "It's as plain as day," he confided to Slater. "That son-of-a-bitch killed Ada Court and Daryn Johnsrude as sure as I'm standing here talking to you. I wonder if he has killed anyone else?" Les couldn't wait to get back to Burnaby, where he was anxious to compile his own Olson profile. He would do this alone, as Sid Slater was going on vacation.

Meanwhile, Olson was nonchalantly checking out

Les Forsythe was the first investigator to try to develop a co-ordinated effort to research missing person files. The failure of his personal initiative to overcome bureaucracy exposed some malfunctions in the communication links of the RCMP.

motorhomes at Coquitlam Chrysler in preparation for a California vacation.

★ ★ ★

Back in Burnaby, Les's first destination was the Vancouver RCMP Crime Index Section (CIS), where he drew Olson's criminal records file. The more he read, the more convinced he became. Olson was coming into focus.

He determined that Olson was a career criminal. He had been in trouble with the law virtually all his adult life. Initially he appeared to be no more than a petty thief and fraud artist. Since 1978 Olson had been serving a two-year sentence for fraud, possession of stolen property, and possession of housebreaking instruments. However, a more frightening persona was emerging of late. His recent clashes with authorities, particularly since his release on mandatory supervision in January 1980, had taken on a brutal tone.

Forsythe read the same data that had influenced Darryll Kettles six weeks earlier. The Squamish charges of rape, buggery, and gross indecency further bolstered his opinion that he was on the right track. The Richmond charges—buggery and indecent assault on a male—stemmed from an event that occurred shortly after he had been released on mandatory supervision. When Darryll Kettles phoned CIS in late May, the Richmond charges had not yet been included in Olson's dossier. All of this, together with the May incident at Agassiz with Kathy Sallow and the July indecent assault of Sandra Docker, painted an ominous picture.

Using the same reasoning as Darryll, Les was convinced Olson had committed at least two murders, namely those of Daryn Johnsrude and Ada Court. Did Les have a potential serial killer on his hands? Maybe, but he had not a scrap of hard evidence to prove it.

As Forsythe continued to develop a case against Olson as the person responsible for Ada Court's disappearance, he briefed Inspector Larry Proke, Burnaby's Operational Support Officer, on his progress. Sometime between July 8 and 15, a Burnaby officer, probably Proke, mentioned to Chief Superintendent Bill Neill, the officer in charge of the Criminal Investigation Branch in Vancouver, that they might need help with surveillance on a murder investigation.

"Burnaby might be coming in with a request for surveillance on a murder," Neill said during a casual conversation with the man in charge of special surveillance personnel, Superintendent Bruce Northorp. As the officer in charge of Support Services, it was not unusual for Northorp to hear beforehand of some pending request. It simply came as a result of officers casually discussing cases.

Les decided it was time to alert other police jurisdictions, and the July 14 meeting he had set with the Mission Detachment investigators was the way to do it. In preparation, Les developed a five-page profile on Olson. It outlined Olson's known and suspected recent criminal activities, his trait of offering his intended victims a job for ten dollars per hour, his penchant for borrowed or rented cars, and his known recent addresses in Surrey and Coquitlam.

Over the next few days Les kept busy telephoning police throughout the Lower Mainland and urging them to attend the meeting. Serious Crime Corporal Fred Maile had been on vacation. When Forsythe called Maile, he learned that Maile was to assist Jim Hunter at an interview with a murder suspect at Squamish on July 14. Forsythe rescheduled to the following day, July 15. All those invited were asked to research their missing persons files to establish if any of these cases could possibly be linked to Olson.

July 15, 1981

Needless to say, all this interest in Olson and missing children caused much discussion within the police community. It should not have been a surprise when a BCTV reporter and camera crew arrived at Burnaby Detachment just prior to the 1:30 meeting. The reporter asked to interview one of the investigators on camera. After some discussion, Inspector Larry Proke convinced Les to give a brief statement to BCTV.

"This meeting," Les explained, "is simply a brainstorming session of investigators from around the Lower Mainland who have a common interest in missing persons investigations." When the story aired later, it was viewers' first indication that police were more concerned than usual about missing children in the Greater Vancouver area.

The meeting proceeded with about 24 police investigators present. Vancouver Police, New Westminster Police, and RCMP members from Burnaby, Surrey, Coquitlam, Richmond, Squamish, and Vancouver headquarters' Serious Crime Section were in attendance. Neither Corporal Darryll Kettles from Agassiz nor the Mission investigators who were handling the Johnsrude murder were at the meeting. Instead, members of the Vancouver Serious Crime Section represented their interests.

The Vancouver and New Westminster Police were at the meeting as observers only. They were not aware of any missing persons within their jurisdictions fitting Olson's modus operandi.

In the case of the New Westminster Police, this proved to be incorrect. Judy Kozma was last seen on July 9, and she was reported missing on July 13. A procedural error prevented her name being circulated as a missing person within the New Westminster Police Service prior to the July 15 meeting. Consequently, her name was not placed on the Canadian Police Information Centre. New Westminster detectives did not know she was missing.

Les first outlined the circumstances of the Ada Court disappearance. He described Olson's impaired driving offence at Burnaby, in which Olson was arrested for the sexual assault of Sandra Docker. Forsythe then elaborated on how his inquiries led him to Mission and then to the Crime Index Section. He distributed the profile he had amassed on Olson.

Coquitlam investigators described a May 14 incident. Olson and Joan, his fiancee, were to be married May 15. Joan and her girlfriends went out to celebrate, and Olson was left to care for several children. He sent the older children to purchase bubble gum while he remained alone with a five-year-old girl. The five-year-old alleged Olson sexually assaulted her. Of course Olson denied the accusation, and police were unable to gain sufficient evidence to charge him. Unfortunately there was no corroborating evidence, and the girl was too young to testify. The Coquitlam police concluded, "Olson remains the strongest suspect in the Johnsrude murder, particularly after the incident involving Kathy Sallow at Agassiz. Olson is also suspected of shoplifting from department stores in the Coquitlam area."

Richmond detectives described a February 10, 1980, incident in which Olson lured a Vancouver Island youth into a Richmond Hotel, then forcibly confined and sexually assaulted him. They commented, "It took a year to track him down."

"Olson could be a possible suspect in the murder of twelve-year-old Christine Weller," Richmond investigators added. "She was last seen in Surrey on November 19, 1980, but not reported missing until November 25. Her body was recovered at Richmond on Christmas Day, 1980." However, Richmond had two suspects who looked better than Olson for this murder. His name came up early on in the investigation, mainly because he lived in close proximity to where the girl went missing. Nothing had been uncovered positively linking him to the Weller murder, but those at the meeting agreed the Weller case fit the profile.

A Squamish investigator briefed those present on their case, where Olson committed gross indecency and raped sixteen-year-old Kim Werbecky at Squamish on January 2, 1981. He picked her up, fed her alcohol, and promised her a job cleaning condos at Whistler. "We kept him in custody for three months on our charges until Crown Counsel, in his wisdom, decided to stay the charges. We protested vigorously but it did no good. He is still charged with two firearms offences."

The abduction of Christine Weller in November 1980 was not tied to Olson for some time. This is the only murder that preceded his Squamish assault on Kim Werbecky, and it remained unsolved until Olson's confession.

Surrey investigators reported charges were pending on the sexual assault of Sandra Docker.

Vancouver Serious Crime investigators, on behalf of Mission and Agassiz, identified Olson as a suspect in the Johnsrude homicide. They preferred to keep an open mind on suspects and were not prepared to concentrate totally on Olson. They acknowledged Olson could be considered a good suspect, but they had one or two other suspects in mind that looked just as good or better than Olson. They speculated he could have rendered Johnsrude defenceless by forcing him to consume alcohol laced with chloral hydrate, as he did with Kathy Sallow.

"It was an interesting meeting," said Fred Maile. "Burnaby and Serious Crime were the only ones interested in Olson. VPD [Vancouver Police Department] was not worried. Richmond had the Weller case, and we would have pushed that further, but they said they had a strong suspect. They had located blood of the same type as the victim's in the suspect's apartment. He had been polygraphed and the examiner said he was the guy, so that seemed pretty convincing."

Les Forsythe's meeting in Burnaby lasted about an hour and a half. All parties agreed Olson had to be a strong suspect in any recent homicides, particularly those involving teenagers and young children. At the end of the meeting, Larry Proke told those who didn't already know that he was moving over to General Investigations

(GI) at Vancouver headquarters and would be there, after taking some time off, in a couple of weeks. "We should work on the profile," advised Fred Maile, who would soon be reporting to Proke at GI. This was the same profile requested by Mission in May. No reason was provided for its limited progress to date. Participants at the meeting were to provide any pertinent information in their possession to be included in the profile. They agreed that the Burnaby Detachment should keep a close eye on the suspect. Forsythe and colleagues were to contact the officer in charge of Support Services at headquarters to enlist aid from their crack surveillance unit, Special "O" Section.

July 16, 1981

Forsythe attempted unsuccessfully to locate Olson. Late in the day, still unable to establish his whereabouts, Les and Constable Brian Wornstaff staked out Olson's Coquitlam residence. When this still did not turn up the suspect, Les, desperate for news of Olson, decided to take control of matters. Posing as an insurance agent, he visited Olson's parents, who lived in an apartment building close to Olson's residence.

"I sold Cliff some life insurance recently and I have to give him his policy," he told them. "I have been trying to contact him, but he doesn't seem to be around. Could you put me in touch with him?"

Olson's parents were wary. "We don't see much of Cliff nowadays," they eventually told Les. "He and his new wife and baby are in California on vacation. They won't be back until next week."

Les was both disappointed and relieved at the news. On one hand, the Burnaby plainclothes unit was critically short of staff and this would buy him some time to get assistance. Conversely, Les was anxious to get started on Olson. He wanted to put this deranged killer away for good.

It appeared that the United States border monitoring system allowed career criminal Clifford Olson to enter their jurisdiction with impunity. This was not his first venture into the U.S.A. He and his wife of two months had previously vacationed in Hawaii.

Up until now, Corporal Forsythe had been reporting his progress to Inspector Proke, but now Proke left for Manitoba to visit his ailing father. On his return, when he assumed new duties as the officer in charge of General Investigations, he would be in charge of the Serious Crime Section as well as many other support units.

If Proke had remained in Burnaby, it is entirely likely Les Forsythe, using Proke's influence, could have prevented further murders. Proke's last words to Forsythe were, "Get the paperwork done and everything will go smoothly."

How simple it seemed then. Enthusiastically, Les filled out the surveillance request and gave it to Staff Sergeant Bill Howitt, the new supervisor of Burnaby's General Investigation Section, who had just arrived from the Vancouver Integrated Intelligence Unit (VIIU). Howitt had been in Burnaby before as a plainclothes investigator. While in the VIIU he ran several very successful stolen property sting operations using both Vancouver Police and RCMP personnel. Now Les had to bring him up to speed on the Olson investigation.

Three
Line Change

Transferred

"Transferred" is a term that appears often in the work biography of the typical Mountie. Most members can expect to go through the process a half dozen times in their career. A transfer in the RCMP usually means picking up family and belongings and physically moving from one jurisdiction to another. Sometimes a member may be fortunate enough to be able to change jobs without actually changing homes.

The reasons why Mounties regularly face transfer have been justified for over 125 years and many of them are good—based on the need for promotion and broader experience. One problem that makes them "not so good" is the issue of disorientation. New members in new jobs might not know what's going on for a period of time. Untimely transfers in the Vancouver RCMP in the summer of 1981 might have given Clifford Olson more time to kill.

The Royal Canadian Mounted Police in British Columbia is a multifaceted organization with federal, provincial, and municipal policing responsibilities. Federally the RCMP is Canada's national police force, responsible for the enforcement of various federal statutes. The RCMP is divided into divisions coinciding with provincial boundaries. British Columbia is designated "E" Division.

In eight of Canada's ten provinces, including British Columbia, the provincial government contracts with the federal government for the RCMP to carry out provincial policing needs. To further complicate the situation, many communities also contract with the federal government for the RCMP to perform municipal duties.

In 1981 the British Columbia RCMP headquarters was situated at Victoria with a Deputy Commissioner in charge. The province was divided into two districts, each with an Assistant Commissioner as the Commanding Officer (CO). District One, headquartered in Vancouver, consisted of the B.C. Lower Mainland from the Sunshine Coast to Hope. District Two, with its headquarters at Victoria, encompassed the remaining portions of the province.

Within District One, the large municipal detachments at Burnaby, Surrey, North Vancouver, Richmond, Coquitlam, Langley, and Maple Ridge, with commissioned officers in charge, reported directly to the Commanding Officer in Vancouver. Depending on the size of the detachment, a Superintendent or an Inspector was in charge. Those detachment commanders were referred to as Officer in Charge or OIC. For instance, Superintendent Norm Fuchs was the OIC Burnaby Detachment. Two subordinate officers, Inspectors Dave Mortimer and Larry Proke (until his transfer), assisted him. Large detachments would be organized further into specific sections such as Administration, a Traffic Section, three or four General Duty watches, an Identification Section, General Investigation, and perhaps other sections. For example, Staff Sergeant Bill Howitt, Sergeant Sid Slater, and Corporal Les Forsythe were members of the Burnaby General Investigation Section (GIS), with Forsythe being in charge of a further subsection, the Sex Crimes Unit.

Also reporting to the Commanding Officer were two Sub-Division OCs, the Officer Commanding Vancouver Sub-Division and the Officer Commanding Chilliwack Sub-Division.

The OC Vancouver Sub-Division was responsible for those smaller detachments situated in the western portion of the Lower Mainland having non-commissioned officers in charge (NCOs i/c). Non-commissioned officers are Staff Sergeants, Sergeants, and Corporals. The number of personnel assigned to the unit determines rank. Some of the Vancouver Sub-Division detachments

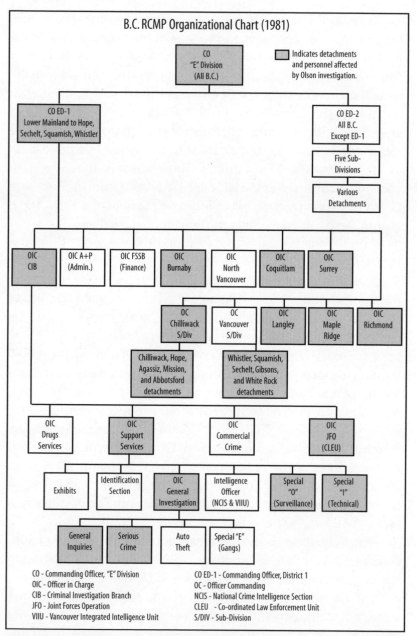

B.C. RCMP Organizational Chart (1981)

Indicates detachments and personnel affected by Olson investigation.

CO "E" Division (All B.C.)

CO ED-1 Lower Mainland to Hope, Sechelt, Squamish, Whistler

CO ED-2 All B.C. Except ED-1

Five Sub-Divisions

Various Detachments

OIC CIB · OIC A+P (Admin.) · OIC FSSB (Finance) · OIC Burnaby · OIC North Vancouver · OIC Coquitlam · OIC Surrey

OC Chilliwack S/Div · OC Vancouver S/Div · OIC Langley · OIC Maple Ridge · OIC Richmond

Chilliwack, Hope, Agassiz, Mission, and Abbotsford detachments

Whistler, Squamish, Sechelt, Gibsons, and White Rock detachments

OIC Drugs Services · OIC Support Services · OIC Commercial Crime · OIC JFO (CLEU)

Exhibits · Identification Section · OIC General Investigation · Intelligence Officer (NCIS & VIIU) · Special "O" (Surveillance) · Special "I" (Technical)

General Inquiries · Serious Crime · Auto Theft · Special "E" (Gangs)

CO - Commanding Officer, "E" Division
OIC - Officer in Charge
CIB - Criminal Investigation Branch
JFO - Joint Forces Operation
VIIU - Vancouver Integrated Intelligence Unit

CO ED-1 - Commanding Officer, District 1
OC - Officer Commanding
NCIS - National Crime Intelligence Section
CLEU - Co-ordinated Law Enforcement Unit
S/DIV - Sub-Division

The RCMP chain of command underwent dramatic upheaval in the spring and summer of 1981. In the ranks on the West Coast there were widespread staff shortages and low morale. All these factors affected day-to-day operations and, unfortunately, coincided with Clifford Olson's killing spree.

were Squamish, Sechelt, Whistler, Gibsons, White Rock, and others. Staff Sergeant Fred Zaharia and Constable Jim Hunter were located at Squamish Detachment.

The OC Chilliwack Sub-Division, Superintendent Cy Thomas, supervised the smaller eastern detachments including Agassiz, Mission, Hope, Abbotsford, and others. Sergeant Dwight Gash, Corporal Darryll Kettles, and Constable Bill Hudyma were at Agassiz Detachment.

The officer in charge of the Criminal Investigation Branch (OIC CIB) at Vancouver was responsible for all criminal operations in District One. A number of Superintendents and some other ranks reported directly to the OIC CIB. The OIC Support Services, the OIC Drug Enforcement, and the OIC Commercial Crime, to name only a few, were under his span-of-control.

The OIC Support Services had a number of Inspectors and NCOs under his direction. These included the OIC General Investigation Section, the OIC Special "O" Section, the District Intelligence Officer, the NCO i/c Special "I" Section, and others.

Taking it one step further, the OIC General Investigation directed units such as the NCO i/c Serious Crime Section, the NCO i/c Polygraph, the NCO i/c General Inquiries, the NCO i/c Auto Theft, the NCO i/c Special "E" Section, the Division Dive Supervisor, and one or two other groups. Staff Sergeant Arnie Nylund, Sergeant Jack Randle, Corporal Fred Maile, Corporal Ed Drozda, and Constable Rick Boyarski were some of the Serious Crime Section members.

The role of the Vancouver Serious Crime Section should be further clarified. When the British Columbia RCMP reorganized in 1975, creating District One and District Two, the Serious Crime Section was formed and located at the District One headquarters in Vancouver under the direction of the OIC General Investigation. After examining major crimes case-management systems used by police agencies across North America, the Serious Crime Section adopted a Tips system developed by the Michigan State Police. Coincidentally, Bruce Northorp had adopted similar procedures when he was in charge of criminal investigations in Burnaby.

The mandate of the Serious Crime Section was to ensure that homicide investigations throughout the Lower Mainland were

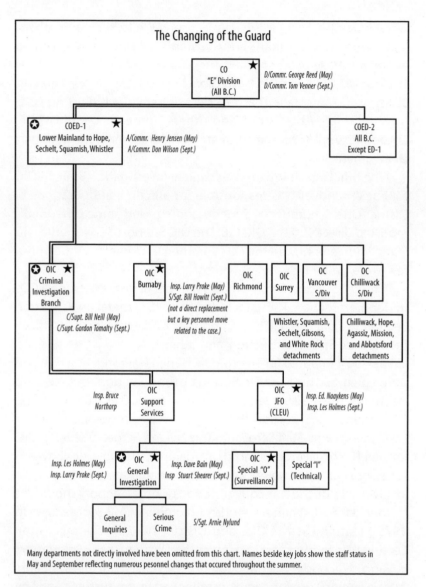

The Changing of the Guard

CO
"E" Division
(All B.C.)

D/Commr. George Reed (May)
D/Commr. Tom Venner (Sept.)

COED-1
Lower Mainland to Hope,
Sechelt, Squamish, Whistler

A/Commr. Henry Jensen (May)
A/Commr. Don Wilson (Sept.)

COED-2
All B.C.
Except ED-1

OIC
Criminal
Investigation
Branch

C/Supt. Bill Neill (May)
C/Supt. Gordon Tomalty (Sept.)

OIC
Burnaby

Insp. Larry Proke (May)
S/Sgt. Bill Howitt (Sept.)
(not a direct replacement
but a key personnel move
related to the case.)

OIC
Richmond

OIC
Surrey

OC
Vancouver
S/Div

OC
Chilliwack
S/Div

Whistler, Squamish,
Sechelt, Gibsons,
and White Rock
detachments

Chilliwack, Hope,
Agassiz, Mission,
and Abbotsford
detachments

Insp. Bruce
Northorp

OIC
Support
Services

OIC
JFO
(CLEU)

Insp. Ed. Naaykens (May)
Insp. Les Holmes (Sept.)

Insp. Les Holmes (May)
Insp. Larry Proke (Sept.)

OIC
General
Investigation

Insp. Dave Bain (May)
Insp Stuart Shearer (Sept.)

OIC
Special "O"
(Surveillance)

Special "I"
(Technical)

General
Inquiries

Serious
Crime

S/Sgt. Arnie Nylund

Many departments not directly involved have been omitted from this chart. Names beside key jobs show the staff status in May and September reflecting numerous pesonnel changes that occured throughout the summer.

The chain of command was in constant change around Bruce Northorp through the summer of 1981. As illustrated by the symbol ★, seven shifts of command occurred at postings key to efficient management of the investigation into child abductions eventually attributed to Clifford Olson. The ✪ symbol shows a position vacant or partially maintained at the critical period of the investigation. The link between Northorp and Arnie Nylund represented the most stable communications channel in the organization hierarchy.

being handled in a uniform manner and the systems in place were being used properly. It also gave support to smaller detachments that were unable to take on major cases with their existing personnel. The Serious Crime Section was not sanctioned to assume full control for major crimes, acting instead in a support role to the detachment charged with the overall responsibility. In actual practice, this relationship often broke down. Serious Crime Section investigators often pursued a case to its conclusion with minimal input and direction from the host detachment, but even in those instances, case responsibility remained with the detachment. Large detachments such as Burnaby, Coquitlam, Surrey, Richmond, and North Vancouver functioned more as city police forces. They usually had sufficient personnel, so rarely required assistance from the Serious Crime Section.

Summer 1981

The Olson case caught the RCMP on a "line change." Everywhere one turned, individuals were changing jobs. This is one of the inherent problems with the RCMP transfer system.

Deputy Commissioner Tom Venner had just arrived in Victoria as the ranking officer for British Columbia. The District One commanding officer, Assistant Commissioner Henry Jensen, had been transferred to Ottawa. Chief Superintendent Bill Neill, the officer in charge of the Criminal Investigation Branch, was covering Jensen's position for a portion of the time. Neill would soon become the commanding officer of "F" Division, the province of Saskatchewan. To further complicate the situation, Neill underwent minor surgery on July 27, leaving Bruce Northorp as the acting OIC CIB. During this most critical period, Northorp's two immediate superior officers were absent.

Inspector Larry Proke, the officer soon to be OIC General Investigation and thus responsible for the Serious Crime Section, had not yet arrived to take up his new duties. Staff Sergeant Bill Howitt came from the Vancouver Integrated Intelligence Unit to head GIS in Burnaby. Inspector Les Holmes, who had been transferred from OIC General Investigations to Joint Forces Operation (JFO), was on leave, and six months later would go to

Toronto. Staff Sergeant Arnie Nylund was left covering the Vancouver HQ General Investigation units until Proke arrived. Inspector Ed Naaykens, the OIC JFO, and Inspector Dave Bain, OIC Special "O," were also transferred at this crucial time.

Most were local transfers that could be completed in only two or three weeks, but it would take time for the officers to get to know their new staff and pertinent issues. Out-of-province moves took longer, particularly if there was the sale of a home involved, unless the move involved senior executive ranks. Those officers transferring to chief superintendent and higher positions were usually directed to proceed forthwith, leaving their families to deal with the logistics of the household move. On occasion, if an inspector or superintendent was urgently required at his new posting, he would be ordered to precede his family.

To say the command level of the RCMP in Vancouver was in transition and understaffed is putting it mildly.

Part of the reason for the major shake-up was to quell a growing mood of restless dissatisfaction among the commissioned officers in British Columbia. Although it defied tradition, officers were taking a vociferous stand against personnel shortages, unpaid overtime, the emphasis on bilingualism, and the perception that transfers had become more a form of punishment than a move up the ladder.

In Eastern Canada, Inspector Chris Sampson refused an ordered transfer to New Brunswick and was ultimately discharged from the RCMP. This served as a warning to others who balked at moves.

Officers had expressed their displeasure to the Commissioner at a tumultuous meeting in the Vancouver headquarters during 1980. It was no secret the commissioner was unhappy with the officers for speaking their minds. A well-informed colleague gave warning, "He's going to get you guys." And he did. In short order, Vancouver's senior officers were sent packing to Ottawa, Regina, Winnipeg, Toronto, and elsewhere.

There were transfers and low morale in the NCO ranks as well. For example, Sergeant Jack Randle was transferred to JFO, to be replaced at the Serious Crime Section by Sergeant Fred Coombs.

Even when Vancouver headquarters was at full strength, RCMP members usually had more than one job. Many were also members of Emergency Response Teams, members of Tactical Troops for riot and crowd control, hostage negotiators, etc. Some Serious Crime members were trained by Corporal Bob Teather, the head of the Division Dive Team, in the use of metal detectors to assist in dry-land searches at crime scenes. It was not unusual to be called out, without notice, on any number of emergencies.

The extra demands in themselves were never the main issue of discontent. It is fair to say that RCMP recruits have long embraced the legends of predecessors overcoming great odds and obstacles to get the job done. Long hours, low pay, and the ever-present criticism of a watchdog press were part of the job. Real problems could surface, however, if members started to feel that they were being mistreated or ignored from above. Then the classic bonding of the force broke down and blind faith took a back seat to individual expression.

Four
Watching Olson

Surveillance

**Surveillance is the close and undetected obser-
vation of a suspicious person. In the RCMP, the
rules of surveillance are more complicated than
one might think. Special situations call for
Special "O," a headquarters unit of highly trained
officers that is available to all detachments on
an "as needed" basis. A Special "O" unit is
assigned under specific terms and conditions,
and it is up to detachment commanders to accept
or reject those conditions. For the media, the
absence of Special "O" in the Olson case raised
one of the major questions of police procedure.**

Week of July 20, 1981

As Les Forsythe briefed his new boss, Bill Howitt, on the July 15
meeting with the Serious Crime Section and other detachments, he
emphasized the need for a tail on Olson. Howitt agreed to seek
outside support, as staff limitations meant that it would be
impossible to organize surveillance immediately.

In an attempt to collect information on Olson's recent activities,
the Serious Crime Section was busy contacting local police agencies
not represented at the July 15 meeting. Corporal Ed Drozda, on his
first day back after a three-week vacation, was assigned to work on
the Olson profile. One of his first stops was the Delta Police station,
where he was told detectives were dealing with a complaint of fraud
against Olson.

On July 22, Surrey Detachment charged Olson with indecent assault as a result of his actions with Sandra Docker on July 3. A summons was issued, requesting that Olson appear in court at a later date to answer the charges.

The same day, Drozda returned to the Delta Police office, where he met with three detectives. He learned from Detective Dennis Tarr that Olson had offered to act as an informant regarding thefts and possession of stolen property offences. Drozda saw an immediate opportunity to get more information on Olson. He asked Tarr to re-establish contact with Olson and explained that Olson was one of several suspects being considered by

On July 23, Raymond King left home on his bicycle, hoping to find work at Canada Manpower. He was never seen alive again. His body was found in early August, near where Judy Kozma's remains were discovered on July 25.

the RCMP in the disappearance and possible murder of some children. After hearing Drozda out, Tarr said he would assist. Drozda's notes indicate Tarr said Olson was willing to sell information on Lower Mainland murders.

Les Forsythe and Brian Wornstaff continued to monitor activity at Olson's residence. Les had been sweating Olson's whereabouts, and he only breathed a sigh of relief when their vigilance finally paid off on a drive-by. They saw Olson's rented vehicle parked in front of his apartment.

Les wanted to get the Special "O" Section working on Olson immediately. Howitt, who was unfamiliar with the case, told Les he would contact the officer in charge of Support Services.

On Thursday, July 23, Raymond King Jr. was reported missing from New Westminster. Last seen shortly after noon, his body was later found near Agassiz, in the Weaver Lake area.

Drozda, this time with Corporal Fred Maile, met with Detective Tarr. Tarr reiterated that he had been investigating Olson for fraud in late June. Olson had attempted to set himself up as an informant in relation to stolen property on the condition that he be paid a hundred dollars for each charge laid.

Tarr agreed to co-operate with the RCMP in any way possible. Drozda and Maile asked him to make contact with Olson. He did so later the same day.

Drozda believed Detective Dennis Tarr had given them a new option for getting to Olson. "We worked out a plan with Tarr to cultivate Olson as an informant. What did we have to lose?" asked Drozda. "If he was involved, maybe we would get something. If not, maybe we would get some information from him." Olson might lead a surveillance team to a murder scene. There, they might locate physical evidence linking Olson with unsolved homicides. If he was not involved in those crimes, he might provide the name of a suspect. The Serious Crime Section decided the investigation should proceed with Burnaby's surveillance coverage in place on Olson and their own continued contact with him through Tarr. They were unaware that surveillance was a problem.

★ ★ ★

At 1:35 p.m. on July 23, Staff Sergeant Bill Howitt, at Les Forsythe's urging, contacted Superintendent Bruce Northorp, OIC Support Services. Howitt knew Bruce well. He had worked for him at the Burnaby plainclothes section when he was a constable and Bruce was in charge of the unit.

"Hi Bruce, this is Bill Howitt. How's the chance of getting the use of Special 'O' on a suspect in a murder? He might also be tied in to some missing children."

Previously alerted by Bill Neill to the possibility of a request from Burnaby for support, Bruce had pondered how surveillance might assist in an after-the-fact homicide investigation. Was it possible the subject was a serial killer? If so, could the police allow a member of the public to be placed at risk while they were watching him? Bruce knew the answer: No!

"Okay," Bruce told Howitt, "I'm prepared to accommodate it with one rider and one tail car per shift. How about coming to my office with the request forms and we can discuss the conditions of surveillance?" As was his custom, Bruce jotted down Howitt's contact in his notebook. His notes read—

23/7/81–1:35 p.m. Bill Howitt phoned re use of Spec "O" for Olsen [sic]—murder suspect—I explained problems.

He didn't waste time with needless questions, and apparently didn't even ask how to spell the suspect's name. In his notebook he spelled Olson with an "e."

Asked to elaborate seventeen years later, his old notebook before him, Bruce said, "I was told that Olson was a suspect in a murder and possibly the disappearances of some children. Surveillance was requested and I was given a brief rundown." It was impossible, based on this short call, to fully grasp the details of the cases under scrutiny by Howitt and others, but Bruce was satisfied it was a serious request on a murder suspect.

"It wasn't my job to supervise cases but rather to provide surveillance if a request was justified and proper," Bruce declared. He stressed that supervision and intimate case knowledge at Burnaby was the responsibility of the line officers there. (In the RCMP, a line officer is in charge of investigative units, while a staff officer provides support for the operational sections. Northorp was a staff officer but on occasion became a line officer for situations such as a penitentiary hostage-taking or for the Olson case.) "There's no question the request was both justified and proper," he confirmed. "Seldom are the police in a position to consider surveillance on a person who may be committing murders. The request took the highest priority as there were no other cases of that magnitude. It was easy for Howitt to get an approval.

"My notes were very brief as there would or should be full detail on the request form when Howitt came in. The notation merely records a contact from Burnaby. I'd okayed his request and asked him to come in to work out a few details, beyond one rider and tail car, that would be required to ensure innocent lives would not be at risk. In all likelihood, surveillance would have commenced on the morning of the 24th after Special 'O' had been briefed on all aspects, including the very strict conditions which would apply to safeguard lives. It was the strict conditions, which would have to be written up, that were the problem. Only Howitt or his crew would be able to tell me about Olson's known pattern in order to consider any special measures."

22/7/81 3.30 PM

Stu Thompson ret. d my call
+ I queried him re pros. use
d spec "o" re missing bag

23/7/81 8.20 AM to 1.00 PM

Out to Citizenship Court
+ address Feds re political
labour strategy — Gerald
Donegan, Dept d Justice
preceded me as speaker

23/7/81 1.35 PM

Bill Howitt phoned re use
d Spec "o" for Olsen —
murder suspect — I
explained problems

23/7/81 1.50 PM

Bill Howitt called back to
say he was considering
giving project to J F O

23/7/81 1.55 PM

Phoned Ed Nauyfen to
advise concerns re the above
target

Bruce Northorp's archive on the Olson murders contains his original notebooks from 1981. Page 15 of his July memo book documented his conversations with Bill Howitt.

Northorp had heard enough to anticipate a potential problem. His worst nightmare would be a crack surveillance team watching a killer claim another victim. He wanted no foul-ups.

The requirement of a rider and the use of tail cars were not unusual procedures. Senior investigators were familiar with them, and certain characteristics of the surveillance unit dictated the need for them. For one thing, Special "O" was an assistance unit; it did not take over cases. Northorp was very protective of it in this regard. In the past, some unit heads had accused Special "O" of making a wrong move and screwing up their cases. On this procedure Northorp went by the book. He required that an investigator from the unit in charge of the case ride along and make any major decisions. (In instances of an intelligence probe, however, when the team was simply determining the movements of suspected or known crime figures, he would not require a rider.)

The tail car was to be available in the event some immediate and overt police action was required. To obtain quality results, the surveillance section had to take extraordinary measures to maintain its members' anonymity. Few RCMP officers knew the location of the Special "O" Section base. It was given out on a need-to-know basis. This precaution ensured that those who suspected the police were watching them couldn't gain any information as to the style or licence numbers of their vehicles. The use of a tail car was simply an extension of this concept to maintain anonymity—the police in the tail car would confront the suspect if necessary, leaving the surveillance team out of sight.

As well, every effort was made to keep surveillance specialists out of court. They operated in the shadows, preferably unknown to both suspects and most other police officers. They were not to be encumbered by arrests, which resulted in court appearances where they could be identified by the criminal element.

Howitt did not mention to Bruce Northorp that he felt he did not have sufficient personnel to accompany the surveillance team. It seemed everyone was short of personnel at this crucial stage. Understaffing in Agassiz and Mission had prevented Darryll Kettles from attending Forsythe's July 15 meeting. Now Howitt felt hamstrung by a lack of personnel. If Olson was to be followed for two shifts, a minimum of four personnel would be required to accompany surveillance, two per shift: one rider and one tail car. (It would be preferable to have one rider and two in the tail car, but that would have been Burnaby's decision.)

As Howitt hung up the phone, Les Forsythe saw that he was visibly disappointed. Although Les did not hear the exchange between Howitt and Northorp, he later commented, "I certainly got the impression from Howitt that Northorp was putting up roadblocks for us to get Special 'O'."

In desperation, Les asked Howitt to seek an alternative solution. He suggested that they contact the Joint Forces Operation (JFO) in Vancouver in an attempt to get enough personnel to accompany the Special "O" Section. The staff at JFO were mainly RCMP and Vancouver Police, with a smattering of police from other jurisdictions. A target such as Olson was clearly outside their mandate. Nevertheless, Les and Howitt set up a meeting with JFO personnel the following day, July 24.

Howitt phoned Bruce again fifteen minutes later. "I won't need Special 'O'," he said. "I'm considering giving the project to JFO."

The Joint Forces Operation of the Co-ordinated Law Enforcement Unit, known as JFO or CLEU, was situated at 250 West 7 Avenue in Vancouver. It did not do after-the-fact investigations but rather worked targets to develop new cases against known or active crime figures. JFO worked differently than Special "O" when doing surveillance. As JFO was the investigator, it did not require a rider or tail car. It would take overt action if necessary.

A target, for the purposes of Special "O," was simply a person who was being followed on behalf of a unit having case responsibility. In police parlance of the day, and for the purposes of JFO, "target" meant a subject they had been assigned to investigate. For JFO, this meant case direction, not assistance. Bruce later recalled that Howitt said he "considered Olson a target."

"I just assumed Howitt wanted JFO to take over the Olson matter from Burnaby," Bruce said. Howitt had not indicated he was understaffed and that Northorp's surveillance conditions caused him a problem.

When asked why he thought Howitt turned to JFO, Bruce replied, "He had just been transferred from the Vancouver Integrated Intelligence Unit, which is housed in the same building as JFO. Maybe he was trying to get rid of a headache. He may have forgotten JFO weren't after-the-fact investigators.

"There's also a chance he may have felt I would ask too many questions for which he didn't have answers," Bruce added. "He'd worked for me at Burnaby and knew I was thorough."

"I was surprised at Howitt's decision, but it was his to make," Bruce said. "It was a Burnaby case and their option. Based on what Howitt said, I phoned Inspector Ed Naaykens at JFO five minutes later. I told him of my concerns about ensuring the safety of any innocents Olson might pick up while under surveillance." (Naaykens was scheduled for transfer, to be replaced by Les Holmes when Holmes returned from vacation. Meanwhile, Staff Sergeant Tom Charlton was the Acting Inspector.)

★ ★ ★

While Forsythe and Howitt struggled to satisfy their surveillance needs, Serious Crime investigators focussed on their new Delta Police ally. Making plans to get closer to their target, Maile and Drozda continued to liaise with Detective Tarr. During the evening of July 23, Tarr went to Olson's residence in Coquitlam where he met with Olson and his wife, Joan. Tarr later expressed his surprise, "The apartment was spotless."

Tarr and Olson exchanged small talk. The discussion then moved on to the purpose of the meeting: to ascertain if Olson was still interested in supplying information on criminal activity. Olson had suggested he could assist police with investigations into crimes ranging from robbery and stolen property to burglaries and homicides.

Olson made no commitment. However, he referred to a newspaper article about Simon Partington, a missing boy from Surrey.

"How reliable do you think the witness is in this case?" he asked. He was referring to the description of a suspicious blonde male accompanying a young boy answering Partington's description. Tarr was unfamiliar with the case.

"I've got three ideas," Olson continued. "It was a hit-and-run with the body dumped. Two, it was a kidnapping, or maybe it was a pervert." Olson then ruled out kidnapping as he felt Simon's family had little money.

"If you possess information on major Lower Mainland crimes, I will introduce you to an RCMP contact," Tarr suggested.

"I will try to help," Olson replied. "But it will be difficult and it will cost money."

After they agreed to meet again on the morning of July 29, Tarr left. He reviewed the meeting, and the plan to reconvene in six days, with Maile and Drozda. Drozda's notes show Olson was already backtracking on the promise of murder information.

★ ★ ★

Corporal Forsythe and Staff Sergeant Howitt met with JFO investigators on July 24 to discuss putting Olson under surveillance. The initial intent was for JFO to supply assistance to Special "O" in the form of riders and "tail-end Charlies."

As the meeting progressed, Howitt appeared to alter his position, showing more willingness to get further from the case. JFO members feared a dump job when Howitt asked them to take on Olson as a target, with full responsibility for the investigation. They declared that this fell outside their mandate. JFO agreed to take the case only as a "filler," a term used to describe their work on assistance cases between projects.

Sergeant Fred Coombs, who was at the meeting, wrote in his notebook:

> It was decided Burnaby RCMP will co-ordinate the material held by themselves and the Serious Crime Unit who are compiling a complete profile on Olson. There is information Olson is to meet with a Delta P.D. member to supply information of murders on Wednesday, July 29th. Our initial objective is to surveille Olson's movements and have JFO personnel in atten-

dance to conduct investigations with regard to potential victims. For example, persons on the street approached by Olson. As well, have JFO and/or Serious Crime Unit personnel continue with Special "O" as Olson moves about. Staff Sergeant Howitt or Corporal Forsythe will contact Sergeant Fred Coombs during the early part of week July 27th to the 31st.

Burnaby was to complete an operational plan to obtain the services of the Special "O" Section. The plan would dictate what steps were to be taken should Olson pick up a potential victim.

RCMP Inspector Ed Naaykens, OIC JFO, contacted Chief Superintendent Bill Neill, the OIC Criminal Investigation Branch, to obtain authority for JFO to assist Burnaby on the Olson case. Approval was granted immediately, with Naaykens providing only brief details. When this was done, Naaykens left JFO for the last time. He was going on annual leave and would then assume new duties as the OIC Coquitlam Detachment.

★ ★ ★

Unknown to police, Clifford Olson, still without surveillance, stalked another victim. He picked up German tourist Sigrun Arnd at the Cariboo Hotel lounge, assaulted her, and killed her in Richmond. She was not reported missing until August 24, as she had been travelling alone in Canada.

★ ★ ★

During some of the critical days in the last week of July, the command level was understaffed and Bruce Northorp was severely overworked. It was not the Olson case plaguing him, however. One issue that was more political than criminal had taken on a new priority.

The Department of Indian Affairs (DIA) office in Vancouver had been occupied by some protesters holding a sit-in. The DIA, through its Ottawa headquarters, requested action by the RCMP. After the RCMP established contact with other federal, provincial, and civic agencies that were involved, Bruce's day dragged on until just before 2 a.m. on July 25, when a four-hour meeting ended.

The list of those in attendance—B.C. Attorney General Allan Williams, Assistant Deputy Attorney General Alan Filmer, Deputy Chief Tom Herdman of the Vancouver Police, and four of Herdman's officers, one representative from the federal Justice Department and one from DIA, plus RCMP Deputy Commissioner Tom Venner from Victoria headquarters, Vancouver CIB's Bill Neill, and his OIC Support Services, Bruce Northorp—indicated the level of concern. The buck got passed to Northorp.

The meeting concluded after it was decided a further meeting of RCMP officers was needed on Saturday from 11 a.m. to 2:20 p.m. Bruce was told that if the Vancouver Police refused to act, he was to head the RCMP contingent responsible for removing the protesters.

It seems a sad state of affairs when one peaceful group of demonstrators can demand so much attention, ranking in priority ahead of what seemed, to some, more pressing matters.

★ ★ ★

While Bruce Northorp attended the Saturday meeting about the sit-in at Indian Affairs, members of the Agassiz Detachment roped off a crime scene. The body of a young woman, later identified as Judy Kozma, had been found in the Weaver Lake area. The local RCMP set the usual identification procedures in motion. No immediate clues were found to indicate the identity of the girl's killer.

★ ★ ★

For Bruce, Sunday July 26 was another non day-off. He was occupied with phone calls on the sit-in issue from 1:40 p.m. until 6:55 p.m, a small indication of the responsibility held by the HQ staff.

The sit-in took on an added dimension for Bruce. He would not embark on an assignment unless he could see a clear legal authority to do so. In this case, B.C.'s attorney general made it clear he did not wish the RCMP to act, and in the absence of a directive from the attorney general, Bruce did not believe the RCMP had authority to act. In his view, acting without authority would deprive the RCMP members involved of protections offered by Section 25 of the Criminal Code of Canada to peace officers when they were authorized or required by law to execute a process.

Bruce dictated a memo to the federal Justice Department. He asked for a legal opinion, in writing, advising how the RCMP were authorized or required by law to act in this instance.

"In the absence of a written legal opinion confirming the federal stance, I will ask to be relieved of the assignment," he said to Neill. "Failing that, I'll likely decline.

"For the first time in my career, I was prepared to refuse an order," Bruce recalled later. "This would likely have meant my dismissal from the Force.

"I started the week not only tired, but mentally fatigued due to the dilemma I faced all weekend. I had no idea I was about to face the toughest assignment of my career, without a real break for almost seven weeks. I went into that week with my batteries low and in need of a full charge."

Week of July 27 1981

Olson started his day by picking up fifteen-year-old Terri Lynn Carson in Surrey. He drove her to the Agassiz area where he assaulted and murdered her. She was reported missing by her mother the next day.

For Bruce, much of the day was taken up with the sit-in issue. The situation finally evaporated when the Vancouver Police advised they would act on the occupation later in the day. No RCMP action was required. What turned out for Bruce Northorp to be a non-event had fully occupied him from 9 p.m. Friday until mid-afternoon Monday.

Les Forsythe's day took a turn for the worse when he learned the body of a young female had been discovered near Agassiz. Could this be Ada Court? A few quick telephone calls established it probably was not the girl he had tried so long and hard to find.

Driven by a new sense of urgency, Les urged Howitt to ask Joint Forces to commence surveillance on Olson forthwith. This tactic would allow breathing time for Burnaby to prepare a formal surveillance request for the Special "O" Section. A meeting at JFO was quickly arranged.

Those at the meeting agreed that if Olson, while under surveillance, picked up any young people, either female or male, he was to be arrested immediately and Burnaby Detachment was to be informed. JFO consented to provide immediate coverage of Olson.

As a result of the meeting with JFO, Les asked Surrey Detachment to issue a warrant for Olson's arrest on the charge of the July 6 indecent assault of Sandra Docker. The purpose of the warrant, which replaced the outstanding summons issued on July 22, was to protect a potential victim by providing a reason to arrest Olson if no other grounds existed. This warrant was not placed on the Canadian Police Information System computer. Instead, it was simply held by Surrey for execution should the need arise. (The summons, which was an order for Olson to appear in court on a certain date, did not give the police the power to arrest or detain Olson.)

JFO, like most other police units, was suffering from staff shortages. The JFO team assigned to Olson had to borrow personnel from other teams in order to mount an effective surveillance. It became operational during the noon hour. Olson was not located until about 4 p.m., when his car was seen near his apartment. No questionable activity by Olson was observed during the balance of the day. What the police didn't know was that he had already murdered a teenager earlier that day.

★ ★ ★

Surveillance of Olson finally started mid-morning on July 28. It had been five days since Howitt entered the loop and thirteen days since Forsythe undertook the mission of watching the suspect. As Olson drove to New Westminster that morning, it soon became apparent he would be difficult to surveille. He drove the way he lived his life, constantly breaking the rules, exceeding the speed limit, and driving in an erratic manner.

To add to the apprehension of the JFO team, hitchhiking was a popular way for young people to travel in 1981. There were literally dozens of youths hitching rides. Olson was constantly stopping and attempting to entice teenagers into his vehicle. Just after noon, surveillance was dropped as he detected he was being followed. During the time he was being watched, Olson picked up two people, one male and one female. Neither pickup was in Olson's car when the other was present, and no assault took place.

At about 1:30 p.m., RCMP Staff Sergeant Tom Charlton of JFO phoned Northorp to ask if they could have a spotter aircraft to assist in their surveillance. Bruce was unaware their discussion was academic. When Olson appeared to notice them, the JFO team had withdrawn from the field

"I can't supply an aircraft, as the only one I have is tied up with a Special 'O' team," he explained to Charlton. "If I give you the aircraft it means their personnel will be working with police officers they don't normally work with, reducing team effectiveness. There'll be difficulties with compatible radio frequencies, and lastly, to move the aircraft would leave Special 'O' teams without one." In other words, the equipment stayed with the unit.

"I'm prepared to give you a total Special 'O' team, which includes an aircraft," Bruce said. "I've already told Howitt that, and I can't understand why he opted for JFO when he could have my unit."

"No request for my Special 'O' unit was made then or later by either JFO or Burnaby," Bruce lamented. "To move an aircraft would simply be moving a problem. It may have solved one but would have created another."

Bruce later had a visit from Sergeant Ron Paull of the Special "I" (Technical) Section, who wanted to discuss the placement of a beeper (a tracking device frequently referred to as a birddog) on a car. He said he was inquiring on behalf of the Serious Crime Section, and it was in relation to Olson.

"No," Bruce told him. "We can't do a beeper. Our new policy prohibits it." This was part of the fallout of the McDonald Commission's inquiry into alleged wrongdoing by the RCMP. The feeling was that such an installation would be illegal, as it would involve a trespass (on the vehicle) and theft of electricity from the vehicle to power the device.

Two things arose from the conversation with Paull that were disturbing. "What is Serious Crime doing asking about a beeper?"

Bruce asked. "I thought this was a Burnaby case." Ron Paull did not have an answer.

Bruce was aware from his discussion with Howitt that Burnaby was actively investigating Olson. He remembered Howitt had gone to JFO for surveillance assistance. Now the Serious Crime Section was involved as well, inquiring about a beeper for Olson's vehicle. Bruce was well aware of the truth of the old adage: too many cooks spoil the broth.

"The other thing that bothered me," Bruce confided after the fact, "was why use a beeper when physical surveillance was being used? Was there a chance a suspected killer would be lost while a pickup was in his vehicle and they'd have to try and locate him by that means? A target lost or minutes lost might cost a life."

That evening JFO attempted, without success, to relocate Olson. Around 6 p.m., Ed Drozda contacted Tarr and asked him to confirm their meeting with Olson the following day. At 9:30 p.m., Tarr phoned Drozda to tell him the meeting had been moved up: he was meeting Olson in an hour at the Cariboo Hotel lounge. Olson was to bring along someone called Randy, from Mission, who would provide information on robberies. Drozda and Maile were to cover Tarr at the meeting. Drozda called Forsythe to ensure Olson would be under surveillance. Maile and Drozda were surprised to learn surveillance on Olson had only started the previous day. They had been at the July 15 meeting and had expected that the RCMP would have been watching the suspect since shortly after that date.

On their arrival, Maile and Drozda saw Larry Silzer, who was on the JFO team. About 10 p.m., Olson showed up accompanied by a young male. They walked to a nearby restaurant where Olson and Tarr had a discussion in the absence of the youth. Tarr talked about information concerning the Lower Mainland missing children cases.

"I'll be able to give you information that will make you a lieutenant," Olson said. "Pick a number between one and ten."

Tarr picked nine.

"I'll give you something relating to locations and you'll find something at each point," Olson said. "What you find will be your own business."

After further discussion about Olson's willingness to be an informant, he agreed to meet with Tarr the next morning, July 29. Tarr left, convinced Olson was the killer the RCMP was seeking.

Detective Tarr and the RCMP Serious Crime members made their way to the Delta police office. The JFO team watched as Olson and his associate drove to Whalley, where another male joined them. Almost at the stroke of midnight, the trio stopped in Surrey to pick up two young female hitchhikers.

Moving quickly, the JFO team stopped the vehicle. The girls, aged fifteen and sixteen, were in possession of beer. They claimed Olson had instructed one of the male occupants to give it to them. The two juvenile girls were interviewed and sent home in a taxi. Olson was arrested for contributing to juvenile delinquency. (The JFO officers did not tell Olson about the existence of the warrant. They didn't need it. They were able to arrest him on a charge involving the two girls he had picked up.)

The two male occupants were released after questioning. The first young man claimed to be an employee of Olson and gave the police a name later determined to be false. He was Randy Ludlow (a.k.a. Randy Cook). The other youth was just a casual pickup and had no relevance to the investigation.

Sergeant Fred Coombs, the JFO road supervisor, contacted Les Forsythe and filled him in on the evening's activities.

"Take Olson to the Surrey RCMP lockup," Les suggested. "Seize his vehicle and tow it to the Surrey Detachment garage for a forensic examination."

On his way to the lockup, Olson went through his now familiar routine of describing his role as an informant in the Gary Francis Marcoux murder trial. Of more interest was his offer to serve as an informant on two drug-related murders.

As the early morning hours passed, the phone lines were buzzing as members of the JFO team, the Serious Crime Section members at the Delta Police office, and Les Forsythe were in constant contact about Olson. The Serious Crime members wanted Olson and his vehicle to be released. They hoped Olson would keep his appointment with Tarr later in the morning. They were optimistic the pending meeting would uncover evidence that could result in murder charges against Olson.

This reasoning astounded Coombs, who was taking his direction from Les Forsythe in Burnaby. Coombs and Forsythe strongly opposed Olson's release. After several heated phone calls with Ed Drozda, Les Forsythe, much to his chagrin, finally agreed to Olson's release on the guarantee that he would be kept under constant surveillance after his morning meeting with Tarr. This proved to be the beginning of considerable animosity held by Les and Fred Coombs toward Fred Maile and Ed Drozda.

Drozda recalled it somewhat differently. Referring to his notes he said, "I was contacted by Larry Silzer [JFO]. Silzer told me Olson had been arrested after he picked up a couple of kids. He said they were investigating Olson for impaired driving, and after they checked him out he would be released. It didn't matter to us whether or not Olson was released, but we did want to see what he said at the meeting on the morning of the 29th. I don't remember talking with Les Forsythe."

Maile similarly recalled, "I received a telephone call from Dave McAree [JFO] who said they had Olson in custody for impaired driving. As far as I was concerned, JFO was calling the shots. I remember joking with McAree about having to cancel our meeting with Olson the next morning. He was going to get out anyway. If we couldn't hold him on the Squamish and Richmond sex charges, we sure couldn't hold him on an impaired driving charge. We laughed about him being out on the Squamish gun charges. He was going to get out. I even commented if he stayed in jail overnight, it was a good place for JFO to set up on him when he got out. I didn't talk to Forsythe and I didn't talk to Coombs. They may have talked to somebody, but it wasn't me."

Dave McAree does not remember speaking with Maile, but he said Olson had been arrested for contributing to juvenile delinquency and not impaired driving. He was also aware Forsythe and Coombs wanted to keep Olson in custody.

Dave McAree and fellow JFOer Ted Lucas lodged Olson in the Surrey cells. Lucas then joined Larry Silzer in the Surrey compound, where they searched and recorded the contents of Olson's vehicle and briefcase. McAree recalls seeing Olson's address book. It was their custom to record the contents of such items, but they had insufficient time to complete the task before Olson was released after 3:20 a.m.

★ ★ ★

Bruce drove west along Marine Drive from his home in suburban Burnaby to the RCMP HQ located in southwest Vancouver's Marpole district near the Fraser River. He had nothing more on his mind than navigating the heavy morning traffic. "I was blissfully ignorant of the events about to unfold," he reflected. "The stage was set for one of the most difficult assignments in my thirty-plus years of law enforcement."

At 9 a.m., Sergeant Fred Coombs, the road supervisor, briefed JFO managers. Unhappy with the overnight developments, they decided to terminate their surveillance of Olson. Olson's early morning release alarmed them. If Olson was as dangerous as some believed, they felt they could not condone a situation where they could not take immediate action if Olson enticed a young person into his vehicle. They were worried that Olson might elude surveillance with disastrous consequences. Burnaby and the Serious Crime Section were told of their decision.

The JFO decision demonstrated that with actual road experience, they had come to realize what Bruce Northorp had seen on July 23 when he insisted on a tail car. He was not creating roadblocks. He was simply proceeding with an abundance of caution.

In Burnaby, Forsythe felt he had been abandoned. He was desperate for assistance to cover Olson's movements. JFO did agree, if requested, to assist by covering Olson's meeting with Tarr, which was slated to take place between 11 and 11:30 a.m. Serious Crime investigators decided they would not require assistance to cover the scheduled meet.

Another day was starting for Staff Sergeant Arnie Nylund, the acting officer in charge of General Investigations at the Vancouver headquarters. Unlike Bruce, he was well aware of the activities of his Serious Crime Section and Burnaby Detachment members. Nylund was a quiet, unassuming, but highly qualified and well-posted investigator. He didn't enjoy dealing with the media, but this certainly did not detract from his top-notch investigative credentials.

It was likely Northorp's role as senior media liaison officer that brought Nylund to his office at 9:30 a.m. Bruce's 1981 notes outline the content of the meeting with Nylund.

> *29/7/81 9.35 a.m. Arnie NYLUND to office re missing*
> *young people - discussed:*
> ① *Media aspect*
> ② *Suspect OLSEN & coverage aspect*
> *plus speaking to him with Delta*
> ③ *Incidents*
> *1/Agassiz - girl's body found*
> *2/ Coquit miss boy - body found in Mission*
> *3/ NWPD - miss boy*
> *4/ Surrey - "   "*
> *5/ Bby -   "   girl*
> *6/ Yale -   "   girl*
> *7/ Langley - miss girl*

Nylund told Bruce he had been contacted by the media about missing young people and he wondered how he should respond to their questions.

"I never gave advice or direction without satisfying myself as to what the situation or problem was," Bruce said. "I told him he better give me some more details."

"There's a boy who went missing from Coquitlam who was found murdered in Mission," Arnie elaborated. "And a girl who's just been found murdered in Agassiz. There are five other missing young people and we think they've met with foul play. There's a suspect named Olson and there's been some surveillance on him. A Delta Police officer met with him yesterday. He might be able to provide information pertaining to bodies and we plan to have members of the Serious Crime Section introduced to him."

The manner in which Nylund laid out the facts was a real eye-opener for Northorp. "The phone call I had from Howitt just days before didn't resemble Nylund's layout. Howitt said nothing to trigger any alarm bells in my mind. There were only three new factors since I talked to Howitt: a boy missing from New

29/7/81 9.35 AM
Annie NYGUND & Steve re
missing young people —
disorder
① Media aspect
② Suspect OLSEN &
coverage aspect plus
speaking to him Oweth
~~DELTA.~~

③ Incidents
  1 Agassiz — girls body found
  2 Coquit miss boy — body
          found in Mission
  3 NWPD — miss boy
  4 Surrey —   —
  5 Bby   —   — girl
  6 Yale —   — girl

1 Langley — miss girl

Daily documentation of key events is a common part of efficient policework. Some colleagues felt Northorp took the practice to new heights. At this point he still did not know the spelling of the suspect's name.

Westminster, a girl's body being found in Agassiz, and the meeting with the Delta Police officer." Northorp had no problem grasping the gravity of the situation as explained by Nylund.

To this day, Bruce has no recollection of how he answered the media question. "It was totally overshadowed by a major issue that demanded prompt attention," he said. "I took a worst case scenario approach. There were at least ten police units involved, under mainly separate commands. What should be done, presuming there was a connection between two murders and five missing person cases, which might be homicides?

"I saw the need for co-ordination," Northorp recalled. "Neill was away, but I intended to discuss the matter with him first thing the next day. Clearly someone had to be in charge, calling the shots."

★ ★ ★

About the same time Northorp and Nylund had their discussion, Ed Drozda met with Dennis Tarr at the Delta police office. At Drozda's behest, Tarr phoned Olson to confirm the meeting scheduled for that morning. Olson said he wanted to put it off until the following morning. Tarr accepted the delay but suggested that he would like to bring along a couple of RCMP investigators.

"Sure," Olson replied. "I don't mind meeting the RCMP." He didn't bother to say that he had been their guest in a Surrey lockup most of the night.

Maile and Drozda contacted their office and were told the body found at Agassiz on July 25 was Judy Kozma. They went to the New Westminster Police office to get further information.

During the evening, Olson, freed earlier that day at the Serious Crime Section's insistence, plied his young friend Randy Cook with drinks at the Cariboo Hotel lounge. For the second night in a row there was no active surveillance in place.

★ ★ ★

Detective Tarr attended his early morning meeting with Olson at a hotel on the Surrey/Delta border. Drozda and Maile covered him.

After some discussion they moved to a nearby White Spot restaurant where they met Maile and Drozda. To ensure no information was forgotten, they were equipped with a hidden recording device. After introductions, the matter of rewards was raised.

The following was recorded at the meeting and entered in evidence at a 1984 civil trial.

Maile: "Well the way we work is, ah, naturally on all these murders there, first off, there's rewards."

Olson: "Right."

Maile: "We're interested in quite a few homicides. And the rewards can go anywhere from $5,000 and one's over $100,000."

Olson: "Yeah, there's some girl on Vancouver Island."

Maile: "We're prepared to pay for whatever you're able to tell us."

Maile questioned Olson about the location of bodies. Drozda's notes show Olson wanted to go on the payroll but he did not want to go to court to give evidence. Maile told Olson they did not simply want to know who was responsible for the murders; they wanted physical evidence as well. Olson said he knew who was responsible, but now he indicated he had been talking about drugs not bodies. By the end of the meeting, Olson was saying he would check around but made no guarantees.

★ ★ ★

At the same time, Nylund was telling Bruce that some members of the Serious Crime Section planned to meet Olson in the company of a Delta Police officer.

"Ensure all dealings with Olson are recorded," Bruce instructed, but then, when Nylund made a comment regarding a warrant for Olson's arrest, he became more concerned. "What the hell are we doing meeting with him when there's a warrant for his arrest?"

"I'm not sure there is," Nylund replied, "but I'll check it out."

"Make sure they don't meet him if there's a warrant," Bruce said.

"Don't worry," Nylund responded. "I'll take care of it."

Both Northorp and Nylund were unaware this meeting was already underway.

When Maile and Drozda returned to the office for a briefing, they learned there was a warrant at Surrey for Olson's arrest. Nylund informed them the warrant had to be cleared up. Drozda telephoned Tarr to arrange for Olson to turn himself in at Surrey.

★ ★ ★

After speaking with Nylund, Bruce raised the issue with Neill, describing the various Olson inquiries he was aware of and relating his brief conversation with Howitt.

"We'll make Burnaby responsible," Neill said initially.

"I wouldn't recommend that," Bruce countered. "I'd suggest it be handled from here, but you should hear Nylund first." Bruce was not satisfied he had enough grasp to explain all that was going on and allow his boss to make an informed decision.

They couldn't arrange a meeting with Nylund until after lunch, so it wasn't until just before two o'clock that Neill heard Nylund's outline. Then he wanted Burnaby's side of the story. "I'll phone Norm Fuchs," he said.

Fuchs was OIC Burnaby Detachment. Bruce sensed from Neill's questions and comments that his idea to have Burnaby head all of the investigations pertaining to Olson had changed. Nylund and Bruce were present for the conference call with Fuchs. Neill gave him a brief rundown on the cases as they had been outlined to him. Fuchs was certainly aware of the Ada Court investigation, but he had limited personal knowledge of the other cases.

"The Lower Mainland HQ is going to assume responsibility for case direction," Neill said, then pointed at Northorp. "You are in charge."

Bruce's jaw dropped. The appointment came as a total surprise. "I'd neither expected nor recommended it," he reflected.

Neill then gestured toward Nylund and ordered, "Serious Crime Section will assume responsibility for any dealings with Olson."

★ ★ ★

Vancouver RCMP headquarters had taken the unusual action of assuming direct control of these cases. At times, the reason for a decision is not communicated clearly, and the more times the message passes through the chain of command, the more vague it becomes. When Les Forsythe finally heard the news, he was incensed. He was now mentally exhausted and totally disgusted with this turn of events. He had done his best to mount an effective offensive against Olson. Like Darryll Kettles, Forsythe had persevered despite overwhelming difficulties, considerable opposition, and lack of support, only to have the Ada Court case rudely snatched from his hands.

Maple Ridge police were told that Louise Chartrand had been abducted while hitchhiking to work along Dewdney Trunk Road about 7 p.m. on July 30, 1981. This was less than two days after Clifford Olson had been released from custody following a heated strategy debate between RCMP investigators over that release.

The corporal mistakenly believed that Northorp, as the OIC Support Services, had been fully briefed on Olson after the July 15 meeting. Now the investigation was moving into high gear and Les, who did not agree with certain tactics used to date, found himself excluded. He began to distance himself from the Serious Crime Section and the RCMP's Vancouver headquarters.

When Northorp later suggested that Les become part of the Olson task force, he was unaware of Forsythe's frustrations. Sick and despondent over his treatment, Forsythe took three weeks leave. Prior to his departure he suggested Constable Brian Wornstaff act as Burnaby's delegate.

★ ★ ★

While the RCMP was sorting out its internal matters, new forces of evil were at work. Before dusk, amid the long shadows of a summer evening, Louise Chartrand, a seventeen-year-old from Maple Ridge, vanished. She was last seen after dinner, hitchhiking to her place of employment. Chartrand never arrived at work. Her sister reported her disappearance to the Maple Ridge RCMP within hours.

Five
Bruce Is In Charge

Co-ordination

Co-ordination involves the pursuit of order and the goal of harmony. In the case of co-ordinated law enforcement it means sharing information and synchronizing police activity across a range of jurisdictions.

In British Columbia's Lower Mainland, the concept manifested itself through a body called the Co-ordinated Law Enforcement Unit (CLEU). Representatives of municipal police forces and the RCMP in its broad capacities as urban, provincial, and federal police belonged to this group. They helped the Vancouver Police Department interact with surrounding communities in cases of common interest. However, this body seldom had anything to do with cases strictly under RCMP jurisdictions. If RCMP detachments alone needed co-ordination, it was believed headquarters would handle it.

Recognizing the need for co-ordination was not always an easy task. Such was the case in matters surrounding Clifford Olson.

Friday July 31, 1981

A large group of investigators assembled at the Vancouver RCMP headquarters. "Investigators briefed me on two murders and five missing children cases," said Northorp, who chaired the meeting. "The names of at least three suspects were raised, Olson being one of them."

Northorp pondered the feasibility of having Olson dealt with as a dangerous sex offender in the event nothing could be found to implicate him in either of the two murders. He then made it clear that any resource of the RCMP in the district was available.

"The matter of surveillance was covered," Bruce added. "I approved it immediately. Some conditions, to safeguard innocents who might be picked up, were to be drafted by the Serious Crime Section based on my verbal guidelines."

The meeting covered the murders of Daryn Johnsrude and Judy Kozma. There was also the disappearance of Raymond King from New Westminster on July 23. Earlier, Simon Partington of Surrey went missing on July 2. Ada Court vanished between Coquitlam and Burnaby on June 21. On May 19, Sandra Wolfsteiner of Langley dropped from sight, and Verna Bjerky of Yale was last seen on May 2. Most of these children had been promptly reported missing to the various police forces. (Bruce now realizes that Les Forsythe, in late June and early July, developed much of the pertinent information presented, although that credit was not voiced at the gathering.)

Bruce made few notes at this meeting, instead concentrating fully on what was said. "I had two stenos taking minutes," he recalled.

There was no hard evidence to show Olson was the killer. The fact that he had approved surveillance did not mean Northorp had decided Olson was responsible for either murder or any other case. He saw it as an attempt to implicate or eliminate him. "Subsequent actions, and steps taken by the police, clearly show such was the case," Bruce emphasized. All bases were covered. Moves were taken to warn the public, develop other suspects, and compile data by the use of computers.

"The media were aware of the meeting," Bruce said. "It was a major story and newspapers, radio, and TV were all awaiting a response." The RCMP issued a printed release outlining the cases under consideration: the two murders and the five missing children who were felt to be the victims of some criminal acts.

The release stated:

> Despite a co-ordinated investigation there was no evidence to indicate a common thread and it would be sheer conjecture to assume the same person was involved in the cases.

It also carried a warning.

> Children should be wary of any contact by strangers.

"Later," Bruce remembered, "the media made much of the point that I wouldn't admit the cases were connected. Obviously, I felt they were, including Verna Bjerky. However, we had no evidence, which is what we had to go by." It turned out the Bjerky case was not connected.

Dealing with the news media in the following days became a major undertaking. Although they had no direct bearing on solving the cases, reporters were informing the public of the dangers, and they distributed police requests for information.

A key issue of the meeting was surveillance. Quickly said, it sounds simple, but in this case it had to be discreet enough that Olson couldn't detect or suspect it or the exercise would be futile. In other words, it had to be a little on the loose side, but it could not chance the loss of life. The police had to ensure no bystander was injured or killed—even if it meant evidence of a major crime was not secured or the target, Olson, because of some necessary police action, was alerted to the fact he was under surveillance. Investigators would have to accompany the surveillance team to keep informed and, more importantly, to make any necessary case decisions. In order to keep surveillance units in the background, it was essential to have a regular detective car following as a tail-end Charlie, ready to move in if some overt police action was required.

Bruce put it in perspective. "Consider a gang of robbers, armed with weapons, planning a major robbery or, as in this situation, a person suspected of perpetrating a murder. Here you have the added complication of not knowing when he might commit it or who the intended victim might be."

A month after the May 19 disappearance of Sandra Wolfsteiner (left) in Surrey, an ex-landlady was certain she talked to Sandra at Guilford Shopping Centre. Verna Bjerky (right) went missing about the same time as Daryn Johnsrude disappeared in early May.

"Those were the main considerations," said Northorp. "I had to develop a contingency plan for every possible eventuality. The public would have to be safeguarded, and the interests of the members assigned to surveillance protected. Police members should not be placed in impossible positions and left holding the bag if something goes awry." In this case, the buck would stop with Northorp. "I simply knew surveillance was necessary, and I did everything humanly possible to ensure innocents were not harmed. If it backfired, I knew there'd be a lot of armchair quarterbacks to fault my lack of foresight."

About 4 p.m., Bruce signed a directive approving the surveillance with guidelines he had verbally dictated. By 8 p.m. Special "O" was actively seeking Olson's location.

To the surprise of all, Olson had left for Alberta that day with his wife and infant child. He had not made his plans known to Tarr or Maile.

July 31 was a Friday and the beginning of a holiday weekend, but it was no holiday for those who were to become part of the task force. It did, however, give Bruce time to think.

Nylund was Northorp's command link to Serious Crime, so it was left to Arnie to directly oversee the investigation until Larry Proke returned from leave. Nylund named Fred Maile the chief investigator.

Monday August 3, 1981

It was the last day of the long weekend, and any hope for some quiet family time was short-lived. Bruce phoned Nylund at home and asked him to contact District Two with respect to a fifteen-year-old girl missing at Duncan.

Coincidentally, Nylund had just heard from Maile. "Some clothing has been found near Whistler," Nylund told Northorp. "It apparently belongs to Louise Chartrand."

"Keep me posted," Bruce instructed.

Corporal Maile phoned Bruce before supper. "The clothes found near Whistler are identical in size and description with those worn by Louise Chartrand," he reported.

Maile's description of the condition of the clothes left little hope that the girl was alive. He also reported that police divers would search a nearby lake. It was shocking to think the teenager may have been abducted from Maple Ridge and murdered miles away in Whistler.

In the quiet of home, Bruce looked ahead. He had signed the initial surveillance directive, but he now felt it should be more complete. "I wrote out what became a two-page typed document," he said. "It set out the area and hours of operation."

The myth that surveillance is conducted by a couple of men or women in shabby overcoats is just that. Without disclosing strategies, a more likely number would be ten undercover officers using nondescript vehicles. In most cases an aircraft assists the ground units.

In the Olson case, Northorp had to resolve how far afield the suspect would be tailed. The assigned officers would need to know whether they might require personal effects for overnight trips. For instance, Olson might try to travel to the U.S. In that case, a plan was developed whereby Olson would be thwarted, without becoming aware that he was being watched. The final directive (see Appendix IV) outlined several situations that might arise and when the situation would have to be considered critical. Essentially, the directive was to ensure no one would be placed in jeopardy.

"At the outset," said Bruce, "when Olson wasn't in town, the coverage was two shifts, seven days a week, restricted to the Lower

Mainland. When he returned, it was altered to 24 hours a day, seven days a week, anywhere in B.C. This involved what could be considered to be a small police agency. The numbers were staggering. The logistics in moving from the Greater Vancouver area, if required, were formidable."

Another dilemma faced Bruce. Clifford Olson and his family had disappeared, and a surveillance team could not make itself visible to help determine his whereabouts. Northorp decided that an all-points bulletin (APB) was unwise. Word of such a bulletin could easily leak to the media. Based on experience, Bruce noted that "the further afield you go, the greater chance there is for your case going sour." An APB could do more damage than good. Patience was a better option.

Bruce further noted that they knew from the empty apartment that Olson was with his family.

At this stage of the investigation, Bruce could not afford the luxury of presuming Olson was their man. Accordingly, he had to ensure that all of the police resources in the province knew firsthand just what the position was in Vancouver. He did not want them to rely on the bits and pieces they might hear through various news outlets.

Tuesday August 4, 1981

When Bruce arrived in the office following the holiday, he had his handwritten notes typed up into messages. The first was directed to all police departments and RCMP units in B.C. and contained a media release. It requested that the Serious Crime Section be advised if any information was received as a result of media saturation.

The media release was directed to all major news outlets in B.C. by way of a commercial news service. The message advised that the RCMP and the New Westminster Police were seeking public assistance in the cases of Johnsrude, Bjerky, Wolfsteiner, Court, Partington, Kozma, King, and Chartrand. Brief details of each case were included. It also warned that the person or persons responsible might attempt to pick up other children and solicited public co-operation.

It was important media releases be accurate for the benefit of all concerned. Locally, this massive investigation became the main news story. Days later it made the headlines nationwide. Northorp found it frustrating to read that the RCMP had been treating the disappearance of Judy Kozma as a routine missing persons case. "Judy's case wasn't our responsibility," Bruce exclaimed. "It was that of the New Westminster Police. She had been missing for weeks before her body was found in Agassiz and her case became an RCMP responsibility."

Early on August 4, Northorp had a lengthy phone call with Inspector Ed Cadenhead of the New Westminster Police Force. "I wanted to ensure he was fully aware of the approach being taken," he explained.

New Westminster Police had an interest in the King and Kozma cases. King had not been located. It was essential that each force was aware of what the other was doing.

Northorp had to apologize to Cadenhead just two days later when a member of the Serious Crime Section failed to notify the New Westminster Police that Raymond King's body was found. "That failure had no impact on the investigations. However, it did little to show we were sharing information," Northorp recalled. "King's body was in the same general area where Kozma's body was found in late July."

There was still no sign of Olson. The balance of Bruce's day was spent dealing with the media and myriad other problems that needed to be resolved. He set a meeting for the next day for all commanders or deputies of units that had cases related to the co-ordinated investigation. The Vancouver Police Department was also invited, though it had no related cases. Bruce felt it would be ludicrous to have the VPD unaware of matters that could conceivably affect it.

Inspector Larry Proke, back from annual leave, stepped into the maelstrom when he arrived on transfer from Burnaby to take up the headquarters position of OIC General Investigations. He replaced Arnie Nylund (Nylund had been wearing two hats, acting OIC General Investigations in addition to his full-time role as NCO/i/c Serious Crime Section) as Northorp's contact with the Serious

Crime Section. Proke's service record was impressive. He had been a detective at the RCMP's New Westminster Sub-Division and Coquitlam Detachment prior to his start in Burnaby. He had expertise as a polygraphist and in interrogational techniques.

Wednesday August 5, 1981

Exactly three weeks after Les Forsythe gathered a group of police investigators in Burnaby, Bruce Northorp repeated the process at Vancouver headquarters. Proke and Maile were among the few who had attended both meetings.

Northorp explained his strategy and set out to establish operational priorities. Subjects covered included the use of computers to process information, the communication requirements, and the need for special patrols.

Patrols were set for key areas where persons had gone missing and where bodies had been found. The patrol schedules were based on known times of previous activity. Patrollers were to be on the lookout for a lone male suspect and potential pickups, young males or females. They hoped these strategies would turn up a suspect. In addition, they would act as a preventive measure

All patrols were to check hitchhikers and warn them of a potential danger. The patrols would submit check sheets to the HQ on all persons stopped, whether they were hitchhikers or suspicious persons. All units were to submit copies of any complaint that was sex-related.

Each detachment reviewed its outstanding local missing persons files for 1981 to determine if any might be a case of foul play. Within days the Surrey RCMP produced the names of two girls who had been reported missing. Foul play was not suspected, and a Surrey NCO refused to compromise his stance that the girls were runaways. Northorp disagreed.

"I overrode his opinion on August 19," Bruce remembered, "when I announced to the media that we had added Colleen Daignault and Terri Lynn Carson to the list of cases we were looking at." Colleen was reported missing on April 21, though she was last seen on the 15th. Terri Lynn was last seen on July 27 and reported missing the next day.

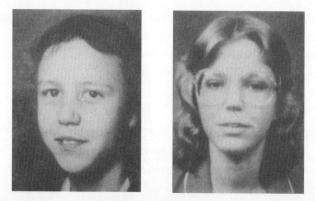

Surrey teen Colleen Daignault (left), a 5'1", 100-pound thirteen-year-old was last seen on April 15, one week after rape charges were stayed against Olson and he was released from custody.

Terri Lynn Carson (right) went to Surrey's Guilford Shopping Centre 3-1/2 months later, on July 27, and disappeared. That was the day Bruce Northorp's priorities had been redefined by his bosses and the Department of Indian Affairs because of a sit-in. In Burnaby, Les Forsythe was still pleading for surveillance support.

After the August 5 meeting, Bruce prepared reference notes for the inevitable deluge of media queries he knew would follow the meeting. "I believe all police agencies in the Lower Mainland are alert to the situation and are prepared to do everything possible to solve the cases and concurrently take preventive measures," he announced. "We have concern and suggest the general public should also have concern, not panic. With co-operation from the public I believe we can identify the person or persons responsible for the homicides and disappearances."

By this time the media focus on the investigations was gaining momentum. It was Bruce's custom to handle media contacts on a one-on-one basis, mainly by phone. This became impossible as it was taking too much time from his primary function. "Eventually, I had to adopt a procedure I'd never done before," Bruce said. "I held media briefings once a day or more as required. I was unable to take phone calls. Out-of-town media were told they would have to liaise with local media outlets to get information."

To relieve the pressure, official releases were transmitted to a commercial news service that sent them to every major media outlet in B.C. This eased the strain on senior personnel.

Thursday August 6, 1981

"The 6th was a momentous day," Bruce declared. "It was the beginning of the events that have probably taken Olson off the streets of Canada for the rest of his life." It was also the beginning of several days of methodical police work.

The surveillance team reported it had located Olson and went into high gear. Surveillance was increased to 24-hour coverage provincewide. There was still no evidence to connect Olson to any homicide or missing child.

"Never once did any subordinate suggest we re-establish contact with Olson," Northorp remembered. "Certainly I never considered such a strategy. As far as I was concerned, Olson was a suspect, not a source." It seemed the Serious Crime Section had finally come to the same conclusion.

August 7 to 11, 1981

The Lower Mainland District HQ was not operating in a vacuum. Bruce kept the commanding officer of the British Columbia RCMP at Victoria informed, as well as the many police agencies throughout the Lower Mainland.

Northorp felt Ottawa should also be informed of what was transpiring in B.C. He sent a lengthy message to national headquarters giving brief details of the cases and the strategies being used. Bruce knew that if he were sitting in Ottawa, he would not like to get information on a major investigation through the news media. The national coverage was extensive and not unlike that given the Yorkshire Ripper case in Great Britain and the killings of young blacks in Atlanta, Georgia. Some members of the media were beginning to compare the local situation to those cases.

"I felt all bases had been covered," said Bruce, "but I requested RCMP HQ in Ottawa make contact with British and U.S. agencies outlining the steps being taken here to determine if anything had been overlooked. About three days later Proke announced to the media that this request had been made." Some of the questions fired at Proke and Northorp implied that the local police were incompetent. "The media never did learn the replies we eventually received did not provide any new avenue of investigation or strategy which could be applied in the B.C. cases. We'd covered every conceivable base."

Over the next few days police received hundreds of tips, all of which had to be checked wherever possible. Many sex offenders were questioned. None of these efforts produced a thing. In one case a polygraph examination was arranged for an acquaintance of a missing child. In another, hypnosis was arranged for a possible witness in an attempt to gain a viable lead.

Bruce learned, through the media, that a spokesman for one or more of the families involved was less than happy with the progress of the police investigation. "The man reportedly said the RCMP weren't doing enough," Bruce related. "He had a host of fantastic ideas. He wanted the army brought in to search and supposedly he'd hired three private detectives to work on the cases. He made a comment to the effect that federal RCMP resources should be assigned to the investigation. He reportedly told the media the killer probably drives a van and likes to make his deadly pickups on Thursdays. He was a colossal irritant.

"Bringing the army in was ludicrous," Northorp declared. "The only useful thing he did was bring the missing children to the public's attention through a massive poster campaign which included photos of Ada Court, Raymond King, and Simon Partington." At the same time, however, it was dangerous to suggest people watch for one style of vehicle or one day of the week. The spokesman was, in effect, telling the public not to worry about anything but vans and Thursdays. Of the ten homicides in 1981, five victims were picked up on Thursdays. In the other cases, every day of the week was involved except Wednesday. The hours of pickup ranged from 10:30 a.m. to 6:40 p.m., and Olson never used a van.

The vocal critic grabbed the attention of the RCMP at Ottawa. On August 10 Vancouver HQ received a message indicating the national office had heard or read the reports criticizing the RCMP. Ottawa wanted to know if a commissioned officer had been assigned to the cases and if contact had been established with the parents and their spokesperson.

"I was taken aback," Bruce said. "I felt Ottawa should have had more confidence in the District and, failing that, a quick phone call would have sufficed." Had they not read the message Northorp sent three days earlier? "Of course contact was being maintained with the parents." There was no contact with the spokesman, nor was any planned.

Northorp surveyed RCMP units and was unable to pinpoint specific dissatisfaction emanating from any of the children's families. To his knowledge, the spokesman never made contact with the RCMP to determine any facts. This was just another time-consuming distraction from the main objective. The last thing Northorp needed was somebody in Ottawa second-guessing him. The only thing he ever said to address this spokesman's remarks was an indirect comment to the media to the effect that the RCMP was doing everything humanly possible to solve these cases and to prevent others from occurring.

Olson was under surveillance and he was on the prowl. Bruce described one incident that clearly supported his surveillance strategy. "On the 7th, the surveillance team was certain they protected a thirteen-year-old girl walking on a street in the Marpole area of Vancouver. It was obvious he had his sights on her. A tail-end Charlie scooped her off the street and took her to the safety of a nearby fire hall. I never did hear if the girl or her parents were aware of the close call she may have had with a killer. I had enough to do without pursuing what didn't transpire."

The same day, Olson followed an attractive young woman on foot until she eluded him. She was a police officer working his surveillance. This was a factor Bruce hadn't considered, and he issued new instructions. "Female officers were not to get into a car with Olson if he approached them." They would avoid conversation with him, because the goal was to follow Olson, not to engage in anything that might be construed as entrapment. It was also possible an officer might be taken by surprise and be wounded or killed. The potential problems were just too great. The police had enough to deal with without becoming embroiled in a serious side issue that could be avoided.

In one incident Olson entered a senior citizens' home in Burnaby and stole a large sum of money from a room. It was just four blocks away from Northorp's own home. On the 11th he went into a residence in Vancouver while the occupants were in their garden, and stole a small sum of money. Later the same day he went to another home in Vancouver claiming to be a builder looking for work. He distracted the elderly resident and managed to steal some money.

To the obvious question—Why wouldn't the police arrest Olson when he was observed committing the crimes?—Northorp explained that, from discreet surveillance, the police would not know if he had a legal purpose in being at or near any of the premises. It was only after he left that police were able to determine if a crime had taken place. Inquiries, made immediately after Olson left the various premises, revealed the occupants, most of whom were elderly, had not been harmed. He had entered either by stealth or subterfuge. It is pointless now to consider if there would have been sufficient evidence to convict him of any of these crimes.

Wednesday August 12, 1981

From August 6 to 11 the RCMP failed to implicate or eliminate Olson as a suspect in any of the missing/murdered children cases.

"We weren't surprised to confirm his actions in relation to picking up young people," Bruce said. "That was one factor that brought him forward as a suspect. It was noted no children who fit the pattern of those under investigation had been reported missing. That was at least something positive."

Fortunately, police didn't have to wrestle with the thought of Olson entering private premises for any length of time. "Shortly after 8:30 a.m. I was told he was headed to Vancouver Island via a BC Ferry. Although the authority to travel provincewide had been granted earlier, this was a minor complication. He was travelling into another RCMP jurisdiction, District Two."

Victoria HQ was advised and told that the police unit following him were at their disposal. In the event of any crime being committed in District Two, based on jurisdiction, it would be up to Victoria to make decisions. Northorp awaited further developments.

"I had no idea this would be the day when the big break would come," declared Bruce, "nor did Olson have any idea this would be his last day as a free man."

Mid-afternoon there was an update. Olson was thought to have committed two burglaries in a Victoria suburb, after which he drove north on Vancouver Island. Near Nanaimo he picked up two young female hitchhikers. That was the last word Northorp received until much later.

The trio continued north, past Nanaimo, and eventually turned west, driving through Port Alberni toward the west coast of the Island. The road was a winding stretch of two-lane blacktop, and surveillance managed to stay in touch. Olson pulled off the road in a bush area near Tofino. He and his passengers were drinking, and one of the women got out of the car. The surveillance team was right on top of him, so close they could hear conversations. The situation had all the earmarks of disaster and required intervention.

The surveillance team moved in. Olson tried to speed away but was blocked by a police vehicle and was arrested at gunpoint. The charge, impaired driving.

Olson must have been in a state of shock when a small army of police officers descended upon him. He was taken to the Ucluelet RCMP office and locked up. His rental car was seized and searched. An address book was found. One name and address, among scores of others, stood out: Judy Kozma's. It was the first real link between Olson and one of the murdered children.

After receiving reports from the field, Proke phoned Northorp at home that evening to update him on the arrest and suggest a course of action. "We have an address book from his car and Judy Kozma's name and phone number are in it," he said. "We're going to photocopy it and put the original back. Olson will be in court tomorrow on impaired driving, and his release on bail won't be opposed. After his release we'll continue the surveillance."

Alarm bells went off in Northorp's head. He couldn't understand this rationale and instinctively vetoed the release plan. "No, we'll have to talk about it," he directed.

"After I hung up, I gave the issue further thought," mused Bruce. "Olson hadn't met with any RCMP investigator since he left for Alberta without notifying anyone. I had the feeling that if he were involved in the murders, he was simply buying time in an attempt to figure out a scheme to provide body locations without incriminating himself." Considering Olson's background, Bruce wondered if he was attempting to manipulate the police. He also couldn't forget the fact that Olson had been released in Surrey without anything being accomplished. "I knew my decision about holding Olson would be both critical and controversial. I wanted some moral support. I may be wrong, but I detected a lack of support on my direction from below," Bruce recalled.

Many things were difficult in the Olson case. Bruce ran into a roadblock when he tried to phone his boss at home. Chief Superintendent Neill's phone was out of order. Northorp contacted the Delta Police and they sent a car to Neill's home to make contact. When Neill phoned, Bruce asked if he would meet him at the office.

Northorp and Neill discussed the developments and reached a decision before any other personnel arrived. Northorp told Neill, "Olson will have to be questioned in relation to the murder of Judy Kozma at some point, and the sooner the better. As time passes it'll be harder to pin him down on specifics. As for other potential but unknown witnesses, their memories will be fading with every passing day." They agreed that Olson would be held on any charge or charges available and that he would be questioned about the murder of Judy Kozma. He would not be released.

When Proke and members of the Serious Crime Section met at the HQ to discuss the issue, "there was no argument regarding the course of action put forward by Neill and myself," Bruce recalled. "Olson would be held and questioned in relation to Judy's name being in his address book." Local investigators spent almost two hours talking to their counterparts on the Island, writing down every name in Olson's address book. The meeting ended and it was well after midnight before Bruce returned home.

Northorp's notes included the analysis he presented to Neill:

1. *In view of Olson's crime activities of theft and break, enter and theft, there was a potential danger to innocent persons when he entered premises.*
2. *The surveillance was developing neither leads nor evidence.*

3. *Olson had not gone to any obvious crime scene, nor to any location where the effects of missing or murdered children were found, nor to any location where anyone was being held prisoner.*

4. *Olson was under surveillance by JFO on July 28th and they had burned him when he was subjected to a dramatic arrest later at Surrey by a team of detectives. Now he had been arrested at gunpoint in an isolated locale when he had no awareness he was under surveillance. If released he'd be totally paranoid. Even if no surveillance were on him he would see imagined police officers at every turn. It was highly improbable he would engage in any unlawful activity in that state of mind. Hence, what was the purpose in further surveillance?*

5. *The investigators may have again wanted Olson free so they could approach him as a source, yet they were convinced he was the killer or at least a prime suspect. To that point Olson had only hinted at some knowledge, there was no hard evidence to connect him to any crime. Now there was a direct link to one of the murder victims. It was time to handle him as a suspect, not a source.*

6. *The final point was evidence. A photocopy of the address book would be second-best evidence. The actual book might be disposed of by Olson if it were returned to his vehicle and he suspected the police had examined it or had some interest in it.*

Had he been aware of it, Northorp could have added one more reason for holding Olson. The fact that he had changed his original story, from claiming to have knowledge of body locations to claiming he had been referring to narcotics, was another factor that reflected negatively on the situation. Although the prime investigators were aware of this, Bruce had not been informed. He was, therefore, unable to include this in his analysis at that time.

"It appeared to me the men were just too close to the issues or so tired they failed to analyze their proposal and plot their future course logically," he said.

Bruce never regretted his veto of the plan to release Olson, nor did he forget the tendency to treat Olson as a source of information. In the Green River serial murders, which occurred a short time later in Seattle, it turned out that the police had treated a source as a suspect. This was not at all helpful to the police investigations. It is vital that the status of each subject be determined and dealt with appropriately to avoid errors.

At the time, Northorp did not contemplate what might have happened to the two young women at Tofino if Olson had not been under surveillance. It was not an issue. With many years' hindsight, however, after considering all Olson's known activities, he declared, "I'm convinced, had we not intervened or been present, it would have been a first for Olson. He would have killed two persons in one incident."

"The surveillance unit did their job well," said Bruce. "Once located, Olson was worked continuously for seven days. They only lost him once, for about fifteen minutes." Placing surveillance on a potential killer was a tough decision, but with the conditions laid on at the outset, it worked. Olson never once tumbled to the fact the teams were on him. In addition, they developed criminal charges against him as they were tailing him. It was the Special "O" team's actions that led to the final arrest in Olson's criminal career and set the stage for the events that followed.

It is significant to note that the appearance of Judy Kozma's name in Olson's address book influenced Northorp's decision. He might have been less decisive had he known Judy's name was in the book when Darryll Kettles first copied it on May 26. (Darryll later regretted that he did not make two copies of the book. In retrospect, he said he would have studied the book in detail, and considering how events unfolded, he would have made the connection to Judy much earlier. As it was, Darryll gave the one copy he made to the Mission investigators, where it languished in a file.)

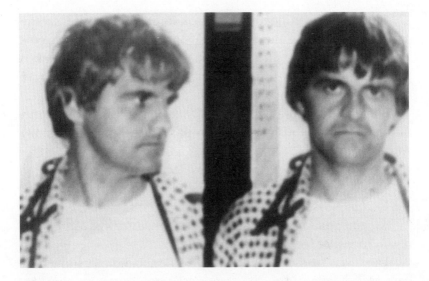

Before being exposed as a monster, Olson exhibited a capacity to charm or con his way through life. Even after his August 1981 arrest, his handling of events was unpredictable. He ended up a spider caught in his own web.

August 13 to 17, 1981

With Olson in custody, it was time to involve Crown Counsel. The murders and suspected murders were in various jurisdictions, but it seemed logical they be handled by one person. B.C.'s Ministry of the Attorney General appointed John Hall to act as special prosecutor.

Bruce had met Hall in connection with a commercial crime case and was impressed with his work. The prosecutor was highly regarded in police circles, and Bruce was delighted he had joined the investigation.

The next step was to have Olson charged with the two burglary offences he committed while being tailed. He was flown to the Lower Mainland on August 13 and held at the Burnaby RCMP detachment.

In the afternoon Bruce made an announcement to the media, informing them that the RCMP had arrested a suspect in the murder of Judy Kozma. "I refused to elaborate," he remembered, "as it could seriously prejudice a prosecution later. I made no connection to the upcoming matter in Burnaby and did not give the sex or age of the suspect."

Bruce had been heading the task force for two weeks. "The pressure was intense," he confirmed. "One of my greatest concerns was for the public and the safety of their children. Parents had taken the police warnings seriously. Streets and playgrounds were strangely empty of children."

Bruce was encouraged by an editorial in the *Vancouver Sun* on August 13. It obviously referred in part to the so-called family spokesman.

> It is not as if there were any evidence that the police are not doing their job. On the contrary, the way they have assembled the largest and probably best-equipped investigative team in the history of the province has been most impressive.

There was further support the next day. Radio talk-show host Rafe Mair spoke out in the strongest terms, even naming the spokesman, and criticized him harshly.

> First of all, who the hell are you anyway and what is your expertise in police matters? What is your track record in the solving of crimes, particularly crimes of this nature?
>
> How many years of experience do you have to bring to this self-appointed role of critic that you play before a willing news media? What schools did you go to, what colleges did you attend, what police academies did you graduate from? What the devil do you know about technology and training and expertise and all of those things that go into police work?
>
> Why should I, why should the public accept that you know as much, let alone more than the 150 policemen, who being mothers and fathers as well as skilled practitioners of the art of crime detection, are working their butts off day and night under the most difficult of circumstances, including I might say your ignorant and ill-advised grandstanding?
>
> How come you're so much smarter than the RCMP, the most respected national police force in the world? What makes you more knowledgeable than the members of some of the oldest and most experi-

enced police forces in Canada, including those in Vancouver and New Westminster?

What do you know about so-called bureaucracies and their workings that entitles you to cast doubt upon the professional competence of at least three police forces and the entire Attorney General's Department? Don't you realize [name deleted] that what you've been saying about the police forces can only hurt the ability of the investigators to do all that we want done? Don't you see that they can't tell you everything that they're doing? Don't you see they can't confide in the public every move they're making? Don't you see that you're accomplishing only one concrete thing and that is making an infernal nuisance of yourself without any redeeming benefit?

What makes you think you're helping? Oh yes, it's true Mr. ... that you are in a no-lose position. So long as these terrible tragic cases remain unsolved you can rant and rave against the police and then when they are solved you can take the credit for having prodded them into action. But tell us some of the concrete things that you propose that will really help.

The massive investigation was really no different than others in one respect: the police could not disclose confidential matters. Mair, a former lawyer, said it all in his commentary.

Years later, Bruce remained grateful to Mair for his expression of support.

On August 14, Olson appeared in court at Burnaby and was remanded into custody on the burglary charges. Mr. Hall appeared for the Crown.

★ ★ ★

Northorp was ready to use all the manpower he could muster. The Serious Crime Section's Corporal Brian Tuckey and his crew returned from the Fraser Valley where they had conducted careful examinations of the known crime scenes. Tuckey obtained a search warrant for Olson's residence and was pleasantly surprised when he searched the apartment. Many searches are done in filthy conditions, but "the Olson residence was immaculate," Tuckey said. "There wasn't a speck of dust anywhere, not even under the bed. It was perfect. Olson's clothes were lined up as if in a military closet. The slacks and shirts were lined up and nicely pressed. Joan was the exact opposite of Olson. He was loud and crass whereas she was quiet and polite. She was in denial."

The questioning of Olson began on August 13.

"I wasn't hopeful," Bruce reflected. "The only thing we had to grill him on was Judy's name in his address book. It wasn't a thing that would cause him to break down and confess. We were dealing with a criminal who knew the rules."

The first stage of questioning, under the direction of Arnie Nylund, began on the evening of August 13 and went through to August 17. First, Corporal Tuckey and Constable Sandy Sandhu interviewed Olson. "I was surprised when Arnie asked Sandy and me to interview him," declared Tuckey. They obtained nothing of consequence.

Prosecutor John Hall, who was at Burnaby when Tuckey and Sandhu completed their questioning, stated, "Well, it doesn't look as if he is going to talk."

Maile and his team set up an interview strategy and a schedule. Maile and Drozda went first. "When Olson was being interviewed, we had a member monitoring everything and investigative teams standing by," revealed Maile. "As soon as Olson said where he was on such-and-such a date, we had a team checking that out. If he said he was at a doctor's office, for instance, we would check it out right away. That's how we started to break down his alibis. We could hit him with his inconsistencies during the same interview." As of August 17, nothing concrete had been gained.

As the questioning continued, the teams observed that Olson seemed to be responding to Maile. "They suggested I might have more success," commented Maile. "I sat in the stuffy, unventilated room for hours and hours while Olson smoked White Owl cigars. The smoke almost made me puke."

Olson's stance was typical for an experienced con. His responses were "I don't have to answer questions" or "I can't be connected to anything" or "I don't have to prove my innocence."

When the police suggested using the polygraph (lie detector), he sidestepped the issue by stating he would have to discuss it with his lawyer. At another stage he declined because, "they [polygraph tests] don't stand up in Canadian courts." Olson knew the police had nothing or they wouldn't be talking to him, but one thing was accomplished: he was feeling the pressure.

★ ★ ★

During this same period Bruce was busy ensuring other avenues of investigation were underway. He felt sure Olson was their man, but there was no evidence to make a charge stick. He also arranged a difficult meeting.

The disappearance of Simon Partington had stirred the sympathy of most of the Lower Mainland. The picture of this young, blonde-haired innocent could melt the hardest heart. Even the supposedly hard-nosed superintendent felt the pain the boy's parents must be feeling. "It was unprecedented for me," Bruce said. "However, I wanted to meet the Partingtons."

He arranged to talk to them on Sunday, August 16, which, barring an emergency, was Northorp's one day off. He did not expect to gain anything that would assist the inquiry, but he had other reasons for the meeting. "As head of the task force, I felt his parents might gain some comfort through talking to me. This discussion was private, but I did answer all their questions," Bruce recalled. The meeting ended with Northorp inviting the Partingtons to phone him if there was anything they wished to know. He knew it was highly unlikely Simon would be found alive. However, he never expressed that view.

The last, and most difficult conversation Bruce had with Mr. Partington was on August 27 when the body of a young male was found in Richmond. At the time, the identification could not be verified. "I was saddened to tell this distraught father I felt it was his son."

Tuesday August 18, 1981

Olson's status had not really changed since August 12, when he was arrested on Vancouver Island. He had continued to be evasive about

Possibly due to the timing or the image of the 4'3", 82-pound, blonde nine-year-old, the July disappearance of Simon Partington heightened the anxiety of all who were familiar with the missing children files. With the recovery of Raymond King's body (crossed out in the poster, left), hope was fading for other parents with missing children.

the presence of Judy Kozma's name in his address book. This was about to change.

Olson appeared in court in Burnaby on the burglary charges on August 18 and was again remanded into custody. His lawyer, Robert Shantz, made no bail application.

Reporters interviewed John Hall, Crown Counsel, and Shantz. Hall told reporters, "Olson has now been charged with three sex offences dealing with an incident in Surrey in May and will be appearing in court there on the 20th."

Shantz told reporters that Olson was a suspect in the cases of murdered and missing children. "I don't have the information the police do, but from what I understand it's very unlikely that they will charge him with these murders. I think they've got the wrong man is what it amounts to." When asked for his client's reaction to speculation he was involved in the child killings, Shantz replied, "He's very upset about it."

★ ★ ★

Questioning Olson was not the only avenue of investigation being pursued by Bruce Northorp's investigation team. Anxious to build a strong enough case to keep Olson in jail, officers Don Brown and Cliff Kusmack were seeking out Olson's known acquaintances. These efforts paid off when the RCMP team tracked down one of the two young men questioned with Olson on July 29. Randy Ludlow (whose use of an alias in July presented an added obstacle to the officers' mid-August search) was fighting his own demons at the time. During an August 18 interview, Brown and Kusmack took a statement from Ludlow that would prove significant in breaking Olson. Randy outlined how he had been present on July 9 when Olson picked up Judy Kozma in his car. He spent several hours with them before he was dropped off at a Burnaby shopping mall.

Maile and Sandhu took another try at Olson. This time they had more ammunition, and confronted with the information from Ludlow, Olson began to shift from total denial. "Where's that bulletin sheet with the pictures on it?" Olson asked Maile, referring to the missing children material.

Maile had one brought up and handed it to him. Pointing, Olson said, "This one…this one…this one." He said "No" to Verna Bjerky, who was also on the list, and when the case of Marnie Jamieson, who had been killed at Sechelt in 1980, was raised, he stated, "No, all were local." He implied that some bodies could be found by some person and began discussing what might happen to the person responsible. He suggested the person might be willing to talk if he could be locked up in a psychiatric hospital versus a prison. Eventually, Olson was talking as if he were responsible for the killings.

When Maile told Olson he was unable to guarantee that the responsible party might be housed in a psychiatric hospital, Olson replied, "I need to talk with somebody with some authority. You can't make any decisions."

"I talked to Arnie," declared Maile. "I suggested he go in, but he thought it should be Inspector Proke. Proke went in and Olson talked with him for some time."

Olson's proposal was advanced to Northorp, who rejected it forthwith. There were no means whereby such an arrangement could be made. Bruce was told Hall would not agree to such a proposition either.

Ludlow's statement was supplied to Bruce the same day. He read it carefully. "It had the ring of truth," he said. "Ludlow's words gave me the clear impression that Olson tried to play down what had happened to Judy after Ludlow left their company."

Northorp was now convinced Olson was responsible for Judy's murder. However, he knew there was insufficient evidence to obtain a conviction. Nonetheless, he instructed a charge of first degree murder be laid, subject to Mr. Hall's concurrence. Serious Crime members did not support this move. Although it was Proke who told him this, Northorp was sure he was just parroting the opinions of Maile and Drozda.

"They thought it would have a negative effect," Bruce said. "I made no attempt to justify my instruction. However, I knew the charge could always be withdrawn if strategically prudent. The matter was discussed with Mr. Hall and he agreed." Olson was told he'd be charged with first degree murder that same day.

Later in the day, Proke interviewed Olson. "I felt he might be successful due to his greater experience," Bruce declared. "Plus, we had jolted Olson with the fact he was now being charged with first degree murder. As well, three other charges had been laid in Surrey."

The status had advanced from the 12th. Olson had now had lots of time to think about how a street-smart wheeler-dealer such as himself had been busted at gunpoint. He'd be wondering, "Just what evidence do they have?"

It was no surprise there was some movement. However, the actual developments were astounding.

August 19 and 20, 1981

Bruce was briefed on the outcome of Proke's interview, which had continued past midnight into the early morning of August 19. He was told that some remarks were made under warned and some under unwarned conditions.

Generally speaking, before any oral or written statements given to the police by an accused can be entered in evidence at a trial, they must be found to be voluntary. Part of the definition of a voluntary statement is that it is given after the accused has been cautioned by the police officer. The caution or warning varied over

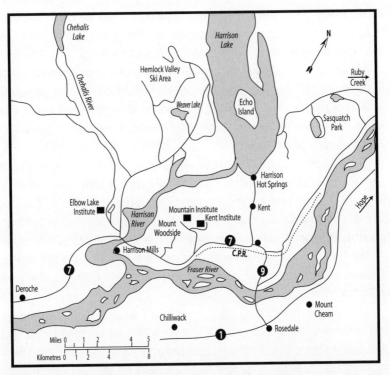

Olson took many of his victims to the area around Weaver Lake, which was also the site of several detention facilities. (Numbers in black circles refer to highway numbers.)

the years, however the one that was probably in effect in 1981 was: It is my duty to warn you that you are not obliged to say anything, but anything you do say may be given in evidence.

An officer must give this warning if he or she has arrived at a state of mind where he or she believes a subject is guilty of the crime being investigated. This state of mind might be reached if the subject has been arrested for the crime or if the officer has decided a charge should be laid. In Olson's situation, the questioner would have given a warning or warnings at various intervals, depending on the direction of the questioning and the information that Olson was revealing. Other conversations would have taken place without a warning. To further complicate matters, Olson talked in the third person at times.

During Proke's interview, Olson indicated he was responsible for the murders of King, Johnsrude, Kozma, and Weller (children whose bodies had been located). He also implied he killed Carson, Partington, Court, Chartrand, Wolfsteiner, Daignault, and a girl from West Germany who had not been reported missing.

He asked for a deal if he co-operated and led police to bodies or evidence. He wanted a guarantee he would be able to serve his time in a psychiatric hospital instead of a penitentiary, but the police could not ensure hospital confinement. Sentencing was the responsibility of the court.

"I had told Olson the previous day he would be going to a mental institution, but what I hadn't told him is that it would only be for a 30-day psychiatric assessment," admitted Maile. On the 20th, Maile told Olson exactly what was happening—that he'd go to a hospital for an assessment but not necessarily for his sentence.

He had no sooner uttered those words than Olson turned to him and said, "I'll give you eleven bodies for $100,000. The first one will be a freebie."

For this amount of money he said he would give statements and evidence, things only the killer could know. He said he would give the police a body, which he referred to as a "freebie," to show his good faith. After this, the RCMP would hand over $10,000 to his wife. When he had verified with his lawyer that the payment had been made, he would go on to another body.

Olson then spoke to Shantz, his lawyer, and insisted an agreement be drawn up before he lead the police to anything. Later the same day he spoke of completing the deal without any lawyer involvement. Drozda's notes say, "Arnie Nylund's signature would be sufficient for Olson."

"The 20th is the first day a $100,000 payment was raised by Olson," observed Bruce. "I have no doubt why he chose $100,000. That figure had been mentioned at his meeting with Maile, Drozda, and Tarr on July 30."

Finally, that day the RCMP issued a news release stating Olson was charged with first degree murder in relation to the death of Judy Kozma. Not only did the police have an obligation to release such information, but it also served other purposes. When Olson heard of it, it would apply more pressure to him. As well, it would give the public some sense of relief.

Six
Doing the Unthinkable

Prudence

Prudence is a matter of applying wisdom and common sense. In police practice and many other real-life situations, to be prudent is to choose a course of action only after careful deliberation. The course is not necessarily one based on precedent. On August 24, 1981, given the options available, Bruce Northorp and a round table of interested parties sought the prudent course. It was not a route the RCMP had ever gone before. And it was a route many would second-guess for a long, long time. Then and now the decision made is best described as prudent.

Friday August 21, 1981

On the morning of August 21, Olson appeared in Chilliwack court on the murder charge. He was given a 30-day remand for a psychiatric examination and was sent to the Forensic Psychiatric Institute in Port Coquitlam.

By this point, Bruce Northorp had been heading the task force for three weeks. With no guidelines to follow, it had been a formidable task just to assemble the approximately 150 officers who were now working the case. In addition he was attempting to absorb all the information gathered before he had taken over his assignment, plan strategy, deal with the ever-hungry media, and consider a host of other details.

However, if he felt the three weeks he had just endured were challenging, he would find they were a proverbial piece of cake compared to this day and others that followed. "At 8.35 a.m. I got a real jolt," said Bruce. "I learned for the first time of the $100,000 deal put forward by Olson."

Superintendent Cy Thomas of Chilliwack Sub-Division, Inspector Larry Proke of OIC General Investigations, and Staff Sergeant Arnie Nylund of General Inquiries asked Northorp to approve an arrangement in which $100,000 would be paid to Olson's wife for Olson's co-operation. The fact that three senior officers came forward with the request suggests that they felt their proposal might need a lot of support. They argued that this payment was perfectly acceptable because it was to be paid to the wife.

However, the fact that it was suggested by Clifford Olson was enough to make people react against it. Northorp found the proposal repugnant and refused to sanction such an arrangement. He simply said, "No, put him off." He was not alone in his thinking. He found out later in the day that John Hall was also opposed to the idea.

Northorp told Deputy Commissioner Tom Venner, the commanding officer of "E" Division, about the proposal and informed Venner that he had rejected it.

Many people, including Bruce, found the proposition repugnant because it is a basic concept that a criminal should not profit from the crime. "I found it unthinkable he should be paid to provide evidence," Bruce elaborated. "The proposition to pay Olson's wife was simply splitting hairs. She was not separated from him, and Olson stood to gain even if monies were paid to his wife. The situation may have been different if she were separated and were supplying information as to past criminal activity. That was not the case."

★ ★ ★

The day was to bring forth another surprise. At 1:25 p.m. Bruce received a phone call.

"This is Ernie."

Northorp immediately recognized the voice and the code name from the late 1960s. It was an informant he had used some twelve to thirteen years prior when he headed the Burnaby GIS.

Ernie said, "I've done time with Olson at the B.C. Pen and I'm ready to help you."

The man's offer was noted, but the situation at that moment did not lend itself to that type of assistance.

The call from an old source may have been heartening for Northorp, but it did not distract from the major issue at hand. The burning question was whether or not the RCMP should enter into an agreement with Olson as he suggested. Bruce Northorp had let Cy Thomas, Larry Proke, and Arnie Nylund have their say. As Northorp wrestled with his options, he could come up with no precedent for such an undertaking. Certainly none of the proponents had provided one. From August 21 to 23 there was much internal discussion about the proposal. For Northorp it meant sleepless nights. The discussions did not resolve anything to his satisfaction.

Serious Crime members, in the main, supported payment. They saw it as a quick fix and they attempted to rationalize payment, saying that it would not be much different than paying an informant if Olson's wife convinced him to provide evidence. Some argued the police would pay the costs of relocating Joan Olson in payment for the information her husband would provide. Others commented that if Joan were to receive the money it would obviate the necessity of paying her welfare. Some suggested the payment would be cost-effective considering the costs being incurred by the task force, particularly in wages.

"I would not accede," declared Northorp. "I simply felt the proposal was distasteful and went against all acceptable principles in the investigation of crime. More to the point, I felt Olson would eventually crack as the pressure on him increased."

It was gut-wrenching for Northorp and senior personnel. They felt Olson was their man and to go with his proposal would wind things up. They were tortured by the anguish so many parents and relatives were enduring and by the state of mind of the community with a child predator on the loose.

Was there a remote chance that Olson was not their man? If the $100,000 was put up and Olson failed to produce, the police could then concentrate on other avenues of investigation.

Monday August 24, 1981

On the morning of August 24, Bruce sent a message to RCMP headquarters in Ottawa. He updated them on the case and stated that the proposed deal was unthinkable. A copy of the message was provided to the Serious Crime Section so there would be a clear understanding of the District One position.

It seemed to be a stalemate. In an attempt to gain evidence, Bruce directed Proke to have his members approach the Regional Crown Counsel to apply for a court authorization to intercept (wiretap) Olson's conversations. Maile was assigned the task and mentioned Olson's proposal during his discussion with that office.

Drozda and Maile met regularly with a core group of Serious Crime investigators. One of the things they discussed was how to make it appear to Olson they were paying him when in fact no money was being expended. They worked out an elaborate scheme where $10,000 would be deposited in a bank in the presence of Joan Olson after each body was located. That $10,000 would be withdrawn and the same $10,000 would be used again and again. At this time the strategy was speculation only, as they had not been authorized to proceed with payment in any form. "I was to be the guy to make the payments but as it turned out, it didn't work," said Corporal Brian Tuckey.

In their numerous encounters, Maile noticed Olson talked a lot to his wife on the phone. He recalled, "I got the idea that we should get a Privacy Act Authorization [a court order allowing the interception of private communications of a suspect]. I suggested that and got the okay to proceed. Ed Drozda and I first went to Crown Counsel Mac Norris in New Westminster, who told us Sean Madigan, the Regional Crown in Vancouver, was handling it. He sent us to his office at 815 Hornby Street.

"To get an authorization you have to make full disclosure." This meant revealing the $100,000 proposal currently being considered. "As we told Madigan what happened, he said he knew Olson from many encounters over the years. Madigan commented that he couldn't see Olson doing something like this." They continued to talk as Madigan took down the information. Suddenly Madigan said, "Don't leave the office. Wait right here, I'll be back."

Madigan returned shortly with Alan Filmer, the assistant deputy attorney general. "Tell him exactly what you have told me," instructed Madigan.

After listening to their story, including the idea of the money scam, Drozda and Maile paused for Filmer's comment. "Filmer said 'The Feds have no guts.' He told us not to waste their time on an authorization as it wasn't required. 'Proceed with the money deal. Don't worry about the money problems. We'll look after that as well as the legalities when seizure is made.'" The conversation had taken a major leap.

Maile recognized they were getting ahead of their bosses. As soon as they left Madigan's office Maile instructed Drozda to stop at the first telephone booth they saw. "I have to make a phone call to Arnie. I think we are in deep shit." Maile made his call. "When we arrived back at the office we met with Northorp, Superintendent Henschel, Holmes[the officer in charge of JFO], Proke, and Nylund. It was agreed we would proceed with the deal."

It was not easy to gain this consensus. The possibility that Olson would have access to the money was the main stumbling block.

"In the afternoon, I heard the deal had been approved by the attorney general of British Columbia," observed Bruce. "It now, for the first time, included a scam. [The Serious Crime Section] had never proposed a scam to me. Scam, to me, meant any monies paid to Joan Olson would be seized from her when our goal had been accomplished. I had no problem with the scam payment proposal. I would not go along with an outright payment to Joan Olson."

Legal opinions were obtained from Special Prosecutor John Hall, the Attorney General's Ministry, and the federal Justice Department. Hall didn't think any payment to Mrs. Olson would cause a problem pertaining to the admissibility of evidence. Federal and provincial lawyers felt there was a 50/50 chance a civil action to recover the monies from Mrs. Olson would be successful in the event the payments could not be physically seized. It was enough to make the money deal more palatable to Hall and Northorp, though both still had their conditions.

"I then phoned Assistant Commissioner Randy Schramm, the director of Criminal Investigations (DCI) at HQ Ottawa, and recommended $100,000 be expended on the deal as it then stood," said Northorp. "The RCMP and Olson, or his lawyer, would sign a document [agreement]. The plan included recovery of monies after bodies and evidence had been found." Recovery and recovered were words Northorp would hear over and over again in the following days.

Tuesday August 25, 1981

In the morning, Bruce sent a message to Ottawa confirming his verbal request. The matter was to proceed as follows: The RCMP and Olson would sign an agreement to pay Olson's wife $100,000. The deal was broken down as a payment of $10,000 for each of seven bodies, and $30,000 for the personal effects of the four victims whose bodies had been recovered. Bruce recalls his message included words to the effect that "We are signing an agreement knowing it is not legally binding and with the knowledge we intend to seize the monies at an appropriate time."

Both Bruce's verbal and written messages underlined the fact that monies would be recovered.

At 8 a.m., Randy Schramm phoned Northorp from Ottawa and told him that the $100,000 had been approved. A message confirming this approval had been sent. The agreement would have to be signed by the police before Olson would take them to a body. At 10:30 a.m., Northorp received a phone call from Schramm's immediate superior, Deputy Commissioner Henry Jensen, in charge of Criminal Operations for the RCMP. It was he who had the financial authority to spend the $100,000. He wanted to personally verify his understanding that the message Bruce had sent was correct. At 11:25 a.m., Northorp placed a conference call to the director of Criminal Investigations. Hall and Proke were present at the Vancouver end. Schramm agreed to Bruce's proposition. It was clearly stated that the $100,000 was at risk of being hidden once delivered. Recovery of money would be secondary to finding the bodies.

At 1:30 p.m., Nylund went to Northorp's office and told him how Olson would lead the police to bodies. Olson was calling the shots. Northorp was told at the outset that Olson did not want to take them to the Partington boy's body as he knew that was a particularly bad case, his youngest victim. In addition he suggested he would be giving the police two for one. The German girl's body was in the same general area as Partington's, and Olson felt if he disclosed the location of one, the other would be found and the police would double-cross him. His proposed schedule was:

1. Chartrand at Whistler
2. Daignault at Surrey
3. Carson at Chilliwack
4. Four locations where evidence would be found
5. Court at Agassiz
6. Wolfsteiner at Chilliwack
7. Partington at Richmond
8. German girl at an unspecified location

At 3 p.m., Northorp had a conference call with Schramm and his assistant, Chief Superintendent Jim Riddell. They discussed recovery of the monies and the federal Justice Department's suggestion that recovery might be made under authority of a search warrant. Other avenues of recovery were to charge Olson with extortion and then seize the funds gained by criminal means. Civil law offered another option. If the agreement was entered into under duress, the RCMP could argue that it did not have an obligation to pay.

"I felt the intense pressure over the ensuing hours," Bruce said. "We were so close [to breaking the case]. But could Olson really be so stupid as to enter into an agreement that would likely result in his spending the balance of his days in prison?" Northorp spent much of the day on the phone to the RCMP in Ottawa, the B.C. Attorney General's Department, and the federal Justice Department office in Vancouver.

Proke and others were busy dealing with Shantz and another lawyer, E. James McNeney, brought in by Shantz to formulate the agreement. Two early drafts were rejected. One included a clause that the RCMP would not attempt to recover any monies paid to

Olson's wife. This clause was not acceptable to either the police or the Justice Department. It was not included in the final document.

At 4:20 p.m., Bruce phoned Proke at McNeney's office. "The agreement has to be adequate to protect RCMP monies in the event Olson does not produce. Equally important, it should clearly set out the monies are not for the benefit of Olson."

"The investigation was without precedent," declared Northorp. "There was no handbook to follow in the many delicate situations that arose. Common sense was my standard, erring on the side of safety and working within the law."

★ ★ ★

Bruce's main focus now shifted to the locating of bodies and recovery of evidence. It was time to look ahead and consider how this might affect the victims' families. They could be devastated, unless Bruce took some unusual steps. Events were unfolding with such speed Bruce had no time to reflect on the horror of this surreal drama. He was determined to be a steadying influence, guiding the course of action as best he could. That night his kitchen table was strewn with papers as he composed messages that would be sent to the parents if the media became aware that bodies were being found.

"In early 1982," Bruce related, "I learned some of the victims' parents were upset at the manner in which they had been notified of their child's death. These occurrences were before I was assigned the case. Given the circumstance, I had given the issue of notification serious thought. Our procedure was as sensitive as possible."

Wednesday August 26, 1981

Bruce Northorp knew that Olson's willingness to deliver bodies would still leave one lingering question. "In the morning I phoned Proke and told him we had to know how Olson lured persons into his car. I also wanted to know how he managed to keep them, especially in the cases of Court and Johnsrude. We had to be satisfied he acted alone."

A second factor to deal with was the new face in the Olson camp. "Shantz called in another lawyer, McNeney, and after he became involved we didn't know what was going on. We were isolated," said Maile. At this point it was not clear to many whether McNeney represented Joan Olson, Clifford, or both.

The final draft of the agreement (see Appendix V) was signed by McNeney and Nylund, not Olson. The $100,000, in cash, was then turned over to McNeney. The agreement stated that the $100,000 would be paid as follows: $10,000 for each of seven bodies which had not been found and $30,000 for personal effects of the four victims whose bodies had been located.

One clause of the agreement read:

> It is acknowledged by Sergeant (sic) Nylund that the making of any payment or payments referred to herein are payments solely for the benefit of Joan Olson and her son aforesaid and are not for the benefit of Clifford Robert Olson.

Northorp, Hall, and others felt that this clause placed an onus on McNeney to ensure no monies went to Clifford Olson.

On the morning of August 26, Olson set out to locate the first body. Northorp explicitly ordered that he be escorted under tight security. "I knew he'd escaped [from custody] on at least six occasions from 1957 to 1968," Bruce said. "While on his gruesome tour, Olson was to be handcuffed to a police officer. Additionally, a police service dog and handler were to accompany them. All Olson's conversations were to be taped."

At 1:15 p.m., Bruce phoned Schramm in Ottawa to let him know that Olson had commenced his dreadful task and the police were, in effect, committed to paying $100,000. The DCI replied. "The matter is in your hands and your judgments will be supported." This was quite a change from Ottawa's initial inquiry. Northorp's efforts to keep everyone informed of developments were reaping benefits. There was no second-guessing at this stage. Bruce also mentioned how the police intended to approach Joan Olson and ask for the return of the monies and discuss relocation monies versus the $100,000.

At 2:50 p.m., Nylund reported they had located the remains of Louise Chartrand near Whistler.

Seven minutes later, Proke phoned with more detail. "Olson showed no reaction when locating the body," stated the inspector.

"He claimed he'd been out to see Shantz and had picked her up while in the area."

Bruce passed this information to the provincial attorney general's office.

"I have the greatest regard for the police officers tasked with his escort and recovery of evidence," Bruce said later. "It was an abhorrent assignment, made all the more so by the vulgarities of this poor excuse for a human being [Olson]. He seemed to relish recounting the details of each murder."

As the searches progressed, Olson would point out the location of a body and say who the victim was, or who the officers should be looking for. However, they did not rely on his word to make any notification to next-of-kin. Relatives were contacted only after a medical examination confirmed an identity.

Olson was calling the shots. He dictated in what order he would point out the locations of bodies. By 5:40 p.m., a convoy of police vehicles was making its way to White Rock. They were going to attempt to locate Colleen Daignault's body. The bodies of Simon Partington and an unidentified female at Richmond would be next. Or perhaps they would go elsewhere; Olson kept changing his mind.

"At 9:15 p.m., I was told there had been a problem in White Rock," recounted Bruce. "They were now in the Queensborough area of New Westminster. Olson said he'd point out two bodies but only after he phoned his lawyer."

It was shortly before midnight when Proke reported the searches in Surrey and Richmond were futile. It had been an agonizing day for the RCMP, particularly those travelling with Olson. They now had sufficient evidence to ensure Olson's conviction for murder, but the grisly nature of their task was overwhelming. They had to steel themselves to be ready to go again at six the next morning.

Thursday August 27, 1981

At 8:07 a.m., Bruce was told that Simon Partington's remains had been located. The body of the unidentified female was in the same area, likely in a ditch, weighted down.

Bruce retrieved the messages he had drafted nights before and penned a slight modification to suit the existing circumstances.

From 8:24 until 8:35 a.m. he personally phoned every unit commander involved—at Langley, Burnaby, Maple Ridge, and Surrey Detachments—and asked them to carry out the following instructions immediately.

> *Would you have someone, preferably a General Investigation Section investigator, attend at the next of kin of (the name of the missing child or children which applied) and advise them we may, emphasize may, have bad news. Tell them we have located some bodies and we don't want them to hear about it through the media first. Tell them they should not tell anyone else what we have told them, as this could seriously impair our investigations. They are to be assured that as soon as we have anything positive they will be advised at once and in any event we will update them by 5:00 p.m.*

Northorp's phone call to Hope varied from the others, as investigations did not lead police to believe Verna Bjerky was one of Olson's victims. "I told the staff sergeant at Hope to advise Verna's next of kin there was absolutely no reason to believe her case was connected to the bodies which had been located and would be reported on the news shortly. They too were asked to keep confidential that which they had been told.

"I felt strongly the families of the victims should not first hear any disturbing news through the media. They deserved every consideration available and should know they were not forgotten in the rush of police work."

★ ★ ★

The investigation and solving of crime is one responsibility of the police. Ensuring the safety and well-being of the community is another. For weeks the public in the Lower Mainland had been alarmed at the news of missing and murdered children. Parents were rightly fearful for the safety of their children. Playgrounds were empty and it was obvious that parents were taking precautions.

Bruce knew he would have to address the media on the latest events. This would not just satisfy news outlets, but would also, through them, let the public know some progress was being made and to ease their concerns. He sent a message to all media outlets in B.C., announcing a news conference just prior to noon at the RCMP Training Academy.

Bruce began the conference by saying it was a very difficult day for the police. "Bedlam broke loose when I announced that two bodies had been found, one female in Whistler and one male in Richmond. It was apparent we were breaking the case wide open. I could say little more than what had been found. Anything beyond that would likely have jeopardized the charges which would follow." Events were breaking so fast that he announced there would be another briefing at seven that evening.

When Northorp returned to his office, he phoned both Langley and Burnaby commanders to advise there was nothing to report on either Sandra Wolfsteiner or Ada Court. "I had just hung up the phone when Proke phoned me. He said they had probably located Terri Carson's remains in Agassiz and some personal effects of Judy Kozma at another location."

Nylund phoned Bruce just before 7 p.m. He sounded tired and his news was disturbing. They had located a few remains, likely those of Ada Court.

The superintendent went ahead with the 7 p.m. briefing. "It was probably the most difficult I ever had to conduct." Northorp braced himself as he prefaced his remarks by saying, "The news doesn't get any better. It gets more gruesome all the time. Since this morning our investigators have located another body of a female in the Agassiz area." He briefly described its condition and said that as soon as there was a positive identification, the next of kin would be advised before the name was released.

He also described the location where the male body had been found in Richmond, about one mile west of the point where Christine Weller's body had been found in late 1980. Northorp elaborated that the police in Richmond were continuing a search of trenches in the same area for another body. Other investigators were continuing efforts to locate other bodies elsewhere. He used this opportunity to say the police now had no reason or evidence to suggest the case of Verna Bjerky was connected in any way to the massive investigation.

He then went on to the most difficult part of his release. "Just a few minutes ago, I was informed we found some human remains in the Agassiz area. I don't have any detail beyond that."

Northorp's final words were intended for the public. "If it gives the community any peace of mind, the suspect in these murders is in custody. I won't say anything that will tend to identify that person."

Although Bruce was sickened that so many children had been killed at the hands of such a cowardly killer, he felt a tremendous sense of relief. The killings were solved. More importantly, there'd be no more at the hands of this sadist. He knew the community would breathe a collective sigh of relief, knowing a menace had been removed from its streets. Sadly, he knew also that others would come along to victimize the innocent. The community should never let its guard down.

Northorp went home to his best night's rest in weeks.

"When I think of this briefing, the whole case wells up inside me," Bruce confided. "I still relive the horror of those events when I am forced to recall the summer of 1981."

Friday August 28, 1981

On Friday morning, Bruce conducted another media briefing to wind up the ongoing major briefings. He announced that RCMP investigations would now scale down and their main job would be to prepare material for Special Prosecutor John Hall. He repeated that Verna Bjerky's disappearance was not believed to be associated with the Olson cases. Her file would remain open at Hope and with the Serious Crime Section.

Despite Northorp's attempts to wind up the briefings, he found himself conducting another in the evening as he reported, "At approximately 4 p.m. today, Richmond RCMP found another body, of a female, in a trench area about 400 to 500 yards from where Simon Partington's body was found yesterday."

The latest discovery was the body of Sigrun Arnd, a German girl who had been vacationing in Canada. As she was on holiday, it

Police were not aware that Sigrun Arnd was missing until Olson confessed to killing the young German student. She had been staying at a Vancouver hostel. Police received Arnd's photo from her parents in Weinheim, Germany, at the end of August.

took some weeks before her parents realized she was missing, so the police were not immediately able to establish her identity.

Earlier in the afternoon, the next of kin of Chartrand, Carson, and Partington were notified that positive identification had been made of their children. Subsequently, the names were released to the media.

At this briefing, Bruce also disclosed that a search had been underway all day in another unspecified area. No body had been found, but other evidence was located. Searchers had secured more evidence near where human remains had been found late the day before. He further advised that investigators were attempting to locate yet another body. Northorp had not specified certain search areas as that would only result in an influx of reporters and the requirement to further control the crime scenes.

Bruce was asked what evidence had been found. He replied, "I won't go into detail. Essentially, they were items which could be established as belonging to each of the four victims whose bodies had been found without Olson's assistance, thus establishing he was the killer. Only the killer would have knowledge of where these articles had been hidden."

The body count was now nine. Four had been found before the task force commenced, and Olson had directed police to five others and to evidence. (Colleen Daignault and Sandra Wolfsteiner were still to be located.) The agreement was being honoured. On each occasion that warranted it, Nylund would phone McNeney to tell him he could release another $10,000. By this time Joan Olson should have received $80,000. In Olson's mind that was $20,000 short. This had an impact in the days to come.

Saturday August 29, 1981

On August 29, Ada Court's remains were positively identified. "By now there was ample evidence to charge Olson with eight additional counts of murder, beyond the count relating to Judy Kozma," Bruce summarized." This was discussed with my subordinates and Mr. Hall. Some felt Olson might be upset if eight more murder charges were laid. They didn't want him in that state of mind."

Olson had hinted to police that he was responsible for three other murders: those of Suzanne Seto on Vancouver Island and Marnie Jamieson in Sechelt, whose bodies had been found, and of a Korean girl at Golden, B.C. (This last likely referred to Oang Ngoc Ha, a nineteen-year-old Vietnamese girl from Banff, Alberta, who was found murdered 80 kilometres from Golden on February 28, 1981.) Some of Northorp's subordinates wanted to solve these three murders and many unknown crimes they suspected Olson had committed. However, Bruce was suspicious of his claims. He thought Olson was just baiting them with other murders, hoping to use them as a means to gain the release of the final $20,000.

"Apparently Mr. Hall was as unconcerned about Olson being upset as I was," observed Bruce."He concurred. Eight further counts of first degree murder would be laid."

Between August 28 and September 1, Bruce was told Olson wanted $15,000 over and above the $80,000 already released. His lawyers were supposedly charging that amount for handling the money transactions. The word "supposedly" is well chosen. Bruce would not believe anything that Olson said unless he could corroborate it independently.

"No payments of money beyond the agreement," Bruce insisted.

Later, Northorp was told Olson had dropped the demand for $15,000, saying he would deal with the RCMP if they dealt with him fairly on the total agreement.

Northorp often told Proke and others, "Put the pressure on him, let him sweat. Hold out the remaining money as a carrot until we've located the two [remaining] bodies covered in the agreement. In the interim, he should supply sufficient information, such as their identities, to satisfy us he has murdered another two persons. After all, it was he who wanted to deal."

Monday August 31, 1981

At 10:40 a.m., Bruce sent out a news release over Canada News Wire. It announced: "Mr. Hall has reviewed our material and has instructed that a suspect in custody will be indicted on eight additional counts of first degree murder. These counts relate to the deaths of Terri Lynn Carson, Louise Chartrand, Ada Court, Daryn Johnsrude, Raymond King, Simon Partington, Christine Weller and an unidentified female."

September 1981

On the afternoon of September 3, an investigator came to Northorp's office and mentioned Olson was back in the Forensic Psychiatric Institute, where he was being held on remand for psychiatric examination. Olson thought police were reneging on the agreement and he was upset. "You're trying to screw me around," he accused. His concern was the non-payment for the body of Daignault. He said he'd done his best. He felt his verbal statements concerning her murder and efforts to locate her body warranted the release of $10,000 regardless of the agreement.

The investigator sought Northorp's authority to release $10,000 in relation to Daignault. Northorp was unconcerned that Olson was upset. "I'll hang in with the wording of the agreement," he responded. "The agreement requires a body being located before any payment. As Daignault's body has not been found, no payment could or should be made. It doesn't say anything about him doing his best."

Northorp was also informed that Olson had said there were two other bodies he would locate pertaining to murders he had committed. He would not proceed unless the $10,000 for Daignault was released. The two, in his terminology, would be freebies when the $100,000 deal was over. The only information he supplied about the two supposed victims was that they were female, about sixteen years old, both buried six feet deep, one buried between Chilliwack and Hope, the other on Vancouver Island. Both murders had taken place during 1980. The personal effects of both victims were supposed to have been placed in plastic bags and buried near the bodies.

Not to be released before: 81-08-31
Time _____ Date IMMEDIATE   Ne pas publier avant:
Houre _____ Date _____

Re: Missing Children/Homicides
Lower Mainland, B.C.

Mr. Hall has reviewed our material and has instructed
that a suspect in custody will be indicted on eight
additional counts of first degree murder.

These counts relate to the deaths of:

Terri Lyn Carson	Raymond King
Louise Chartrand	Simon Partington
Ada Court	Christine Weller
Daryn Johnsrude	An unidentified female

The decision as to when the charges will be laid and
when and where the suspect will be arraigned will be
made by Mr. Hall.

As charges are to be laid, the RCMP will not be making
any further comment and the regular media briefings
will now be discontinued. Supt. Northorp and Insp.
Proke will be available by telephone to respond to
enquiries related to searches for bodies, notification
of next of kin or other like matters.

"I was told that Olson was talking in the third person at times, as if his information had come from someone else," Bruce remembered. "Investigators were convinced he was talking about himself."

Just days prior, Olson had stated there may be three cases and the locations were Vancouver Island, Sechelt, and Golden. Now the only constant was Vancouver Island. Suzanne Seto, the Vancouver Island woman, had been murdered in 1980, but she was twenty-nine years of age, not sixteen. Police later determined, through questioning, that one of the two murdered girls Olson had referred to was Verna Bjerky. She did not meet the criteria he laid out earlier either. She had gone missing in 1981, not 1980.

Bruce recalled, "I'd been pitched to release the $10,000 in question for almost 45 minutes and I now demanded a position paper."

"What if I tell you it's already been done?" his colleague asked.

It turned out the decision to release the money had been made almost three hours before Northorp asked for a position paper. Apparently his subordinates were so enthused about Olson's two-body offer that they authorized the release of $10,000 before Daignault's body was found, and before they raised the issue with Northorp. Now $90,000 had been released.

"I was really angry at this ploy," declared Bruce. "It left a rotten taste in my mouth. I felt I was being set up. If I had agreed and the release of $10,000 beyond the agreement was ever questioned, I'd be the patsy. It turned out Colleen Daignault's body was eventually found [two weeks later] and the payment did not become an issue."

At 4:15 p.m. that same day, Northorp briefed his immediate boss, Superintendent Gordon Tomalty, the officer in charge of CIB, on the circumstances surrounding the release of the $10,000. Bruce also made a brief entry in his notebook, summarizing his displeasure.

★ ★ ★

By the morning of September 4, Surrey RCMP had been searching for Colleen's body for eight days without success. At 10:51 a.m., Surrey phoned to say they had found what appeared to be a human body part. It turned out to be just another false lead.

After noon the same day, Proke reported that Olson had talked to his lawyer. On the 8th he would be ready to give a statement pertaining to Sandra Wolfsteiner. He would then take police to the two new bodies, one on Vancouver Island.

★ ★ ★

On September 8, police divers found a compact and T-shirt belonging to Judy Kozma and Simon Partington respectively.

This was also the day Olson was to lead the police to further bodies. "I was convinced Olson's admission to two more murders was merely a ploy," observed Bruce. "Bearing in mind his many escapes from custody, tight security was laid on. Olson was to be taken in a car with three unarmed police officers, with one handcuffed to him. The car was to be escorted by two other cars, with two officers in each, armed with revolvers, rifles, and shotguns. District Two was alerted that Olson might be taken their way, and I arranged for the use of a police aircraft. If escape was on his mind, he would not succeed."

But Olson had a change of plans. He wanted to look for Sandra Wolfsteiner's body prior to locating other bodies. Until there was something positive on her, he wasn't prepared to go further. Maile turned down his proposition. Olson said he would think about it and let Maile know his decision the next day. "I'm still in a position to deal some more," he said, but ultimately, nothing transpired. Again, Northorp sensed the offer for two more bodies was simply an attempt to get the last $10,000.

★ ★ ★

At 8:40 a.m. on September 14 the first real break came in the Surrey case. Bruce was told some female clothing had been found in the search area.

The next development came on the 15th when Olson was in the Lower Mainland Regional Correctional Centre (Oakalla Prison Farm). "I was phoned at home in the evening and told Olson had agreed to take us to two bodies, no strings attached," said Bruce. "We would just have to assure him of total isolation in Oakalla."

This arrangement was possible. However, Olson changed his mind after two days, despite the fact he was told his request would be met.

"This was another Olson deal which didn't transpire," Bruce declared. "I leave it to you to speculate what he had in mind. Maybe it was just a change of scenery, maybe escape. I can't begin to guess what went on in his head."

Surrey's hard work was paying off. On September 16, police found a hammer believed to be the murder weapon in Daignault's case. Finally, on the 17th, remains believed to be human were found in the area that had been subjected to searches since late August.

Northorp made sure the next of kin of both Colleen Daignault and Sandra Wolfsteiner were contacted. Using dental charts, the remains were identified as those of Daignault. Again, both families were notified and a media release followed.

"I can only imagine the tenacity of the police officers, and others, assisting in the search in Surrey," Bruce remarked. "With a relatively small suspect area, it took about three weeks to locate the body of the victim and evidence. I don't believe any mention was ever made of the tremendous effort put forth in Surrey."

★ ★ ★

Olson's apparent attempts to con the police with promises of more bodies got him nowhere. Next he tried the media.

"On the 24th at 3:56 p.m., I received a phone call from Rick Ouston, a *Vancouver Sun* reporter," Northorp remembered. "I made the following note—

> *24/9/81 3.56 p.m. Call from Rick Ouston who said he had a call from Olson and he described where Wolfsteiner's body was located - he had phoned to complain about conditions [at Oakalla]. I put him on phone to Larry [Proke] and then I spoke to him and asked how he felt about giving evidence and he said he'd cross that bridge when he came to it.*

★ ★ ★

On the afternoon of Friday September 25, Proke was in Northorp's office discussing the Olson case. After various points had been covered, Larry implied that his section had some concerns about the CIB's hands-on case management.

"The last item raised by Proke is shown in my notes," said Northorp. "[There was] a suggestion of interference from CIB level—I discussed some of my concerns re past decisions at that level."

According to Northorp, "Interference would have had to apply to myself, or perhaps the new CIB officer, Superintendent Gordon Tomalty." Bruce thought it the right time to distinguish between this perceived interference and what he felt were legitimate concerns. He pointed out to Proke the reservations he had about the way some members of the Serious Crime Section had handled the case, including:

> 1. *The interference by one or more members in the arrest of Olson on July 29 at Surrey, and the ramifications when Louise Chartrand was murdered. At the time of Olson's arrest on the 29th, the case was Burnaby's, not Serious Crime's, and in Northorp's view, the wishes of Burnaby should have prevailed.*

2. *They considered meeting Olson when there was a warrant for his arrest.*

3. *They planned to have Olson released after his arrest on August 12, despite the fact his address book contained the name of Judy Kozma, a known victim.*

The accusations that he had interfered continued to rankle Northorp over the weekend, so he called Proke as soon as he got into the office on Monday. The issue had to be confronted: was interference real or perceived?

"I was asking Proke to assess what was said and advise facts rather than passing on gossip or grumbling. In effect, someone should put up or shut up," Northorp said. "I also pointed out there was a difference between his staff and myself. I was the one who was responsible and accountable for the Olson case from the time I was given the assignment. The questions seemed to end the issue as I was never provided with one example of the suggested interference." Bruce knew how rumour mills worked. He wondered if the concerns he had raised with Chief Superintendent Neill back on July 30 had been construed by Burnaby Detachment, the Serious Crime Section, or both as meddling.

Recovering the Money

From late August until September 10, Northorp had many discussions with his HQ in Ottawa about the recovery of monies paid to Joan Olson. On the evening of September 4, Proke phoned Northorp at home and told him both Special Prosecutor Hall and the federal Justice Department agreed that seeking the return of the money was a federal responsibility. At an appropriate time, the first step would be to request $10,000 back from McNeney, as Olson had not delivered on one commitment. Then the police would approach Olson's wife in an attempt to gain a voluntary return of the monies from her. Failing that, the department would proceed with a civil action at a time when it would not have an impact on any criminal proceeding.

On September 9, Alan Filmer, B.C.'s assistant deputy AG, phoned to request an update for the attorney general on several matters, including what steps the police intended to take to recover the monies paid out. The next day Northorp received a call from Chief Superintendent Jack Carroll, another Assistant DCI in Ottawa, on behalf of Assistant Commissioner Schramm, who was wondering, among other things, what attempts, if any, had been taken to recover the monies.

The issue of the money was raised again on October 6, but not with Ottawa. At 4:02 p.m. Northorp was talking with John Hall. A portion of his notes quoting Hall reads: "We <u>MUST</u> attempt to

Prosecutor John Hall was against payments to Olson, but once the deal was done he set out to make sure the Crown got its money's worth. He remained more adamant than most that authorities should make every effort to regain the funds disbursed to Joan Olson.

recover the money even if we aren't successful."

Hall was emphatic on this. Although Northorp's notes were usually written, the word "must" was printed in capital letters and underlined.

★ ★ ★

Olson had still not produced anything material in relation to other murders. The final $10,000 payment had not been released, as Sandra Wolfsteiner's body had not been found.

Bruce suggested a think-tank approach be taken to develop a strategy. To this end, several RCMP investigators, considered to be tops in the Lower Mainland, were assembled at the HQ on October 23 to consider what steps should be taken to solve other murders or recover other bodies of alleged victims.

They were told the payment of money was not an option. Both the attorney general and the RCMP had vetoed this. In addition, they were briefed on the circumstances under which Olson had talked. No useful strategy was ever developed by this group. Their first recommendation was to pay more money.

★ ★ ★

By the end of 1981, police had still been unable to locate Sandra Wolfsteiner's body. Some remains were found, but the most that could be determined was they were those of a young female who was the same general age as Sandra.

"As no body had been found which could be proven to be Sandra's," Bruce recalled, "no authority was given to McNeney to release $10,000."

Nylund made phone calls and wrote letters to McNeney requesting the return of the money in accordance with the agreement. It was never returned.

In 1982, after Northorp had retired, he was told by a knowledgeable source, "The money has been written off."

Moving On

On December 30, 1981, Northorp worked his last day as a police officer. This was about eighteen months before he reached maximum service. Some who followed the Olson case had his leaving early all figured out. A male caller to an open-line radio show on which Bruce appeared in January 1982 asked if he had been forced to retire.

Even Jack Webster touched on this on his TV show. "Were there any resignations from the RCMP in connection with the Olson case?" Webster asked Attorney General Allan Williams.

"Not to my knowledge," the AG responded. "The RCMP did, I think, a superb job under Superintendent Northorp."

Bruce was the only key player who had left the Force. It hurt him to think some presumed he was forced to retire or resign because of the case, and he wanted to put the rumours to rest.

"In May 1981, my wife Louisa and I were on a bus tour in England," Bruce explained. "We noticed it was mainly widows on the tour. Then and there we decided I would take early retirement and we'd enjoy some years together.

"I planned on making my last day April Fools' Day 1982. It would be significant beyond being April Fools' Day. It was April 1, 1949, when I joined the British Columbia Provincial Police, and I was promoted to the RCMP commissioned ranks on April 1, 1971.

"Things changed in the fall of 1981 when I read about some proposed changes to the RCMP Superannuation Act [that would have had a negative effect on his pension]. I decided to leave earlier than planned. I made my announcement on November 23, my wife's birthday. My retirement was a present to my wife."

Allan Williams, B.C.'s attorney general, took heat along with the other decision makers when his name was attached to the Olson payoff. Years later he had no regrets.

A letter from the commissioner of the RCMP, R.H. Simmonds, confirmed that Bruce's request to retire from the Force was dated November 23, 1981.

Seven
Justice Then, Justice Now

Justice

Justice in the legal sense is judgment by the due process of the law. To do justice is to treat one fairly or appropriately. In 1982, the court dealt with Clifford Robert Olson. He was certainly treated fairly, but whether he was dealt with appropriately depends on one's point of view. For those taunted by Olson from behind the safety of prison walls, he got away with murder.

January 1982

On January 11, Olson's trial on ten counts of first degree murder commenced at Vancouver before Mr. Justice Harry McKay. The charges included all the children except Sandra Wolfsteiner, whose body had not been recovered. Olson entered a plea of "Not Guilty" to each charge.

Fred Maile and Ed Drozda rode with Olson to court in the B.C. Sheriff's prisoner van. The tapes of Olson's conversations during interrogation were now starting to haunt him. Ironically, the only ear he could plead with was the one he had confessed to. "We can't go first degree murder, Fred. We have to go second degree. You've got to keep those tapes out of court," persisted Olson.

"It's out of my hands," replied Maile. "It's up to John Hall what goes in as evidence."

The presentation of evidence began on January 13 when Detective Tarr took the witness stand. During a *voir dire* (evidence given without the jury being present) Tarr outlined his contacts

Dennis Tarr had agreed to co-operate with RCMP Serious Crimes in late July and found himself at the heart of the Olson case controversy. He was the only trial witness to appear before Olson changed his plea to guilty.

with Olson the previous year. At this time two tapes were played that had been made at the Olson-Tarr-Maile meetings.

"When the tapes started to go in," recalled Maile, "Olson stopped the court. He asked that I come down and see him in the cells. It was then he told me he was changing his plea to guilty.

"We went back upstairs and he wanted to plead guilty to eleven charges, but we only had ten." That's when Olson accepted the Wolfsteiner charge, admitting he had killed the one victim yet to be found.

After the noon recess there was an unexpected development. The two lawyers, John Hall, acting for the Crown, and Robert Shantz, acting for Olson, had a private meeting in Justice McKay's chambers. When they returned the case was adjourned to the next day.

On the morning of the 14th, Olson changed his pleas from "Not Guilty" to "Guilty." In addition, he entered a plea of "Guilty" to the murder of Wolfsteiner, a count that had now been added.

Justice McKay said in sentencing, "I do not have the words to adequately describe the enormity of your crimes and the heartbreak and anguish you have brought to so many people. No punishment a civilized country could give you could come close to being adequate."

sunday

the province

EXCLUSIVE INTERVIEW

Child killer taunts police

By DAMIAN INWOOD and JON FERRY

Olson has always managed to find someone willing to listen to him and occasionally fall victim to his endless con game.

Vancouver Province writers Damian Inwood and Jon Ferry followed this article with a controversial book, *Olson Murders*.

He then sentenced Olson to eleven life terms without eligibility for parole for 25 years.

"I would not normally presume to express my views to the National Parole Board, which has a separate function," he added, "but in this case my considered opinion is that you should never be granted parole for the remainder of your days. It would be foolhardy to let you at large."

Section 745

In accordance with Canadian law, Justice McKay sentenced Olson to life in prison, with no eligibility for parole for 25 years. This is the maximum sentence that can be imposed in Canada, no matter how horrific the crime.

Our courts do not have the power to impose a sentence for each count or to order that those sentences be served consecutively. Nor do they have the power to impose the death penalty. In fact, at the time that Olson was sentenced, the courts didn't really even have the power to sentence an individual to life with no eligibility for parole for 25 years.

"I knew," said Bruce, "as did others, Olson would be entitled to a judicial review fifteen years after the date of his arrest in 1981. It would be his right by virtue of Section 745 of the Criminal Code of Canada, whereby he could apply to have his parole eligibility date lowered from 25 years."

Olson applied for and had his review in 1997, though no one, including Olson, thought he would succeed. He did succeed in making headline news again, and he got another trip to B.C. Olson's judicial review was an appalling joke, perpetrated by our justice system. It was also a colossal waste of taxpayers' money.

Worst of all, it was another tragic ordeal in the lives of the families and friends of his victims. It brought Olson back to the forefront and resurrected their pain. "It's like pulling the scabs off again," one parent said. Many shared their grief, though unable to comprehend the true depths of their agony.

The jury got it right. Jury members took only fifteen minutes to deny Olson's application, and they went even further. They recommended he not be allowed to reapply until he has served his full 25 years.

We can only hope that Olson will never be free to roam our streets again.

"I'm convinced he'll never make parole and his only release will take place when he's carried out in a coffin," said Bruce. "His likely options are death by natural causes, at the hands of another inmate, or suicide."

★ ★ ★

Olson's guilty plea brought the trial to an abrupt end. Olson's lawyer Robert Shantz was quite critical of the payments to Joan Olson, describing them as "improper" and "politically insane." Later he revised his stance.

Dr. Stanley Semrau, an Ontario psychiatrist, was the last witness to testify at Olson's Section 745 hearing. Semrau has dealt with hundreds of psychopaths, murderers, and sex offenders. He described Olson as "the most disturbed personality I have ever encountered."

Olson told him he had sexually assaulted in excess of a hundred children, mostly girls but some boys (though he never admitted to sexually assaulting the eleven children he murdered). He bragged about using drugs, alcohol, candy, and various other means to lure children into his grasp. He told Semrau he was writing a manual on seduction techniques. He admitted to Semrau that as time went on, he began to enjoy killing his victims. It was apparent that Olson found pleasure in describing how he disposed of those he killed.

At the time of the judicial review, Olson was 57 years of age and showing no sign of burnout. Dr. Semrau testified that he is totally untreatable and more dangerous now than he was when he was arrested. He is incapable of feeling remorse towards the families of those he killed.

Semrau suggested it would be reckless in the extreme to allow Olson out in public without being shackled and surrounded by guards.

★ ★ ★

The Olson story will not die until his death, if then. For as long as he lives, he will continue to plague the system with his never-ending claims, complaints, and observations. As this book went to print, Olson was insisting that he was responsible for murders in Ireland and Hawaii.

Eight
Where Shadows Linger

Fallout

After the bombshell comes fallout. Whether it be the slow descent from a mushroom cloud of toxic residue or the general side effects of the latest scandal, fallout should ultimately be a prelude to clarity.

The follow-up to Olson's guilty plea was a questioning media, a sensitive RCMP, and a restless public. Fallout from the disclosures surrounding the Olson case failed to clarify matters and led to myths and misinformation generated by some reporters and a few investigators.

An Efficient Investigation

Two of the problems affecting the Olson investigation were transfers of key personnel and shortages of staff, which resulted in overtaxed police officers. Some left the province, others were transferred to new duties within District One. For example, Inspector Larry Proke was transferred to General Investigation just after the task force commenced. Investigators on the task force did not know him and he was unfamiliar with his new personnel. It made for a difficult situation. By coincidence he had come from Burnaby, where the Olson case originated, but this boon to the investigation was more a matter of luck than planning.

"It is amazing the case proceeded as well as it did under those circumstances," reflected Bruce. "Certainly the RCMP's post-case analysis should have noted those factors. One would expect corrective action would have been taken to avoid problems in the future."

If any lessons were learned, they seem to have been forgotten by RCMP management and its political masters. By 1999, personnel shortages in the Lower Mainland had never been worse. An assistant commissioner from Ottawa visited Surrey in July 1999 and was unable to give any assurance the shortages would be remedied within a year. A Burnaby city councillor spoke to Bruce and touched on the same subject. He too was alarmed at the shortages of RCMP staff in Burnaby. Burnaby and most other communities were promoting the community policing concept. The councillor explained the NCO in charge of a particular zone had just become familiar with the civilians he was working with, only to be transferred. Now a new relationship would have to be developed as the new incumbent went through the learning process. Such illogical management made the public wonder if the RCMP and politicians really cared about local crime.

Back in 1981 there were also problems of jurisdiction and second-guessing, with subordinates criticizing the men in charge. In major cases, an investigator may solicit a range of viewpoints from colleagues, but the overall investigation can rarely be run by consensus. There must be a decision-maker. This was evident from the fragmented efforts that occurred before Bruce Northorp was named co-ordinator of the 1981 task force.

After Northorp became co-ordinator, he became a target for a certain amount of criticism. Bruce commented, "I would hear from Proke that the Serious Crime members felt this or said that, but no names were given. I had the impression he was passing on the opinions of just a few."

"I found out in 1998 that the RCMP's 1982 post-case analysis concluded that the investigation ran very efficiently after I took over. No one in the Force was thoughtful enough to tell me that. I'd been wondering for almost two decades what they had determined."

Bruce noticed a lack of support in other areas as well. "After retiring, I found it stressful to be quizzed on the Olson case. Most issues were matters I had no part in. The RCMP had opted not to make disclosures beyond a certain point. I was forced to go into those issues that tended to reflect on myself. I felt the Force could at least have taken the heat off me."

Where Credit is Due

It appears that other individuals felt slighted as well, and responded by becoming defensive. Bruce remembered, "Sometime in September 1981 I phoned Superintendent Norm Fuchs, at Burnaby. I felt two of his investigators deserved to be commended for their work on the Olson case. At the time, from the little information I had, I thought that Les Forsythe and Sid Slater should be recognized. I suggested to Fuchs he might wish to consider commendations."

At the end of October, Bruce received a memo from his superior. Gordon Tomalty asked for Northorp's comments on a four-page report from Burnaby that was signed by Howitt. The report was obviously the result of Northorp's call to Fuchs, but the questions Tomalty asked indicated something was unclear. This was understandable, as Tomalty had just been transferred in to replace Bill Neill as OIC CIB and knew none of the details of what had transpired during the hectic months of July and August.

When Bruce read the report, he found that it was inaccurate and reflected poorly on himself. In essence, it demonstrated how a communication breakdown can fester into sores of discontent. Although the original report was signed by Howitt, seventeen years later Bruce learned it had been written by Les Forsythe.

Forsythe's perceptions, especially when taken together with Larry Proke's comments about interference after he moved to the Serious Crime Section, indicate there were some serious misconceptions. Les was reporting somewhat defensively based on what he knew or understood from discussions with his superiors Howitt and Proke. Neither Howitt nor Forsythe knew that the purpose of the requested memo was to support Northorp's desire for Forsythe to receive commendation. It was logical that Fuchs would choose not to mention that recognition might be forthcoming in case it did not materialize, but the apparent defensiveness and erroneous conclusions drawn by Howitt and Forsythe say much about their state of mind.

Basically, the Burnaby report outlined how Forsythe and others had advanced the investigation into Ada Court's disappearance. It said, among other things, that after the July 15 meeting at Burnaby,

Proke briefed Northorp about Olson and suggested they might request surveillance. That was wrong. Bruce had no contact from Burnaby until Howitt phoned him on July 23.

"It also reported that Howitt gave me details of their case on the 23rd," stated Bruce. "Details is hardly the correct word. I was given scant information to satisfy myself surveillance was justified."

The report mentioned Burnaby had a manpower shortage and was not able to supply the additional coverage required. No mention had been made to Northorp about a manpower shortage. He told Howitt they could have the surveillance coverage and asked them to come in and work out what extra conditions would have to apply if they were to watch a potential killer. He fully expected Howitt and others to come to his office.

"Absent from the report was any mention of the second call Howitt made, cancelling his request," declared Bruce. "Nor was there mention they had decided to go to JFO based on the fact they considered Olson a target."

Bruce questions the comment about manpower. He headed the Burnaby GIS for years until 1970, when it was much smaller. On a major issue, and for a short term, extra manpower was always available by simply applying extra resources to a problem from within the section and delaying lesser matters for a few days.

"By the 8th of September, Howitt had no problem with manpower or the concept of riders and a tail-car," said Northorp. "He phoned me that day for surveillance dealing with some robberies." His notes read, in part, "They'd supply 2 riders and one car with 2 members."

In retrospect, the fact that Forsythe penned the report seems to indicate that he was left in the dark on some relevant points. Fewer misunderstandings before the report was signed might have helped win him the commendation that he richly deserved.

Media Surveillance

If Northorp thought the internal accusations were misdirected, the external misinformation proved to be even farther off-base. "On January 14, 1982, after I retired," he can now recall with the slightest trace of a smile, "the worst came at 9 in the evening while Louisa and I were watching a CBC-TV special on Olson. I was devastated by what came out of the mouth of their reporter, Chris Bird."

> *From being one of several suspects, Olson became the main suspect. Twice Corporal Forsythe goes to Superintendent Bruce Northorp, the man who will later head the investigation, but Northorp is not convinced.*

The next blow came from reporter Sue Stern, who continued with a vivid if inaccurate retelling of the facts.

> *On July 15, Forsythe organizes a meeting of about twenty investigators here at the Burnaby RCMP Detachment. They discuss Olson as a suspect in the murders of Johnsrude and Weller and in the disappearance of Kozma, Partington, and Court. Forsythe has come up with a profile of the killer and believes Olson is the murderer. Shortly after the meeting, the co-ordination of the investigation is taken over by the RCMP headquarters in Vancouver. It will take two precious weeks and four more murders before senior police officers are as convinced as Forsythe that Olson is the killer.*

The inference was that Northorp refused to provide surveillance, which caused the death of four children. Bruce reacted by retaining legal counsel. His lawyer wrote the CBC on January 19, and his letter included the following paragraph:

> *Forsythe never spoke to Northorp on any matter either in person or by any other means prior to Olson's arrest on August 12th, 1981. Further, Forsythe did not come under Northorp's command structure and consequently would not report to him on any matter... The erroneous statements made by Bird and the inferences raised by Stern, reflect adversely on the ability and competency of Supt. Northorp as a Senior and distinguished officer...It is our position that the remarks are inaccurate, defamatory and actionable. Our client has therefore instructed us to demand an immediate retraction and apology.*

The CBC response was speedy. The broadcaster's letter of January 22 read in part:

> *After I received your letter, I caused inquiries to be made and our sources have either inadvertently or deliberately misled us. A retrospective report on the Olson affair was being prepared when Olson changed his plea and was sentenced all in one day, so that time pressures upon us were intense. This, of course, does not excuse any implication that might be inferred from our broadcast, that Supt. Northorp is anything but a highly responsible and respected Police Officer. We regret very much any distress we might have caused Supt. Northorp; this was not our intention. I would like to take this opportunity to add that Supt. Northorp's relationship with us and, we are told, with other members of the media, was helpful, insightful and co-operative.*

Included with the CBC letter to Northorp was a copy of the apology, which was aired twice.

> *Last week we broadcast a special on the Clifford Olson case. We said that as early as mid-July RCMP Corporal Les Forsythe was convinced that Olson was the killer and went twice to Supt. Bruce Northorp but failed to convince him. It's true that Forsythe was convinced of Olson's guilt in July and that Olson wasn't under full surveillance until the beginning of August, two weeks and four murders later. But Forsythe didn't go to Northorp and Northorp didn't learn all the facts until the end of July. It was never our intention to suggest that Northorp was anything but diligent and we regret any embarrassment we may have caused him.*

"My action in going to a lawyer was to kill the snake by setting the record straight," declared Bruce. "It likely served notice to others, I was prepared to go the distance. Although of little consequence, [the CBC also] erroneously reported that Kozma's case was raised at the Burnaby meeting on July 15."

Bruce Northorp was forthright with the media during a sensitive investigation. Seen here at a press conference, Bruce developed a particular respect for the late Moira Farrow, who wrote for the *Vancouver Sun*.

It wasn't the end of the controversy. Members of the media were picking up various stories suggesting errors had been made. They wanted accountability. A BCTV reporter told Bruce he had heard that surveillance had been refused on Olson. In addition, B.C.'s chief coroner, former RCMP Inspector Bob Galbraith, announced he was ordering an investigation under Section 25 of the B.C. Coroner's Act. He named Dr. Alan W. Askey, a coroner from Cranbrook, to head the probe.

The BCTV interest in surveillance was evident in its news broadcast of January 20, 1982. It reported the RCMP would not allow investigators to speak to the media without permission from headquarters. One of the questions BCTV wanted Les Forsythe to answer was: "Who turned down his request for surveillance on Olson on July 15, the day Forsythe identified Olson as the killer?"

It appears the media's interest in surveillance arose during a news conference held by Superintendent Lyman Henschel and Inspector Larry Proke. During that scrum, CBC reporter Chris Bird had asked, in part:

> You used a surveillance team from CLEU in July, but
> you didn't use your top surveillance organization until

into August. Why was that not done earlier? Why? I mean Special "O" are the experts, even more than CLEU or the Drug Squad or whatever.

Proke had answered the question:

That's correct, ah, there was, ah consider ... there was difficulties in manpower situation, ah, has been expressed to me. I really ... I really can't answer that.

BCTV reporter Alyn Edwards later referred to that news conference in an interview with Northorp, with a remark that suggested why they had been pushing the issue of surveillance.

So when we asked pertinent questions at the first news conference, they're all looking at each other. "Well I don't know, do you know Lyman?" And that's what really got this thing off the rails.

The situation became so contentious that on January 22, 1982, the two top RCMP officers in B.C., Deputy Commissioner Tom Venner and Assistant Commissioner Don Wilson, held an unprecedented media conference to deal with it. To that date Henschel and Proke had handled the media relations. Wilson said he'd answer three questions, which were a slight modification of those raised by BCTV two days earlier.

To the question "Who turned down Corporal Forsythe's request for surveillance following the July 15 meeting at Burnaby?" Wilson replied:

Corporal Forsythe did not make a request for surveillance as a result of the July 15, 1981, meeting held in Burnaby Detachment, although that strategy was discussed. In exploring the possibility of implementing surveillance immediately following the meeting, it was determined that Olson was out of the country, having left for the United States on July 10, 1981. A request for surveillance coverage was therefore not made at that time. Olson returned to Vancouver on July 22.

On July 23 the possibility of deploying specialized surveillance was discussed with District HQ staff. However, due to a lack of manpower to supplement the specialized surveillance team in order to provide

*intercept capability, a formal request was not sub-
mitted. The Burnaby case officers instead elected to
request the assistance from Vancouver Joint Forces
Operation, the JFO, to expedite coverage. This was
done on July 24. Before surveillance could be
deployed, additional profile information and a
contingency plan to intercept had to be drawn. In any
event, JFO manpower was already fully committed to
other targets for the weekend of July 25/26. JFO
surveillance commenced on July 27 and this was
discontinued in the early morning of July 29 when
Olson was checked and became aware of the
coverage on him.*

*On July 28 the JFO surveillance team was experi-
encing difficulty in maintaining coverage on Olson
and discussed with District HQ the possibility of ob-
taining an aerial surveillance unit from our specialized surveillance section to assist them. At that time
difficulties were identified in matching two communication systems and it was decided that if the specialized surveillance unit were to be deployed at all,
it should be with a full crew and not a partial one.
JFO personnel, however, decided to continue with the
surveillance on their own and a formal request for the
specialized unit was not submitted.*

*The decision to deploy the specialized surveil-
lance unit was made following careful evaluation of
all the case facts on July the 31st in a meeting held at
District HQ. When an attempt to implement this surveillance was made on the same date, Olson again
could not be located. It was later learned that he had
gone on a trip to Alberta. He returned to the Vancouver area on August the 6th.*

This was not the end of BCTV's relentless pursuit on the matter
of surveillance—the reporters apparently favoured their instincts
over the explanation of Assistant Commissioner Wilson. A team of
three reporters ended up on Bruce's doorstep in mid-February,

trying to get from him what they seemed to think they did not get from Wilson. Eventually Bruce agreed to an off-camera interview at his home on February 12 with Alyn Edwards.

Both Edwards and Bruce had their tape recorders going. "I pointed out I had no authority or responsibility in any of the cases until 1:50 p.m. on July 30," explained Bruce. "The main issue was surveillance. I saw no need to address this question as Wilson answered it when he said no request for surveillance had ever been turned down and gave details of the sequence of events. I told Edwards there was no substance to the allegation that surveillance was not made available. The interview went on to other issues. Edwards eventually seemed to accept my word that surveillance hadn't been refused."

Bruce did not supply Alyn Edwards with any details about discussions relating to surveillance on July 23. From reports Northorp had submitted, the RCMP was well aware discussions had taken place, but had chosen to answer the issue in the manner they did.

"I was retired, it was their case, and I saw no need to go beyond what I'd said," commented Bruce. "In hindsight, it might have made my life a little easier to explain it fully. However, it might have created problems for others."

This was much the same stance Northorp took with the coroner's office. Bruce was not willing to talk to Dr. Askey's investigator as it was an RCMP case and any questions should be directed to them. Only if they failed to answer was he prepared to comment.

Later, published accounts stated that two levels of the RCMP had not authorized the use of the Special "O" surveillance unit. "Utter nonsense," said Bruce. He also read that the cost had made everyone leery. "Expense had little bearing on Special 'O.' Costs were never a factor in my decision-making as to when the unit would be used. The unit's costs were the same whether they were targeted or sitting still. The only minor variances would be some expenses related to gasoline and, in some instances, out-of-area travel expenses. I made decisions on who to target based on the requests before me, by setting priorities."

The Unexecuted Warrant

Bruce Northorp respected the tenacity of some media members, even though he could have lived without some of their speculation. One of the issues commented on by the media and Dr. Askey in his report to the coroner was Olson's release from custody at Surrey on July 29, even though there was a warrant for his arrest. Three separate units were involved in this situation: Burnaby, JFO, and Serious Crime Section.

"In one way it's unfortunate I was approached by Nylund on the 29th, the same day Olson was arrested and released at Surrey," Bruce explained. "For a time it placed my actions in question. BCTV and [Alyn] Edwards knew a warrant existed for Olson on the 29th, knew of his arrest in Surrey and his almost immediate release the same day without the warrant being executed. Edwards was sure I'd received a phone call in the night to authorize his release. They added two and two, and came up with five.

"They thought it would have taken a high-ranking officer to order Olson's release. In their opinion, I fit their profile since the Serious Crime Section and Nylund were in my chain of command."

As the RCMP was not addressing the issue to BCTV's satisfaction, the unexecuted warrant came to reflect badly on Northorp, and he had to address it to defend his reputation. Edwards questioned him at length.

> Can you help me understand and the people that will be listening to this who have put so much time into it, because we know of the existence of the warrant and we know what happened and I'll just run over this scenario. On the 22nd of July there was a charge of indecent assault relating to an incident that occurred in Surrey on July 6th, so on the 22nd we have a charge and the decision by the prosecutor we assume to proceed by summons against Clifford Robert Olson. On the 27th of July, Corporal Forsythe, we believe, phoned Sergeant Tilley at Surrey and asked him to change that summons procedure into a warrant. Okay, so on the 27th a warrant is issued and Forsythe asked Tilley to keep if off CPIC [Canadian

*Police Information Centre]. On the 27th also
something else happens, that's when JFO surveillance
begins. We assume that the warrant is to be used as a
tool by JFO surveillance. On the 29th Olson is released
at 3:20 a.m. from the cells and at 9:35 you become
apprised of the situation from Sergeant [sic] Nylund.
At about ten o'clock Drozda goes down to meet
Dennis Tarr and asks him to phone Olson about the
warrant. Did you know anything about that, can you
offer an explanation for that?*

Bruce could not attest to the validity of the information put
forward by Edwards. All he could say was that he had told Nylund
his investigators were not to meet Olson if there was a warrant
and that Nylund's response was, "Don't worry, I'll take care of it."
Bruce assumed that if there was a warrant, Drozda and Tarr would
not meet with Olson because the warrant would have to be
executed—meaning they would have to arrest Olson. The
statement about Drozda getting Tarr to call Olson made little sense
to Bruce. He never once thought Olson would be phoned to turn
himself in.

After a lengthy exchange, Edwards seemed satisfied when
Northorp said, "I had no knowledge of the arrest at the time and
had nothing to do with Olson's release."

One of Edwards' final questions was, "Who authorized Olson's
release in Surrey?"

"I don't know," Bruce responded. "When I took on the case I
didn't look into history. I had enough to do going forward."

In fact, JFO was opposed to Olson's release, as it had accomplished its objective of arresting him. Les Forsythe wanted Olson
in custody. Serious Crime Section wanted him free. They felt he was
a source, or at least might provide a lead. Later reports said that
the decision to release Olson was mutually agreed upon. In fact,
Forsythe and JFO reluctantly agreed under pressure from the Serious Crime Section. It was Burnaby's case, and normally the wishes
of Burnaby should have prevailed. However, consciously or uncon-
sciously, Les Forsythe might have believed the HQ unit had more
status than a detachment's General Investigation Section.

Had the summons procedure been followed, Olson would have been served the document, which required him to appear in court at some specified date. He would have been free to roam the streets. This was the reason Forsythe had requested the warrant.

If the warrant had been executed, Olson would have been arrested as ordered by the warrant and placed in custody until he appeared in court. In all likelihood he would have been released on bail or on his own recognizance. The results might have been the same, but the point is that police have an obligation to arrest someone for whom there is a warrant to arrest.

If JFO had wanted to hold Olson for some reason, it could have arrested him at any time by relying on its authority to arrest, without a warrant, a person believed, on reasonable and probable grounds, to have committed an indictable offence. That offence would have been the earlier sexual assault in Surrey.

The murder of Louise Chartrand would likely not have taken place if Olson had been arrested on the Surrey warrant by Maile and Drozda on July 30. However, knowledge of the warrant was not widespread and the Serious Crime officers were apparently unaware of it.

The plan to obtain a warrant seems to have been an abuse of process. Dr. Askey, in his report to the coroner, commented, "The police should not apply for warrants to arrest without the intent of executing them."

★ ★ ★

Serious Crime wanted Olson released because Drozda, Maile, and Tarr saw him as a possible source of information on crimes. From the day Northorp became involved, he had no illusions Olson was a source.

"As far as I was concerned," he said, "he was a suspect and he was treated as such. I only had to look at his long criminal record, and his involvement as a Crown witness in the Marcoux murder case, to realize he knew every trick in the book. He simply was not going to implicate himself. I think it was idealistic to think he would supply anything of value if treated as a source."

The earlier strategy was the option of the investigators at the time. When Bruce took charge, that approach was not used. The results are evident.

Clifford Olson, Non-Suspect

Olson was considered a suspect in the Johnsrude murder in Mission as early as May 27, yet nothing concrete was done to either eliminate or implicate him. Understaffing was part of the reason.

Mission and Agassiz had heavy workloads, which continued into July. Members of these detachments were unable to attend the July 15 meeting at Burnaby. Another factor was that Mission had a better suspect at the outset. It was not until mid-June that Olson moved to the top of the list.

The fact that Serious Crime had an interest in Olson and was supposed to be building a profile on him might have blurred the issue. Mission might have erroneously concluded that it was not their responsibility to follow up on Olson.

Nonetheless, Northorp believes all suspects in any case should be interviewed as soon as possible, unless there is some compelling reason not to do so.

"By mid to late June, Olson should have been questioned," Bruce declared. "It's highly probable the investigators would have learned they were dealing with a killer, as was the case with both Darryll and Les after their contacts with Olson. It may have been sufficient to flag him as a probable murderer and deter him from further killings, or the outcome might have been similar to what transpired with Peter Sutcliffe, the Yorkshire Ripper. He was questioned several times by detectives who obviously gained nothing concrete, and his killings continued.

"Darryll did his best. I'm really impressed with what I now know about his identifying Olson as a suspect. However, the Johnsrude homicide investigation rested with others. It was up to them to further or not further Darryll's deadly accurate suspicions."

Les Forsythe was in much the same position as Darryll Kettles. He uncovered key information and concluded Olson was a prime suspect in the Johnsrude case and that of Ada Court. He did everything he could within his authority, and it should have been up to Howitt or one of his superiors to see the need for co-ordination.

It was a multi-jurisdictional case that cried out for a co-ordinator. Had that been recognized earlier, the events which began on July 30 would likely have commenced after the July 15 meeting.

The Prosecution Process

Were some prosecutors less than diligent in their handling of charges against Olson, causing them to be withdrawn? Controversy has surrounded charges arising from Olson's rape and assault of Kim Werbecky in Squamish on January 2, 1981 (see Chapter 10). Olson was in custody at Squamish until the character of the victim was brought into question.

"Years ago in Burnaby," said Bruce Northorp, "I had a like situation with two men I'd arrested for rape. The prosecutor didn't want to proceed with charges against them. He felt the hippie-looking appearance of the victim, and her willingness to accept a ride, made it almost impossible to obtain a conviction. I prevailed and the charges proceeded. The case went to the jury, who were out for a markedly short period of time before returning guilty verdicts. Clearly they had no problem with the guilt of the duo."

With deviants like Olson, it might be better to look at their total history and consider whether or not it would be beneficial to put the case before the courts and not worry unduly about the probabilities of a conviction. If he had been convicted of the Squamish charges, it is unlikely the ten 1981 murders would have taken place. As it was, the police did their job at Squamish and pressed the issue vociferously. They were simply overruled by the B.C. justice system.

The Pay-Off

It was a shock for many to learn that Olson had suddenly pleaded guilty to the eleven charges of first degree murder. Another surprise was yet to come, sprung on the public by a bold front-page headline in the January 14, 1982, *Vancouver Sun*: "Olson was paid to locate bodies."

"Anybody offering $10,000 for information leading to my whereabouts…?"

Vancouver Sun, January 20, 1982

Respected *Sun* cartoonist Les Peterson and a host of others offered social comment on the controversial decision to bring monetary incentives into play.

(Courtesy—Roy Peterson, *Vancouver Sun*.)

On January 15 the *Sun* headline said, "Olson deal greeted by disgust." In that same paper an article was headed, "Payment to murderer disgusts families of victims."

In the days that followed, most of the media followed the *Sun*'s lead, reporting how Olson was paid and how the deal was a secret, now suddenly exposed. Many members of the media condemned it as improper, scandalous, and precedent setting. Some reported an outcry from the public.

The police did not disclose the money deal before the case went to court because to do so would have prejudiced Olson's right to a fair trial. It was certainly John Hall's intention to present evidence of such an arrangement. However, the idea that it was a secret deal made for a better story.

The papers also made little mention of the facts that the arrangement was intended to be a scam or that the money was not going directly to Olson. (The money was in fact put into a trust fund for Joan Olson under the supervision of her lawyer.)

"I question the media's portrayal of an enraged Canadian public," Bruce stated. "For years after I retired, countless numbers of people, who recognized me from TV, approached me and spoke in a most amiable fashion. None of them had a bad word to say about the investigations, the payment, or anything else."

The RCMP received over a hundred letters applauding Northorp and the RCMP for their actions in this case. Most agreed with the payment; others didn't mention it. Bruce is unaware of any letters criticizing the payment.

The former attorney general of B.C., Alex McDonald, supported the deal. His opinion carried extra weight, as Attorney General Allan Williams, who authorized the payment, was a Social Credit cabinet minister, whereas McDonald was the AG for an NDP government.

Harry Rankin, a top criminal lawyer and former alderman for the City of Vancouver, also came out in support. Anyone who knew Rankin was aware he was not a Socred fan.

Some other reasoned thinking about the payment emerged. On January 27, 1982, the *Wall Street Journal* invited two philosophers, one from the University of Missouri at St. Louis and the other from the University of Calgary, to comment on the payment. The newspaper also asked for the expert opinions of the chief law assistant to the presiding judge of the Appellate Division Second Department of the New York State Supreme Court, and a program analyst in the United States Department of Justice. Three of these four persons regarded the payment as appropriate, even without the scam factor.

There are also a number of people who deplored the payment initially and had second thoughts thereafter.

In early 1982, Olson's lawyer, Robert Shantz, who was as close to the situation as anyone, described the payment as politically insane and said he did not approve of it. He apparently had a change of heart, as in 1985 the *Ottawa Citizen* reported that Shantz debated the issue of the payment with another lawyer who was opposed to it. Shantz took the position the Crown must have the freedom to strike even unpalatable bargains with criminals, and those deals must be kept. He reportedly also said the Crown had only a small chance of success of getting a conviction without Olson's co-operation.

In April 1986, Shantz appeared on the TV show *Front Page Challenge*, where he said, "Well, initially I was very much against the payment, but at this stage I actually think it was the right thing. I'm satisfied that he would not have revealed the locations of the bodies had he not received, via his wife, those funds."

Another prominent personage had second thoughts. In 1982 veteran newsman Peter Worthington, then editor-in-chief of the *Toronto Sun*, was opposed to the $100,000 payment. In 1993 he wrote an article for *Saturday Night* magazine in which he reported, "There is still widespread public anger over the RCMP's $100,000 deal with Olson. As the *Toronto Sun*'s editor-in-chief then, I joined the chorus of indignation. But now that I know more about the case and about Olson, I'm absolutely convinced it was the best investment the RCMP ever made."

Worthington's opinion cannot be taken lightly. He had frequent conversations with Olson over a period of eighteen months.

Even though stories in January 1982 said the families of the victims were disgusted with the payment, some of them, too, must have had second opinions. A November 2, 1984, headline in the *Vancouver Sun* read: "Families not critical of deal with Olson, lawyer says." Dave Gibbons, a lawyer acting for the families of Olson's victims, was quoted in the story. "The plaintiffs are not at this, or any other time, criticizing the attorney-general or the RCMP for having paid the $100,000...In August 1981, it was the best thing to do—it may have been the only thing to do."

Mr. Gibbons was acting for the families in a civil action launched to obtain the monies paid Joan Olson. They were unsuccessful.

The Scam

A story in the January 23, 1982, edition of the *Vancouver Sun* shocked Bruce. Under the headline "Briefing on payoff deal came late to RCMP chief" (a reference to RCMP Commissioner Robert

Simmonds), the article quoted Solicitor General Robert Kaplan as saying that the RCMP would "keep its word" and would not try to recover the money paid Joan Olson.

Northorp could not understand who had given their word to Joan Olson or her lawyer that the RCMP would not try to recover the money. From the outset it had been abundantly clear that the operation was to be a scam. Joan Olson's lawyer was so sure the police would attempt to recover the money that he unsuccessfully tried to put a clause in the agreement preventing such an action.

After the agreement was reached, Bruce had spoken many times to top brass in Ottawa, answering questions about what steps would be or had been taken to recover the money. He also had discussions with the provincial Attorney General's Ministry about recovery. John Hall, Crown

An indication that the federal government would not seek to recover the $100,000 came from Solicitor General Robert Kaplan in Ottawa. "Buying information by police is a 100-year-old practice...the responsibility of enforcing justice is assisted if the people they obtain information from know that their word is their bond."

Counsel, had said, "We must attempt to recover money even if we aren't successful."

To Northorp's knowledge, no one had said that recovery would not be attempted.

After reading the article in the *Sun*, Northorp suspected why recovery action was not taken. The lead sentence of the article said, "RCMP Commissioner Robert Simmonds says he and Solicitor General Robert Kaplan were told of the $90,000 payoff to convicted murderer Clifford Olson on September 10—ten days after it had been authorized." It was the following Monday, September 14, when Northorp detected he was on the hot seat during a conference call with Ottawa. Those present at the Vancouver HQ were Deputy Commissioner Venner, Assistant Commissioner Wilson, and Chief Superintendent Tomalty. Northorp, being the low man on the totem pole, was left to answer Commissioner Simmonds' queries. The commissioner wanted to know how it was possible for the money deal to go from being "unthinkable" when it was first proposed to becoming "fully recommended" in such short order. It was obvious Simmonds was piqued. When Bruce explained the provincial authorities were of the opinion there was no obligation to honour an agreement made under duress, the commissioner snapped, "It's not duress."

Deputy Commissioner Jensen, the acting commissioner, had approved the original arrangement and payment of monies in the absence of Commissioner Simmonds. Word gradually filtered through the ranks that the commissioner was strongly critical of the decision.

Reading between the lines, Bruce concluded Solicitor General Kaplan and/or the commissioner had vetoed the original plan to collect the money. Hence, no attempt was to be made to recover it.

The $100,000 had been provided from federal funds, and although the B.C. government had an interest in the recovery, it seems the federal will prevailed. On February 8, 1982, Bruce met with Dr. Gilbert Kennedy of the provincial Attorney General's Ministry for almost two hours, discussing recovery of the monies. On February 28 he had a twenty-minute phone call from a Duncan lawyer, David Williams, who was working for the AG's Ministry on the same topic.

By all accounts, the issue was shelved after that.

Nine
The Benefit of Hindsight

Reflection

Reflection is the process of taking long and careful consideration of events and drawing conclusions. Thoughtful contemplation can be a necessary but painful process.

It is true that solutions are more evident with the benefit of hindsight. Nevertheless, if we accept only what we are told and neglect honest introspection, we have learned nothing and we are bound to repeat our mistakes.

Darryll Kettles

During my research for this book in early 1998, a serving RCMP member suggested in confidence that Darryll Kettles was the first person to identify Olson as Daryn Johnsrude's murderer as early as May 1981. The tip was so unexpected and shocking that I received it with much skepticism. If it were true, why would Kettles' name not figure prominently in the investigation?

Bruce Northorp, when apprised of the information, shook his head and quipped, "I doubt that. That's a crucial point and it's something I would remember. This is the first I've heard that."

Nevertheless, the new information had to be verified or discounted to ensure there were no loose ends to this story. It was a jolting surprise when I discovered the tipster was correct. Darryll Kettles was indeed the first person to name Olson as Johnsrude's killer. How could this be? Why was this not a well-known aspect of the case? There was just one way to find out for certain—consult Kettles directly.

On our first encounter by telephone, Darryll Kettles met my questions with a long pause. "You have caught me by surprise," he finally said in an emotional voice. "That's a touchy subject. You are the first one who has wanted to talk with me about it. I have agonized for years that all these children died and I couldn't do anything to stop it. I was personally devastated. It's really tough for me to even think about them. I try to keep it out of my mind. I wouldn't talk to just anybody," he added hesitantly, "but you were always a straight shooter and I trust you—Okay, I'll talk to you. So far, nobody has paid attention to anything I had to say about Olson."

We arranged a meeting for the following week. Darryll called the next day, emotionally distraught. "Your phone call has opened old wounds," he said. "I can't sleep and I can't eat just thinking about this. My arthritis is acting up. I can't wait until next week. I have to get some of this off my chest. I would really like to get this over with. It's painful for me to even think about it." The meeting was moved up.

"I had put a lot of effort into the investigation and I was sure Olson was a killer," Darryll began. "I wasn't looking for any glory. All I wanted to do was take a bad guy off the street. Even now," he added, "the last thing I want to do is cause anybody trouble. There's been enough of that."

Olson killed eleven children. We know of several others he sexually assaulted and brutalized. They are fortunate just to be alive. Even now, more than eighteen years later, the pain and suffering continues for the families of those he so callously murdered. These are the obvious victims.

Not so obvious are those such as Darryll Kettles. He found himself *persona non grata* at Vancouver headquarters while others, after Olson's arrest, appeared to bask in the limelight, exchanging pats on the back. Flushed with success, no one wanted to hear anything to dampen the glory or diminish the credit. Olson was in prison where he was likely to stay for the rest of his miserable, rotten life. End of story, or so they thought.

No one wanted to acknowledge the obvious. Darryll, early on, possessed the key to the Johnsrude homicide. Had they listened, it is possible seven lives might have been spared.

There are no winners here—only victims, still suffering for the terrible sins of one individual.

Over the ensuing years, Darryll tried to speak with senior police administrators. He was met with disbelief and disdain as they visualized, with horror, the consequences of Darryll's words, if true. This was a can of putrid worms best left undisturbed. They took the easy road. They did nothing.

It was a great relief for Darryll when he was finally able to unburden himself seventeen years later.

Kettles had no idea that now-retired Superintendent Bruce Northorp had been totally unaware of his suspicions until the spring of 1998. Northorp had always believed Les Forsythe was the first person to suspect Olson was a child-killer. He had reviewed countless files and had spoken to most of the people involved in the Olson case. Not once had Kettles' name been mentioned.

In contrast, Bill Hudyma, now a sergeant at Prince George, confirmed, "I remember the night Olson was arrested at Agassiz. The girl was stoned out of her mind and Olson did a lot of talking. The one thing that has stuck with me all these years was Olson saying, 'You would be surprised what's really going on.' Darryll called me into his office the morning after I administered the breathalyzer test to Olson. 'This is the guy that did Johnsrude,' he said. Darryll was adamant. If you know Darryll at all, you know he is always drawing pictures of what he is talking about. Pointing to what he had drawn he said, 'I lived here, the girl lives here, and Olson lives right there. This is where Johnsrude was last seen and that's where the girl was picked up. It's him. Olson killed Johnsrude.'"

I found that my story was not coming together as planned. The unexpected twists were disturbing. There was the temptation to walk away and forget it. "Are you going to write what happened or are you going to gloss over it?" Darryll asked.

Many RCMP, both serving and retired, thought the whole project should be dropped. "No good can come of it," they said.

Who, then, would speak for Darryll? Everyone deserves to be heard and acknowledged.

Police work is a trying occupation. Police officers work too many homicides and too many sexual assaults. They see too many victims suffer, and too many criminals walk free. It takes its toll. Shortly after the Olson case, Darryll contracted a severe case of rheumatoid arthritis. He attributes this directly to his personal frustration and agony over the Olson tragedies. It took nine long years of suffering before his deteriorating health resulted in a medical discharge. To help him deal with his inner turmoil, Darryll ultimately underwent counselling.

He only wanted to forget about Olson.

Most of those touched by the Olson case have done everything in their power to try and forget. There are no good memories here, only disgust and frustration. Serving policemen are reluctant to discuss the case at all. Some retired policemen would only speak on the condition their names not be used. Those who were close to the case are still haunted by the young, defenceless victims. They still ask, "Could I have done more to save them?"

During early discussions with Darryll it was apparent he did not believe that Northorp was unaware of his suspicions. Darryll still felt anger at the superintendent for ignoring his information.

When I suggested he meet with Bruce, Darryll exclaimed, "I just can't face him right now. I have too many negative feelings about this whole affair. Maybe after we work through some of these things I'll talk with him, but I'm not up to that yet."

★ ★ ★

It took more than a year before Darryll Kettles was ready to meet with Bruce Northorp. The meeting involved visiting various strategic sites.

"I'll first take you to the area around Cottonwood and Clarke Road," Darryll suggested. "You'll see for yourselves what I have been talking about. Olson, Kathy Sallow, and Daryn Johnsrude all lived within a stone's throw of each other. I'll then take you to where Daryn Johnsrude was found near Deroche. Then I'll show you where some of Olson's other victims were left, close to Weaver Lake in the Agassiz area. I'm a bit nervous and apprehensive about this. Anyway, we'll need a four-wheel drive to get up to the Weaver Lake area." A breakfast meeting was arranged at a cafe near Darryll's home.

In 1999, Darryll Kettles (right) and Bruce Northorp made a trip to the Weaver Lake crime scenes with author Les Holmes. All three RCMP officers were long retired at the time. For Darryll it was a day of conversation long overdue.

Over toast and coffee, Bruce explained, "I first heard Olson's name on July 23, 1981, when I approved surveillance on Olson and invited Burnaby to come in to discuss the details and ride-along requirements. Burnaby never did come in. In fact, Bill Howitt phoned fifteen minutes later and said they would be going to Joint Forces. I wondered why they would do that, but it was their decision to make as they had conduct of the case. To demonstrate how little I knew of the case, I spelled Olson as Olsen in my notebook."

As breakfast progressed, it was apparent that Darryll was feeling less anxious. "I have been in Northorp's office," he said later. "I have seen how he writes everything in a steno type notepad. He is very thorough and his notes are meticulous. Up until I spoke with him, I couldn't believe he was not fully aware of what I had been saying about Olson. I wish now I had got in the car and driven to headquarters and asked to speak personally with him. Had I done that, things might have been different."

It is one thing to look at a map and see where Olson, Daryn Johnsrude, and Kathy Sallow lived in relation to Burquitlam Plaza and Mac's Milk at Cottonwood and Clarke Road. To actually drive there and look at these places is even more convincing. One couldn't help but wonder, had Darryll been able to convince the Mission or Serious Crime investigators to physically visit these addresses, as he had suggested many times, would Olson's reign of terror have been shortened?

"Once you took over the case in late July, you did exactly what I was asking the guys to do in May," Darryll informed Bruce on the drive to Deroche and Agassiz. "You put Olson under surveillance. I originally blamed Fred Maile and the Mission investigators," he added. "They didn't push it. They obviously didn't have the same enthusiasm I did. I should have made two copies of everything. I only made one copy that night and gave it to Mission.

"It was Don Tobin who gave them their lead on the Saskatchewan pickup. He checked the vehicle near where Daryn Johnsrude was found, noted the Saskatchewan plate, and saw the clothes in the back. I know they eliminated the driver as a suspect within ten days to two weeks.

"They didn't have any other suspects, except Olson. I was convinced they would carry the ball. If I had a murder file and a suspect I would at least question him. I know it would have been only circumstantial and he probably wouldn't have admitted anything, but at least it might have slowed him down."

Near Deroche, Darryll pointed to where Daryn Johnsrude had been found, south of the highway. "I think this is where he was coming with Kathy Sallow," he declared. "This is where we would have found her had he not run off the road."

The journey continued past the Sasquatch Inn, beyond the Elbow Lake Minimum Security Prison Camp, and up Weaver Lake Road. In 1981 the road was in better shape, Darryll stated as the four-wheel drive churned its way upward. Then police cars could reach the lake without difficulty. Now, without the truck, the rocky and deeply rutted Weaver Lake Road was impassable.

Darryll described how Olson had been incarcerated at nearby Mountain Prison and probably at Elbow Lake Prison Camp. The Elbow Lake Camp is a minimum-security facility. There are no fences and only a couple of guards. The prisoners live in trailers. The inmates supplied firewood to the nearby wilderness campsite.

Kettles suggested a stranger would never find his way up here. Bruce had to agree.

"Judy Kozma was found at the last campsite, just past the bridge," said Darryll, pointing. "There are a few more sites now. Raymond King was found on a side road just before the campground by a couple who were out for a walk. They detected a bad odour and called the police. It was actually a police dog that found him.

"Ada Court was found up that road back of Hemlock Valley," Darryll reflected on the drive back toward Elbow Lake Prison Camp. "You can see how the Burquitlam Plaza, Lougheed Mall, and that area around Cottonwood and Clarke Road was Olson's backyard. This area was also his backyard. He knew this vicinity very well.

"I always believed a criminal operates in an area known to him," Darryll said. "He doesn't commit crimes in unfamiliar territory. I am convinced the whole thing was a trip for Olson from the time he got the kids into the car until he did it. The whole thing was a trip.

"I still can't understand how Olson beat us up so badly that we all have this excruciating pain. I have really struggled just thinking about the families on this. You can't bring the kids back. Olson was such a chicken shit, they would all have been unconscious."

Kettles still regrets asking Olson about the blood on his T-shirt when he first encountered him in Agassiz. Thereafter, Olson always destroyed his clothing after each murder and replaced it with similar clothing. Even his wife did not detect the garment switch.

"I made as much noise about Olson as I was capable of. Do you know how I found out they were going to arrest Olson?" Darryll asked. "I was at a party on a day off. There was a New Westminster policeman there and he told me in confidence that the RCMP believed Olson had killed a number of kids. They had him under surveillance and he had committed a number of crimes. He concluded they would be arresting him soon."

After Olson had been arrested and things were getting back to normal, Kettles travelled to the Vancouver headquarters where he asked Staff Sergeant Arnie Nylund what happened to his information.

"Come with me," directed Arnie as he led Darryll into a room crammed with four-drawer file cabinets. "You want to read the

Olson file? Go ahead. We got ten thousand tips and yours was one of them. We followed them up as best we could."

"I don't think that was a fair comment," said Darryll. "I gave them more than that. It was an embarrassment. They couldn't make it go away, but they could minimize what I did. I'll never get over the deaths of those seven kids. That's a hard thing to live with.

"The last time I saw Olson I was washing my car at Agassiz Detachment. Olson had been travelling around with the Serious Crime guys, smoking cigars, eating steaks, and acting like a big shot while identifying sites where he had left his victims. They borrowed the hose so Olson could wash the mud off his shoes. When he finished he threw the hose at my feet. I felt like shooting him right there. That's when they told me Sallow and I would not be testifying. I was pissed off anyway, but that was the crowning insult.

"I couldn't believe they wouldn't be calling us," Darryll added. "Here we had a young, thin, fair, longhaired teenager who was the epitome of all his other victims. This timid, innocent young girl personified what Olson was: a monster picking on petite, vulnerable, fragile kids. She would have made the perfect witness and she could have given his *modus operandi*, knock-out drops and all."

Looking back, one wonders how others failed to see the situation as clearly as Darryll Kettles. He has paid dearly for his insight. Olson murdered seven children following Darryll's encounter with him. The ghosts of these victims haunt him still. He is tortured by his thoughts, constantly wondering what else he could have done to prevent their deaths. He tries desperately to force them from his mind, but the mere mention of Olson brings it all back. He sees their faces. He feels their tears.

"It's really strange," Darryll added. "I later worked with Mike Lysyk, who was at Mission in 1981. I know it's hard to believe, but we never once talked about the Olson case. He was probably like me and just wanted to forget about it."

Les Forsythe

Burnaby Corporal Les Forsythe felt no relief as the Vancouver task force pursued Olson. He was bitter that he had not received

Les Forsythe (right) found some relief in the process of discussing the events of 1981 with Les Holmes.

assistance when he urgently needed it in mid to late July. He was troubled that more children had been reported missing after he fingered Olson.

During the ensuing weeks, as the full horror of Olson's activities unfolded, Les became more despondent. The enormity of the crimes overwhelmed him. The burden of carrying this case alone, his plea for assistance mishandled, had taken its toll. To find himself out of the loop when the case went to headquarters made matters even worse. Forsythe had lost his appetite for active, front-line policing. He sought solace by transferring to the RCMP Training Section, where he remained for many years. Ironically, when he did return to active policework it was as a road supervisor for the support unit he needed so desperately in 1981, the Special "O" Section.

Like Darryll, after Olson's arrest he found himself unwelcome at the Serious Crime Section. It was apparent senior personnel were uncomfortable in his presence. On one occasion when he appeared before Assistant Commissioner Don Wilson, the CO of District One, he was grateful for his voluminous notes describing the circumstances of Olson's release during the early morning hours of July 29. He could discern from the questions asked that there was some uncertainty as to who exactly had wanted Olson turned loose.

Les Forsythe deserves a great deal of credit for his drive, insight, and persistence. Northorp's suggestion in 1981 that Forsythe be considered for commendation went nowhere. Neither Les nor anyone else has received any official recognition for their efforts.

When asked about the July 15 meeting, Inspector Larry Proke commented, "Les was not all that sure Olson was a killer at this stage of the investigation. Other suspects were discussed at that meeting."

The old adage "Actions speak louder than words" contradicts this observation. Forsythe had Sid Slater arrange for the helicopter, and, they flew off to Deroche to look for fresh gravesites. He quickly researched Olson's past and developed a detailed profile of Olson's current known and suspected criminal activities. Even more impressive, he single-handedly and on his own initiative arranged the Burnaby meeting that included investigators from all of the areas from which he suspected missing children may have met their demise at the hands of Olson. Of course subsequent events proved Les Forsythe to be correct. His intuition and deductive reasoning were exceptional.

In fairness to Proke, he is correct in saying other suspects were discussed at the July 15 meeting. Vancouver Serious Crime Section investigators discussed at least two other suspects. Their presentation took some of the focus away from Olson. But Forsythe called the meeting, and Clifford Robert Olson was the one and only suspect put forth by the corporal. There was no doubt in his mind.

Darryll Kettles and Les Forsythe arrived at the same conclusion with only the barest of facts. They were not satisfied to just do their job as it related to the matter at hand. They sensed that Olson was evil personified. The more they learned, the surer they became. Others who did not speak directly with Olson, or who declined to actually go and view the locations where the children were last seen in relation to his residence, failed to comprehend how these two could be so certain of his guilt.

One of Forsythe's supervisors, who would only speak if promised anonymity, confided, "I have never spoken to anyone about this case. It's too painful. When Les Forsythe first spoke to me about Olson he didn't say, 'This may be the guy.' He said, 'This is the guy who killed these kids.' There was no doubt in his mind. When CLEU [JFO] arrested Olson in Surrey, neither Les nor CLEU felt he should have been released. CLEU abandoned the case the next day.

RCMP officer Ed Drozda (behind Olson) and his partner Fred Maile got as close to Olson as any cops could. They rode with Olson to his trial on the day he changed his plea to guilty.

"I know Les thinks I let him down," he added, "but that's not true. I did the best I could. I just couldn't get any people to help out. I went to several units and was turned down due to personnel shortages. I actually get physically sick when I even think about it. It's probably the reason I quit when I did." He has chosen a self-imposed exile in the shadows.

Now retired, Les tries to banish the Olson case to the dark recesses of his memory. Unfortunately, the shadows linger. "Could I have done more?" he asks. The question haunts him. "It hurts to remember," he said. "Most cases are long forgotten. This case just will not go away."

Fred Coombs

The same questions and memories haunt Fred Coombs, the road supervisor for the JFO team on July 29. Although JFO was acting strictly as a support unit and had no case responsibility on this occasion, Coombs cannot help wondering what more he could have done to change the course of events. He did make it known he opposed Olson's release in Surrey, but the question always remains, "Would it have made a difference if I had argued longer and harder?"

Ed Drozda

Ed Drozda had to learn the ropes in the Serious Crime Section in a hurry. Nothing had prepared him for a case of such magnitude.

"At the time, we had a job to do and you can't calculate the effect it has on you. It left an effect on everybody. We knew Olson was as dirty as they come. You could see he was a manipulator. He was literally feeding his ego. You just steel yourself and do it. I didn't realize how much stress I was under until I retired. We all had a job to do and we went out and did it. We didn't do it alone and we didn't make all the decisions ourselves. Everyone pitched in.

"There seemed to be a security leak when we were dealing with Olson. The media seemed to know our every move. I don't know if it was at Oakalla or where.

"I have been asked to talk with people doing books or articles on Olson over the years. I have always declined because I didn't want to feed his ego."

Fred Maile

"We were all fairly new on the Serious Crime Section," said Fred Maile. "Nothing had prepared us for anything as big as the Olson case." The sheer volume of information coming in was enormous, and then all the other systems such as data entry had to be put in place.

Prior to his transfer to the Serious Crime Section, Maile was stationed at Squamish, where Jim Hunter was the lone GIS investigator. At that time the Squamish locale was known within the Serious Crime Section as the dumping grounds because of the large number of Vancouver-area murder victims found there. It was the usual practice for someone from the Vancouver Police Homicide Unit to accompany a Serious Crime investigator to the scene.

Hunter was unable to handle all of the murders, and Maile was assigned to assist. As it worked out, he spent most of his time working with Hunter on GIS.

In 1980 Maile was promoted to corporal and assigned to the Serious Crime Section at Vancouver HQ. He was known

Philosophical in later years, Fred Maile went "private" and in 1999 was president of the Private Investigators Association of B.C.

within the RCMP as a seasoned and competent investigator, a jovial individual who seemed to be always smiling, and who was well liked by his peers and superiors. His supervisors had confidence in his abilities and he was a welcome addition to the Serious Crime Section.

On January 9, 1981, Jim Hunter called to give his friend a tip regarding the Marnie Jamieson murder at Sechelt. Hunter told Maile that a man named Clifford Olson had indecently assaulted a young woman named Kim Werbecky at Squamish and a teenage boy at Richmond. When Hunter mentioned Olson had been driving a green Ford Granada with opera windows at the time of the Werbecky indecent assault, Maile became very interested. "Hold it right there," he said. "A vehicle of that description was seen picking up a girl of Jamieson's description about the time of her disappearance, and green paint was located on a rock at the site where her body was found."

Maile began to look more closely at Olson. During his inquiries he found that Olson was suspected of credit card fraud and had gone to the credit card office to straighten out a misunderstanding. At the time he had a fifteen- or sixteen-year-old girl on his arm.

In an attempt to garner more information, Maile put out an all-points inquiry asking for any information on Olson. He received three replies that failed to further his investigation.

170

In addition, Maile took a paint sample from Olson's car and had it compared with the paint at the scene of the Jamieson homicide. The RCMP Crime Detection Laboratory found that the paint samples did not match.

When Maile and Drozda assisted on the Johnsrude murder, they were extremely busy. While they were there, the local officers, MacIntosh and Lysyk, were called away to investigate an unconnected homicide in the parking lot of a Mission pub.

"I only included Olson as a possible suspect in the Johnsrude murder because of his assault on the boy at Richmond," said Maile. "We had not run into much of that before.

"Prior to the Olson cases we had been going non-stop for several months. As an example, we were out in the Valley doing an attempted homicide when Arnie phoned and asked us to be in Hope the next morning at 9 a.m. to help with a murder there. We were still working at Hope when Arnie phoned again and asked us to stop at Chilliwack to work on a double murder. Ed Drozda was sick by this time, and I told Arnie to get someone else. We couldn't handle it."

It was out-of-character for him to respond as he did on May 26 when Darryll Kettles phoned him about his suspicions regarding Olson and the Johnsrude murder, but it was perhaps an indication of the stress he was under.

"At one time I spoke to Darryll Kettles. He was distraught and almost in tears about the Olson case." Maile remembered telling him, "Look, Darryll, give me one piece of hard evidence and we can do something. That's what we need, hard evidence."

"He was like us," observed Maile. "He didn't have any. We didn't interview Olson until his arrest on the 12th of August because we didn't have anything." Maile knew Olson was an experienced criminal and was unlikely to talk unless there was some evidence.

"To say the least, Olson was a most unpleasant individual to deal with," asserted Maile, who accompanied Olson on the trips to find bodies. "To make matters worse, we were driving those small Ford Fairmonts. It was hot and Olson insisted on smoking those White Owl cigars.

"When you see that much murder and carnage, it's almost as if it's not real," said Maile. "As a defensive action you laugh about things that are not funny. It was really hard. I could tell by the way guys looked at us when we stopped at detachments with Olson."

Maile's boss, Staff Sergeant Arnie Nylund, commented, "Fred seemed to know what he was doing, and I had never seen anything to indicate otherwise. It is easy to view these things in hindsight and draw conclusions. We had other suspects that looked better than Olson. Don't forget, it was not apparent a serial killer was on the loose. Up until then the guys were busy working on a number of other homicides not related to these cases at all. After Olson was in jail we had all kinds of second-guessers. We did the best we could with what we had. I have nothing but respect for the guys and how they did it. It was terrible, just terrible for those members who accompanied Olson when they were recovering those bodies. It was so bad I had to send one man home. He just couldn't take it anymore."

Larry Proke

Retired Deputy Commissioner Larry Proke was an inspector at the Burnaby Detachment in July 1981. He assumed new duties as the officer in charge of General Investigation at Vancouver head-quarters in early August. Although involved at the height of the murder investigation, he chose not to talk about the Olson affair.

Bruce Northorp

"I had no illusions," Northorp said when I asked how the Olson case affected him. "The case was demanding and I was second-guessed at times. I knew I was as qualified as any of my peers or subordinates. Furthermore, I was able to make objective decisions as I didn't have to worry about how my actions would impact future promotion. I had written myself out of promotion despite urging from the commissioner to make myself available.

"I didn't deal with the Olson case alone," Bruce reflected. "My wife, Louisa, was subjected to the steady barrage of telephone calls, often in the middle of the night. She knew all too well that I was tasked to the limit during the Olson investigation. This concerned her. The public don't see this side of a police officer's job.

"In the long term," said Bruce, "the case will live with me as long as I do."

"In the short term, while the investigations were underway, it was very difficult. The HQ was short-staffed and there'd been a major shuffling of key personnel above and below me. I was thrust into heading an investigation using a group I'd never worked with."

I asked Bruce how he felt when he was told to take over the cases.

After a long pause he said, "I suppose I was immune to most any assignment. I'd had some tough ones. You might say I was a bit numb but not phased."

Over the years Northorp had found there was always a logical approach to any situation. You identify the problem, determine what steps can and should be taken, then you set priorities. When he was in charge of the Burnaby GIS, he learned he did his best on major cases by directing rather than running around doing the legwork. When he was too close to witnesses or suspects, his vision tended to get blurred. When he managed, he remained objective, made better decisions, and often saw issues the investigators did not. In a homicide case he would usually go to the scene and get the actual picture in his mind, but from then on he would manage a team of investigators.

That is the stance he took in the Olson case. He dealt with the main issues. The mechanics of carrying out the day-to-day requirements were under the direction of Proke and Nylund.

"I didn't presume I had sufficient knowledge of the facts to undertake the monumental task ahead. I asked for a briefing from all police officers involved in the cases for the morning of July 31st. Taking on the case was like jumping onto a fast-moving train. I had to digest almost immediately all the information that had been gathered for weeks."

Hindsight has mellowed the strong feelings that existed among the RCMP's chain of command during the Olson trial, and time has healed the raw nerve endings inflamed by months of stress.

Ten
Kim and Randy

Association

Association is the act of connecting, in the mind or imagination, two independent concepts or individuals.

In police work, association can lead investigators to turn possibilities into probabilities as they pursue the criminal. Guilt by association is a good place to start regardless of what any textbook on criminal justice may state. Most rotten apples come from the same barrel.

Sometimes, in police work—as in life—association can trigger a rush to judgment.

If you were a prostitute, the assumption was that you couldn't be raped. And in July 1981, if you rode shotgun for Clifford Olson you simply had to be guilty as sin. Or did you?

After the trial of Clifford Olson, media came to consider Kim Werbecky the sole assault victim to survive his violence. As late as 1994 she believed the reason all later victims were killed was because of his arrest after her rape near Squamish. Kim has never met Randy Cook Ludlow.

Jim, Kim, and the District Crown

Olson picked up sixteen-year-old Kim Werbecky in Whalley on January 2, 1981, offered her a job in Whistler, and drove her to Squamish, drinking beer on the way there. He raped and assaulted her twice. She went to the police the next day.

Olson was on a one-man crime spree. He had argued with a group of young people in New Westminster, pointing a revolver at them, while running his vehicle into an automobile occupied by an older couple. At Squamish, while with Kim,

Squamish Constable Jim Hunter was adamant that the Crown proceed with Olson's rape trial and was pushy enough to draw a complaint from Crown Counsel's office. Ironically, though both he and Don Celle still work in the justice system, they have not met again.

he had a dispute with a number of youths and threatened them with a revolver. She said her attacker took pot shots at the youths. Both incidents were reported to police.

Squamish RCMP Constable Jim Hunter was assigned the case. He could almost feel Kim's pain and discomfort as he photographed her bruised and battered face. Within days he took Kim to the Witness Suspect Viewing System (WiSViS) at the Vancouver RCMP headquarters. Werbecky identified her assailant as Clifford Robert Olson from a selection of over 400 photos.

Hunter noticed Olson had been released on mandatory supervision in June 1980. It gave him great satisfaction to charge the man with rape, buggery, gross indecency, and two counts of possession of a weapon. Working swiftly, Hunter had Surrey RCMP arrest Olson on January 7 at his Surrey apartment. Olson was remanded in custody to Burnaby's Oakalla Prison Farm to await trial. He would remain out of circulation for three months.

Hunter interviewed the sixteen-year-old several times. "Kim didn't try to hide her past. She told me she had run away from home and had been a street kid for a time," declared Hunter. "She also told me she had worked as a child prostitute." Despite her history, Hunter believed she was telling the truth. Embarrassed when speaking of her experience with Olson, she at times left out some pertinent facts during the interviews. Nevertheless, Hunter was confident he possessed all the details of the crime. "She would have made a good witness," he declared.

★ ★ ★

Constable Jim Hunter was furious. It was April Fools' Day, but what he had just heard from a Squamish prosecutor was no joke. Don Celle, the District Crown Counsel, had directed that the charges of rape, buggery, and gross indecency against Olson be stayed. Two weapon possession charges would proceed. Though based in North Vancouver, Celle had been appointed by the AG's office to oversee Squamish, and he routinely approved or quashed charges for prosecution and gave direction to prosecutors on the North Shore and at Squamish.

Hunter couldn't believe it. Olson was a violent and dangerous criminal and Hunter was determined to vigorously oppose the District Crown's decision. He and Staff Sergeant Fred Zaharia, the officer in charge of Squamish Detachment, travelled to North Vancouver, where they met with Celle. "It got pretty heated," said Hunter. "It almost got to me punching him out. Zaharia asked me to leave and then he got into a huge argument with him. I'll never forget what the Crown said. 'I won't prosecute him [Olson] because she is a liar and a tramp.'" In Hunter's eyes, the District Crown's opinion reeked of arrogance and insensitivity.

"I tried to get the Crown to talk with Kim Werbecky," lamented Hunter. "He refused. I had talked with her and her mother several times. There was no doubt in my mind that she was telling the truth. We sent a memo to the headquarters' CIB for permission to talk with Celle's boss, the Regional Crown Counsel at Vancouver. We never did have a meeting. It was obviously handled at the headquarters level.

Alan Filmer, the Vancouver Regional Crown Counsel [later the assistant deputy attorney general] stood behind his District Crown and that was the end of it."

Concurrently, the Richmond charges of buggery and indecent assault of a male were stayed on April 2, 1981, on the instructions of South Fraser Regional Crown Counsel Al Hoem. A year had elapsed between the time of the offences and Olson's identification. Apparently there were procedural problems with the photo line-up used to identify Olson. Clifford Olson had got off again.

Six days later, on April 8, 1981, Crown Counsel Robert Bruce McNair stayed the Squamish charges of rape, buggery, and gross indecency at the direction of the District Crown Counsel. Olson was released on bail, free to prey on unsuspecting youth. Subsequently, the Vancouver RCMP HQ received a letter from the Attorney General's Ministry criticizing the manner in which Zaharia and Hunter had spoken to the District Crown Counsel.

Asked if he had been disciplined by the RCMP as a result, Hunter replied, "No, but prosecutors had complained about me before. If I thought I was right I wouldn't just roll over like some guys. I wasn't afraid to argue with them.

"I was fairly junior in service then," confided Hunter. "Olson was something else, like a salesman. I had never come across anybody like that: cool, polished, full of bullshit. That's another thing, he never denied having sex with her. He got her up there by promising her a job at Whistler.

"The day we arrested Olson, Bill McBratney of the Richmond Detachment was at Squamish. He was investigating the 1980 Richmond indecent assault on male offence and subsequently charged Olson. McBratney discussed the Richmond Christine Weller murder with me. He felt Olson should remain a suspect in the Weller murder, even though they had another very strong suspect. When I sent my exhibits to the Crime Detection Laboratory I suggested they compare the Weller exhibits with mine. I don't know if they did or not.

"I knew Fred Maile, who was on the Serious Crime Section, was investigating the Marnie Jamieson murder at Sechelt the previous summer. I called Fred to tell him he should have a look at Olson for that murder. As it turned out, Olson didn't kill Marnie."

Ironically, Hunter never did come across Don Celle after Olson's confession, even though they have both remained in the justice system to the present time.

Hunter knew Maile from their days in Squamish and feels he never got the credit he deserved. He figures, "It was Fred Maile who was the driving force in the Olson investigation, not those Burnaby guys as we had been led to believe."

Amid the shadows, strong opinions remain.

On Trial

In December 1999, Bruce Northorp interviewed an individual who gave evidence at Olson's Squamish trial on weapons charges on April 8, 1981. This person did not wish to be identified in any fashion.

The first-time witness was most apprehensive about the formal courtroom setting. The witness recalled Kim's mother saying that Kim was also upset and nervous about testifying. The prosecutor did not review anything with either witness before they took the stand. "Just be calm" was the only advice he gave. As usual, all other witnesses were excluded from the courtroom until they were called in to give their evidence.

The unnamed witness was shocked to learn that a person attending court, who appeared to be a lawyer, was actually Clifford Olson. Wearing a powder blue suit, pink shirt, and gold jewellery, Olson displayed all the earmarks of a bigshot. The witness also remembers a pregnant woman in the waiting area of the courthouse, quietly reading her Bible. This was Joan Berryman, who would later marry Olson.

The unnamed witness, after giving testimony, remained in the courtroom while Kim Werbecky took the stand. Soon Kim was crying and visibly shaken. Two questions in Robert Shantz's cross-examination stand out, even today. "Is it true you were a street girl?" and "Could the gun have been a pencil?"

Kim's nervousness was not helped by questions like this, nor by her awareness that the District Crown Counsel did not believe her allegations regarding the stayed sex offences.

Shantz indicated that he had a lengthy cross-examination planned, and the case was adjourned to May 22. Kim had endured enough. She failed to appear on May 22, and a bench warrant was issued for her arrest. The case was set over until September 29, 1981. By then Olson had been arrested and charged with all the murders.

Not My Fault

In 1994, Val Meredith, member of Parliament and the Reform Party's justice critic, complained in the House of Commons that authorities had not charged serial killer Clifford Olson for allegedly raping a prostitute before he murdered most of his young victims. Allan Rock, justice minister at the time, said he would investigate. (Meredith told Bruce Northorp in December 1999 that she did not recall ever receiving a report on the issue, but she thought the matter might have been referred to provincial authorities.)

Meredith's inquiries lead to considerable media coverage, and reporters contacted Werbecky in 1994. Kim told them, "If a British Columbia Crown Counsel had not decided a former child prostitute couldn't be raped, Clifford Olson would have been in jail and not killed the ten children he did in the four months after he raped me. There is a government lawyer who must be suffering and the guilt belongs to him, not me. It's not my fault I survived and that the Crown's lawyer wouldn't even talk to me." Kim firmly believed Olson intended to kill her during their return trip to Vancouver from Squamish.

Jim Hunter agrees with Kim Werbecky. He believes that had the District Crown Counsel taken the time to interview Werbecky, he might have been convinced she would be a truthful, proficient witness and might have allowed the charges to proceed.

"I think we had a good case," Hunter insisted. "We stood a good chance of convicting him." Considering Olson's criminal past, had he been convicted of all or even some of the charges, he probably would have been sentenced to several years in the penitentiary. When the Richmond and Squamish charges were stayed, the B.C. justice system lost its last chance to derail the savage menace Olson had become. Constable Jim Hunter had done his best.

★ ★ ★

As a result of the 1994 publicity, a British Columbia Crown Counsel was dispatched to Calgary where Kim Werbecky was living. During the course of researching this book, a Freedom of Information Act request was sent to Michael B. Hicks, Acting Regional Crown Counsel at Vancouver. His response came in the form of the following letter, dated January 25, 2000:

> In January of 1981 Kim Werbecky reported to the RCMP that she had been sexually assaulted by Clifford Olson. Criminal charges were laid as a result of those allegations. Later in 1981 Crown Counsel directed a stay of proceedings in respect to those allegations.
>
> In 1994 Ms. Werbecky came forward and complained about the Crown's decision to stay those proceedings.
>
> As a result of the issues raised by Ms. Werbecky, Senior Crown Counsel in Region 2 conducted a review of the 1981 charges and the decision to stay proceedings. Both Crown and RCMP files were reviewed.
>
> That review resulted in a determination that there was no substantial likelihood of conviction in respect to those allegations and that the proper decision had been made in 1981 to stay proceedings.
>
> On September 2, 1994, following the conclusion of this review, I, as Deputy Regional Crown Counsel, met with Ms. Werbecky and her lawyer in Calgary to explain this decision.
>
> I trust this information responds to your inquiry.

★ ★ ★

In early April 2000, I sought a meeting with Don Celle, still occasionally active on behalf of the Crown Counsel's North Vancouver office. Celle made a few comments in a phone interview, then agreed to a meeting to discuss the Olson case. Celle recalled that police had sought to subpoena Kim Werbecky at the Crown's instruction but could not find her. Celle, at that point, says he "did what he had to do," electing not to proceed. Celle acknowledged that Hunter and Zaharia were not pleased with the decision. He also allowed that he was "not pleased with Hunter" and told the pair to take it up with the Regional Crown Counsel, Alan Filmer.

"Out of the blue," Werbecky showed up in court, Celle said. Of course by then the sex charges were stayed, but she did testify on the weapons charges.

Before the call ended, Celle decided it best to get the permission of Regional Crown Council Michael Hicks before the meeting. Hicks advised Celle not to discuss the pros and cons of the case, "at least at this stage." This stage, of course, was almost twenty years after Olson's arrest. Hicks also instructed Celle not to talk about "the substantive and the procedural part."

A Whalley Kind of Guy

"I was a street kid, a Whalley kind of guy," proclaimed Randy Cook. "I had long hair, wore jeans, black boots and sported a couple of home-made tattoos. I didn't know my biological father, but I knew his name. He grew up in Richmond and I had been trying to find him."

Randy was hitchhiking on the King George Highway near the Surrey Memorial Hospital. It was mid-April 1981 and he had just turned eighteen. A small white car stopped to pick him up. A briefcase, chequebooks, and papers were strewn over the front passenger seat. The clean-cut driver gathered up his material and tossed it on the rear seat. Randy took his benefactor to be a successful businessman. "He was really friendly," he recalled.

Randy had, for the first time, encountered Clifford Robert Olson.

Life had not been kind to Randy, and he would come to realize that fate had just dealt him another cruel blow. The repercussions of this chance meeting plague him still.

"I'm a success now, but when I was your age I was in a lot of trouble," Olson counselled, looking at Randy. "I grew up in Richmond and I pulled a lot of capers. You may not believe it, but in the sixties I actually spent time in the Pen. I rehabilitated myself and now I run my own construction company."

"My father was from Richmond," Cook declared. "He spent time in the B.C. Pen for some type of fraud. I've been searching for my dad. My dad's name is Larry Ludlow, maybe you know him."

"Holy shit, I can't believe it," Olson exclaimed. "I grew up with him in Richmond. He was my best friend. We got into all kinds of trouble together. We joined the Bridgeport Boxing Club together. We went to kindergarten, grade one, grade two, grade three, grade four, grade five, grade six, grade seven, grade eight, grade nine, and grade ten together. He used to live at the corner of Number 3 Road and Cambie. He married Margaret Fald."

Randy Cook was shocked. All of this took less than three minutes. Here was a total stranger giving him information he knew was accurate. His father had lived at Number 3 Road and Cambie as a youth. His mother's maiden name was Fald. "A complete stranger telling me all about myself blew me away," he declared.

As they neared the Turf Hotel in Whalley, Olson suggested, "Come on, we have to have a drink on this." They had a beer together and Olson promised to help Randy find his father.

Randy agreed to go to breakfast with Olson the following day. "That, in a nutshell, sums up the reason for our relationship," Randy said. "I desperately wanted to find my dad."

Randy Cook was born Randy Julian Ludlow at Surrey, British Columbia, to Margaret and Larry Ludlow. They later divorced. In 1964 Margaret married Leonard Cook. Margaret and Leonard had five children together.

"When I was thirteen I was a straight 'A' student," Randy said. "I didn't get along with Leonard and he kicked me out. He made me a ward of the court and I was placed in a series of group homes. I constantly ran away.

"I don't think Mom and Leonard stayed home more than five nights a year. They were always out. They frequented the bingo parlour, went to hockey games, the horse races, you name it."

Randy knew he could sneak home while his parents were away. There were always other children at the house and he would hide under the bed or some other safe place. If Leonard heard Randy had been around, he would search the house using a flashlight. Randy would then be turned over to the police. As a result, Randy had little regard for the police or our legal and social justice system.

The Guy is For Real

The following day Olson took Randy to breakfast at the White Spot Restaurant on North Road near Burnaby's Lougheed Mall. After breakfast they drove to the same building site Olson would show to Sandra Docker and Rose Smythe on July 3. He told Randy they were his buildings.

Olson parked the car near the foreman's shack while Randy remained in the vehicle. The windows were down and Randy could hear what transpired. There were at least two or three men in the shack and one was talking on the telephone. Olson, playing the role of the business tycoon for Randy's benefit, stomped into the hut and bellowed, "What the fuck's going on here. Get off the phone."

Surprised at this affront, the bewildered worker using the phone hung up. Olson then snatched the phone and made, or appeared to make, his own call. After a further exchange he turned around and walked casually back to the car. As he entered the car he grunted to Randy, "You've got to keep these guys on their toes or they slack off."

Randy was impressed. "If I had any apprehension about Olson, that convinced me; this guy is for real. He is obviously the boss. This is his operation."

Later in the day they drove to the South Terminal at Vancouver International Airport in Richmond. Olson stopped the car near three men who were talking near a hangar. He walked over and spoke to them. Randy now suspects he asked them for directions, but at the time Olson said, "I keep my plane over there a ways. They are working on it."

"Can you imagine how I felt?" Cook asked. "Here I am, a young guy working in a Whalley bakery. I meet this guy who was my dad's best friend. He owns a huge construction business and flies his own aircraft. He is always flashing large bills. He appears to have gobs of money and he takes an interest in me. He even hints he may have a job for me. I was overwhelmed. Can you blame me for thinking my ship had just come in? I didn't quit my job. I just never went back to the bakery. I had something better."

Randy suggests he was with Olson about eight to a dozen times over a three-month period. Olson would usually find Cook on the street in Whalley. He wasn't hard to find. Olson would show up and offer to help him find his father. Olson always had beer in the car. Randy observed, "He changed cars frequently."

Everywhere Randy went with him, Olson knew people. "It didn't matter which bar we walked into, he seemed to be known. He is an extrovert, constantly chatting it up with people. He spent lots of money buying drinks and playing the big shot."

"Olson never hit on the girls when he was with me. In fact, he discouraged me from having a girlfriend. [He said] 'If you are going to work for me, no girls. They become a distraction.'"

One afternoon Randy and Olson were in Abbotsford, at the Key Lounge. It came as no surprise that Olson was known there. Olson asked Randy, in the presence of others at the table, "Who do you trust more, me or your friend Ivan Jones?"

"Ivan of course," Randy replied. "I have known him for twelve years. I've only known you for a few weeks."

Randy's reply stung and embarrassed Olson in front of his friends. He soon rose to go to the washroom. As he passed Cook, he cuffed him hard on the back of his head. Randy got up, pursued Olson into the washroom, and retaliated by pushing him on the shoulder while asking, "What did you do that for?"

Even though Olson was always well dressed when he was with Randy, his constant companion was a folding buck knife, a Buck 110. Olson pulled out the knife, pointing the blade at Randy.

"What, you're going to stab me?" Randy asked as he raised his hands and turned his back to Olson. "Go ahead," he barked, "you haven't got the guts to slice me." Nothing came of the altercation and they returned to the table.

Doting Dad

"I met Joan Olson twice," said Randy. "Both times at their residence. Olson was the doting father, picking up and showing off his son, Clifford Junior."

The second time was on July 8. Olson was going on vacation and he wanted to rent a motorhome. He was taking his family to California and he invited Randy to accompany them. Olson, Joan, young Clifford, and Randy went to Coquitlam Chrysler. Olson was unable to rent the motor home, but he went to California anyway, as Les Forsythe was to learn shortly. Randy did not go with them.

"Between eleven and noon on July 9 I was with Olson," Randy confirmed. "We were driving toward downtown New Westminster. Olson spotted a girl leaving a phone booth on Columbia Street in front of the Royal Columbian Hospital. He obviously knew her because he waved to her. She smiled and seemed to be happy to see him. He pulled over. She came across the street and talked with him."

It was Judy Kozma. She was on her way to Richmond to see a friend and apply for a job at Wendy's. "Hop in," Olson said. "We'll take you there."

Once in the car, Judy exclaimed, "This is good. This will be faster than the bus. I would have had to go all through Vancouver to get there."

They drove to Richmond. Olson had the ever-present beer in the car. All three of them had a beer.

At the time Randy Cook was dating a girl and it was her birthday. He was planning a celebration that night. Olson had promised to loan him his brother-in-law's white Corvette for the evening. Playing the bigshot for Judy's benefit, Olson pulled out a wad of hundred dollar bills and gave it to Randy, saying, "Here, have a good time tonight."

Randy was speechless; there were several thousand dollars in the wad.

They arrived in Richmond long before it was time for Judy's job interview and too early for her to meet her friend. "We went to the Richmond Inn to buy some more beer," Randy continued. "Olson and I went to the washroom. He asked for his money back. I gave it to him. I should have realized this was just a big show to impress her.

"When we returned to the car, Judy sat in the front passenger seat. I sat in back. Olson offered Judy a job cleaning windows at ten dollars an hour."

They returned to New Westminster where Olson bought a bottle of rum at the liquor store near the foot of 10th Street. He returned to the car with the rum, coke, and plastic glasses. On Olson's instructions, Randy mixed drinks for all three.

"Olson encouraged Judy to have another drink," related Cook. "She didn't want more."

Olson persisted. "Give her another drink, give her another drink," he ordered.

Eventually Judy agreed to take a light one. "Olson told me to mix it," said Randy. "I gave her a glass of coke with no rum. I caught Judy's eye and signalled it was only coke."

Judy took a sip and said, "This is really strong."

"Olson looked at me and nodded, indicating I had done well by giving her a stiff drink," Randy continued.

Olson then gave Judy some tiny green pills, saying, "Here, take these, they'll straighten you out. They keep you from getting drunk." She took the pills.

Olson parked in the underground garage at the complex where he lived. Cook and Judy stayed in the car while he went to his apartment. Randy reflected, "This was the only time I detected any anxiety on her part. She was nervous and upset. I put it down to the fact she was fifteen years old, she had been drinking, and she was going to miss her job interview. She was crying and I wiped the tears from her eyes. Olson returned shortly and she seemed her old self again."

Randy thought they were on the way to get the Corvette. Instead, Olson drove to the Lougheed Mall. Judy stayed in the car. As Olson walked with Randy toward the mall he told him, "The Corvette's not my car. You've had too much to drink. I can't let you have it."

"I was ticked, really ticked," said Cook. "Olson bought a sandwich and gave it to me. He peeled $300 from his wad and handed it to me saying, 'Here, have a good time.' I went to Surrey and partied. I never saw Judy again."

"The next time I saw Olson he said he dropped her off at Richmond. I learned much later he killed Judy, then went on vacation the next day."

Hey, Hey, Hey, Pull Over

"Olson picked me up on July 28," Randy remembered. "We later picked up my friend Ivan Jones. It was the first time Olson actually met him, although we had discussed Ivan a few times."

While researching this book, author Les Holmes and his retirement sidekick, Dr. Watson, visited the isolated corridor where Olson took teenager Randy Cook on July 29, 1981.

Unknown to Randy Cook, JFO members had watched him leave the Cariboo Hotel lounge and cross North Road to the White Spot Restaurant where he and Olson met Delta Police Detective Dennis Tarr. After Cook and Olson left the restaurant they were followed by JFO. In Whalley, the police watched as the two picked up Ivan Jones.

Randy continued, "As we drove through Whalley, two girls were hitchhiking. 'Hey, hey, hey, pull over,' I told Olson. The two girls were going to a party at White Rock and we decided to go with them. As usual, there was beer in the car and we gave the girls some. We were soon pulled over by police and Olson was arrested at gunpoint. The girls, Ivan, and I were not detained."

Come Closer, Come Closer

Olson found Randy on the afternoon of July 29. He explained he was arrested the night before for uttering threats against a former business partner. He claimed he was released about three o'clock in the morning once that situation was clarified. Cook accepted Olson's explanation. As far as Randy was concerned, Olson was nothing more than a successful businessman.

187

They went to the Cariboo Hotel's Lougheed Village Pub at North and Lougheed. Cook had been there before with Olson. It was one of Olson's favourite drinking establishments. Randy learned later it was there Olson picked up Sigrun Arnd, the unwitting German tourist he murdered.

Cook noticed Olson was different on this occasion. He pushed doubles and triples at him from the time they entered the lounge. "I have something to do. I need you to help me," Olson repeated time and again.

With so much public angst and anger in 1981, local newspapers were looking for someone else to punish besides Clifford Olson. Little did they know that by targeting Randy Ludlow they were truly adding insult to injury. A homeless teen, he was pictured here above the words "still at large."

"I was really getting blitzed," attested Randy.

Late in the evening Olson commanded, "It's time, let's go."

Once outside, Olson roughly pushed Randy to the pavement, snarling, "Look at you, you're drunk. If you are going to work for me you have to smarten up. You are useless in this condition. You are disgusting."

Olson then changed his tack. "If I have to drive long distances, I take a couple of these to keep me awake," he declared as he gave Randy two greenish translucent pills.

"I was drunk," Randy professed. "They didn't help."

Once underway, Olson claimed he had a friend who owned an appliance store. He claimed to be helping his friend with an insurance rip-off. "I need your help," Olson kept saying.

They drove to a strip mall on the Barnet Highway not far from Coquitlam Centre. Olson parked his car near the appliance store. "We walked into a dark, narrow corridor behind the strip mall. It was about the length of a city block and so narrow if I stretched out my arms I could touch both sides," described Randy. "It was dark. We were walking away from the car and the appliance store. There were weeds, wooden pallets, and other junky items in the corridor." About four stores along, Olson went to the rear door of one of the businesses. Beyond this, a huge pile of foam rubber blocked the passageway. He looked like he was trying to break into the premises.

It was a heavy, solid metal door. A steel plate reinforced the door near the lock. Olson placed the blade of his Buck 110 in the key slot and tried to turn it. "I thought this was hilarious," recalled Cook. "He could have worked on that door all night and never gained entry. While he was fooling with the door he kept saying, 'Come here, come closer. I need you to help me.'

"I was laughing at him, saying, 'You're crazy man, you'll never get in there that way.' I was too far gone to be concerned for my safety.

"Olson told me, 'Shut up, shut up. Come closer, come closer.'

"By this time I am leaning on his shoulder laughing at him. My mind was clear but I was starting to sway and my knees began to buckle.

"'Fuck it, fuck it, fuck it,' Olson suddenly burst out."

Using both hands he threw Cook to the ground. Olson dragged him to the parked car where, without uttering a word, he picked him up and tossed him like a sack of groceries into the back seat.

"It was as if he knew I had lost all my motor skills," said Randy. "I was unable to move my arms or legs. I couldn't bend a finger, open my mouth, or utter a sound. Nothing worked, but my mind was clear and I was aware of everything. Olson drove to his underground parking spot in his apartment complex. He said nothing. He got out of the car and left me there.

"Before long, Olson returned. Again, he said nothing. He removed me from the car, slung me over his shoulder, and carried me into his residence. The hide-a-bed was already out."

Olson dropped Randy on the bed and removed his clothing, except his underwear shorts. He then went down the hall to what Randy took to be his bedroom. To his horror, Olson returned shortly and raped him.

"I was incapable of resisting," lamented Randy. "I was fully aware what was happening. Nothing like that had ever happened to me before. I hadn't realized I was in danger. I just lay there all night, completely helpless, unable to move or cry out."

As the sun began to rise, Randy was relieved to find his body slowly regaining some movement. He knew he had to get away. As soon as he was able to manoeuvre, he dressed and stumbled from the apartment. He was devastated.

Outside, the first thing he saw was the number 666 on the apartment building across the lane. "666 is the sign of the Devil," Cook observed. "I am a spiritual person and I pondered its significance for a long time."

Prison

"I was really messed up after being sexually assaulted. To make matters worse, I was arrested later that day on a warrant for failing to appear on a common assault charge and some other minor matter. A warrant had been issued for my arrest. I was subsequently sentenced to twenty-one days in the Alouette River Unit [ARU]."

When Randy Cook met Olson, he thought his life was finally coming together. Now he was in jail, his dream was shattered, and he was even more despondent from being raped. He was unable to cope with all these problems.

"About August 15 or 16 I managed to get some valium from one of the guys in ARU," said Randy. "I tried to OD. I guess I tried to commit suicide. I staggered through the TV room, where I collapsed. They rushed me to the prison hospital at Oakalla. I was really messed up."

It was August 18 before Cook recovered sufficiently to be interviewed. As RCMP task force members Sergeant Don Brown and Corporal Cliff Kusmack handed their weapons to prison authorities for safekeeping, they were unaware they were about to get the break everyone had been praying for. Their job was simply to interview Randy as an Olson associate.

Cook thought they were investigating Olson for pulling "some corporate rip-off...They showed me a folder with, I think, eight photos. When I identified Judy Kozma's picture they removed a yellow square of paper so I could read the typing under the photo. That's when I learned Judy had been killed."

Randy Cook provided a statement detailing his involvement with Olson. Although Brown and Kusmack showed no outward emotion, they were ecstatic. They had finally netted the elusive link they had all been searching for: a witness who could put Olson with one of the murder victims the day she disappeared.

"It was on the strength of my identification the first charge of murder was laid against Olson," asserted Cook.

Kusmack asked Randy if Olson had sexually assaulted him. "I said no," admitted Cook. "I don't think he believed me. I couldn't bring myself to admit it to anyone. I was too ashamed. It took many years before I could talk about being raped."

As it became clear Olson was a serial killer, it dawned on Randy that Olson intended to kill him behind the Coquitlam strip mall during the early morning hours of July 30. He had been toying with the door lock, knife in hand, to lure Randy within stabbing range. "They would have found my body concealed under the pile of foam rubber," declared Cook. The reason is apparent. "I could put him with Judy Kozma the day she disappeared. He wanted to get rid of all the evidence and that meant killing me.

"I'm convinced that when Olson elected not to kill me, I was the recipient of his last humane act. The reason he spared me is that I bear an uncanny resemblance to my father as a young man. He couldn't bring himself to kill someone who looked so much like his childhood friend."

Bad News

"In January 1982, things took a turn for the worse. There were some articles published which tended to portray me as an accomplice of Olson. I wasn't," said Randy.

"Up until then I went under the name Randy Cook. I had never used another name. Since then I have used the name Randy Ludlow. I'm not trying to conceal my identity."

"The articles brought me all kinds of grief," claimed Ludlow. "Five guys attacked me in Holland Park, located behind Surrey Place Mall. They knew my identity and they were going to carve 'Clifford

Olson' in the skin on my stomach. I still have the scars. That's where I got this," Randy said, pointing to a scar under his right eye.

Ludlow described how two shots were fired at him as he departed a biker establishment in Edmonton. He had been verbally abused and jostled after being recognized as an Olson associate. Fearing for his life, he fled from the club as two shots missed their mark.

"There was a $12,000 contract out on my life over this case," said Randy. "I managed to confront the person who picked up the contract. He had been advanced $4,000. When he heard my explanation, he refused to carry out the hit and refunded the money."

Randy Ludlow said these are only three examples of abuse he has suffered from being linked to Olson. "There are more and they occur even today. I mean actually today," Ludlow exclaimed. "Coming here on the Sky Train, a girl recognized me as Randy Cook. As I left the train her boyfriend shouted, 'Hey, Cook, have you killed any kids lately?' Stuff like that happens often."

In recent years Randy Ludlow has tried to clear his name by telling his story to a number of newspaper, television, and radio reporters.

Dad

"I finally located my dad, Larry Ludlow, in 1989. I learned he frequented the Lumberman's Club on Kingsway in Burnaby. I went there and found out he had a tee-time at the Central Park Par Three Golf Course. I was excited. I had been searching for him for a long time."

Randy Ludlow was due for another disappointment. "Dad's main interest in me was to write a book and maybe do a movie about Olson. He tried to talk me into it. He even introduced me to a guy who would write the book. I didn't want anything to do with it. Most of all, I didn't want to profit from these tragedies.

"Dad confirmed he was best friends with Clifford Olson when they were growing up. He admitted they pulled all kinds of stunts together but tried to minimize his involvement. Dad told me Olson was strictly interested in girls when they were growing up. He speculated Olson developed a liking for boys while in jail.

"Olson and Dad did a caper at a bingo hall in Vancouver or Richmond. Mom never told me, but she was actually Clifford Olson's date that night. Dad was with another girl. Olson and Dad were nineteen, the girls were only fifteen. I am not sure if the girls were part of the caper, but Olson and Dad made lots of money and they were celebrating. They were all drinking. The girl Dad was with was crying about getting in trouble for being out late. Olson berated and verbally abused her. Dad defended her against Olson. Obviously Mom liked what she saw in Dad. They eloped and were married at Coeur d'Alene, Idaho. My Dad actually stole Clifford Olson's girlfriend. Dad never saw Clifford Olson again.

"After I met Dad in 1989, his mother died and left him a lot of money. In 1991, when I tried to locate him, he had disappeared leaving no forwarding address. I managed to find him again, but he told me he wanted nothing to do with me. He didn't want anything I did to affect his life or connect him with Clifford Olson. He even changed his name."

No Angel

"I am not trying to portray myself as an angel," said Randy Ludlow. "I have had more than my share of adversity. All of my problems with the justice system have been relatively petty stuff. Assaulting my stepfather, theft of gas, running away while a ward of the court, and disobeying restraining orders prohibiting me from going home."

Randy admitted he has little respect for authority, and his chronic problem was his failure to attend court appearances. A warrant would be issued for his non-attendance at court, he would be arrested, and he would compound his problems by again failing to appear. His life was a vicious circle, spiralling downward.

Ludlow's first adult conviction was in 1980 when he was placed on probation for attempted theft of gasoline. As a condition of probation he reported every two weeks to Gateway Correctional Services at Burnaby. After his release from Alouette River Unit, he continued to report to Gateway. It was not unusual for Sergeant Brown and Corporal Kusmack to drop him off there. Randy elaborated, "Cliff Kusmack asked Gateway to keep a rein on me. The RCMP were going to use me as a witness against Olson and they wanted me in good shape for the trial."

Reporters interested in Randy Ludlow's association with Olson approached Gateway for information. In Randy's opinion, the media interest caused counsellors to panic. For the first time Gateway expressed concern regarding his mental health and the absence of a strong support network of family or friends. Gateway workers encouraged Randy to enrol in the Outward Bound Program at Keremeos. The next session was starting in October. "My probation period ended September 13, 1981, so technically Gateway had no say in what I did, but I didn't know that," said Randy.

Randy agreed to attend. "It cost Gateway $1,300 to fully outfit me," Ludlow recalled. "Included in my gear was a model 112 buck knife and sheath."

The course was not starting for a week or two, and Gateway suggested Randy voluntarily admit himself into a psychiatric ward. He declined and instead received permission to stay with an aunt and uncle at Pitt Meadows.

He was given medication to calm his nerves. Ludlow did not wish to take the pills, but relented at his aunt's urging. "I was completely out of it all the time I was there," Randy observed.

Later, on the way to Outward Bound, Randy was provided with a less potent medication, which was given to the director of Outward Bound to mete out. When the Gateway people departed, the program director said, "Here, you are old enough to look after your own medication. You have to be responsible for your own actions."

While hiking, Randy stumbled and fell over a cliff. When he regained consciousness, he was lying on a mattress. His right hand throbbed. As he examined his hand, he noted it had been cut, and several sutures closed the wound. The door to the room was ajar and Ludlow walked into the hallway wondering where he could be. He deduced he was in an institutional setting.

"Where am I?" he asked the first person he encountered.

"You're in the puzzle factory," came the reply. "You're in the insane asylum."

"When I examined material on the wall, I learned I was in Riverview Hospital," Randy stated. "It all became clear to me. Gateway suspected me. That's why all the heavy medication. I was paranoid. Were the police involved?"

Riverview staff told Ludlow he was an involuntary admission. He had seventy-two hours to demonstrate he was mentally fit. Riverview had seventy-two hours to show he was mentally unfit. "Okay," Randy said, "what do we do, play word games?" They did exactly that. Three days later he was released.

Randy was furious at Gateway. He walked in the pouring rain all the way from Coquitlam's Riverview Hospital to Gateway in Burnaby. He was angry and conveyed his displeasure to Gateway officials. As his lengthy tirade continued, two people entered the room and sat down. They listened for a short while, then arrested him. They were Burnaby RCMP detectives. "They arrested me for possession of a dangerous weapon," Randy continued, "the buck knife Gateway bought for me. It was in the sheath on my belt. Gateway said I had it out threatening them and cleaning my nails. That was totally untrue. It was never out."

A doctor examined Randy. The court asked for a psychiatric assessment and he was sent to the Forensic Psychiatric Institute in Port Coquitlam for 30 days. He ended up staying only seventeen days. He was found mentally competent to stand trial and released on the condition he stay away from Gateway.

In the News

On January 14, 1982, Olson entered a plea of guilty to eleven counts of murder. Shortly after, Ludlow failed to appear on the possession of a dangerous weapon charge. "News broadcasts said I was a friend of Olson and a bench warrant had been issued for my arrest," said Ludlow. "The news suggested I had a propensity for violence."

Randy claimed he was later kicked, beaten, and called a child murderer by police. "I was a mouthy guy, so that's what you get. They actually put me in the hospital. I was in a wheelchair and later on crutches. I received an absolute discharge on four charges of assaulting a police officer. An internal investigation officer told me he was willing to pursue my complaint of police brutality, but I took off."

By 1994 things had settled down for Randy Ludlow. He and friends attended a National Hockey League Stanley Cup playoff game when Vancouver was in the final against New York. After the game, Ludlow noticed a huge crowd at the intersection of Robson and Thurlow streets. Vancouver's Stanley Cup Riot was about to erupt.

Randy and his party were on their way to a bar. "Maybe we had better get out of here," he suggested. At that instant, his face exploded in pain and he crumpled to his knees in agony. He had been the recipient of a projectile fired from a Vancouver Police Arwen anti-riot gun. It took more than forty stitches to repair his face. He sued the Vancouver Police but no settlement was obtained.

Once again, Randy's name was featured prominently in the news. During the ensuing coverage, reporters linked him to the Olson case.

For many years Ludlow couldn't bring himself to read newspaper accounts of the Olson cases. Finally, in 1994, he decided he had to learn what had been written. Randy was nervous as he entered the New Westminster Library. As he asked for the Olson files, he knew it was only his own paranoia that made him feel as if every eye was looking directly at him. The library attendant complied, giving him an envelope containing the clippings.

"When I read all the things they said about me, I couldn't believe it," Randy remembered. "I was horrified. In my shock and confusion I stuffed the articles under my jacket and dashed out of the library. I obviously looked suspicious. Within a couple of blocks the police stopped me and asked to see what I had inside my jacket. I was returned to the library where I apologized. Although the library didn't pursue charges, I was banned from further entry. The police released me. From then on, if I needed that service I used the library at Douglas College."

Randy's life was getting back to normal until 1997, when Olson's Section 745 hearing resulted in further news coverage of Randy and his association with Olson.

Victimized

"I want to assure the parents of Olson's victims that I had nothing to do with the deaths of their children. I was not an accomplice of Olson. I was a victim and I paid dearly for it.

"After Olson raped me I became an alcoholic and a drug user. Now I have turned my life around."

Some people who have been sexually assaulted choose to retreat within themselves. Others have a need to confront their tormentor. At first Ludlow was unable to admit he had been raped. He now has a burning desire to face Olson. He wants to ask him why he sexually assaulted him. Randy also wants to ask Olson why he didn't kill him behind the Coquitlam strip mall.

★ ★ ★

Today, Randy Ludlow is an articulate man who wears a neatly trimmed moustache, beard, and braided hair. He first contacted Bruce Northorp in 1997 when he was suing a news outlet and others concerning news coverage linking him to Clifford Olson. Randy wished to establish exactly what role the RCMP felt he played in the Olson murders. Bruce cooperated with Randy's lawyer and may be called as a witness in the upcoming civil case.

Bruce interviewed Randy several times in late 1999. Randy, nervous at first, gradually relaxed as it became apparent the sessions would be non-judgmental and concentrate only on what he had to say.

"I recently read the briefing document on the Olson case that appeared in the *Globe and Mail*...It's a very significant document. You [Bruce] only took over the Olson case on July 30. Twelve days later Olson was in jail. Six days after that, he was charged with the murder of Judy Kozma. That's very fast. It's incredible.

"July 30 was a very significant day in more ways than one," ventured Randy. "It was probably the worst day of my life. It's the day I was almost killed by Olson. It was the day he raped me. He killed Louise Chartrand. And you [Bruce] were stuck with the Olson case."

"It's really a relief to sit here and just talk," Randy commented at a later interview. "It's good to be able to unload some of this stuff. I have talked to others, but I had to go over it again and again. You know what I'm talking about right away. I sometimes feel as though you are interrogating me, but at least you understand. This is very therapeutic for me."

After the interview, Randy was on his way to the New Westminster Library. His ban lifted, he planned to do more research on the Olson cases.

Eleven
Did Olson Commit Other Murders?

Self-aggrandizement

Self-aggrandizement is not an uncommon trait in the criminal world. Attempts to exaggerate one's stature can regularly preoccupy even the lowest of lowlifes—predators who prey upon the defenceless. Both inside and outside prison it is fair to say that pathological liars and killers thrive on an overblown self-image. Anyone conned by the lies and bravado of such a person usually ends up feeling gullible and victimized—unsuspecting fulfilment for an insatiable ego.

Clifford Olson had proven himself a master of self-promotion. Few healthy minds can relate to his personal realm of glory, but there is little doubt that Olson wished to rank with the worst serial killers of the past century.

Mind Crimes

At various times since his confession, Clifford Olson has claimed responsibility for assorted atrocities. Did Olson commit other murders? This remains a burning question in the minds of many, and it was an issue Bruce Northorp examined during two time periods: after Olson's arrest until the end of 1981; and after his convictions in January 1982 for the eleven murders. Northorp believed Olson's outlandish claims were exacerbated by the credence police investigators gave them.

Did Olson Commit Other Murders?

On August 13, 1981, the day after Olson was arrested, he began to experience increasing pressure. After the RCMP flew him back to Vancouver from the site of the arrest, he was charged with sex offences committed some months earlier in Surrey. He was then told he was the prime suspect in the murder of Judy Kozma.

First Tuckey and Sandhu, then Maile and Drozda grilled him. Olson's first comments to Maile and Drozda pertained to his first interrogators. Olson complained, "Boy, they really threw the heat on me."

When Maile told Olson they had a statement (from Randy Ludlow) placing him with Judy Kozma on the day of her murder, Olson began to talk. He was given the RCMP's list of missing Lower Mainland children, but denied having anything to do with Verna Bjerky's disappearance. As well, when the case of Marnie Jamieson, who was not on the list, was raised, he answered, "No, all were local."

When he was questioned by Inspector Larry Proke, Olson knew he was getting heavy-duty treatment. During Proke's interview he indicated that he was responsible for the murders of Johnsrude, King, Kozma, and Weller. He also implied he'd killed Carson, Partington, Court, Chartrand, Wolfsteiner, Daignault, and, significantly, a girl from West Germany.

"Those two statements are significant. His devious mind hadn't yet formulated a plot. He was still trying to get himself out of the immediate mess. He didn't want any more murders being laid on him than those he had committed," Bruce declared.

Now Olson's focus shifted to making a deal so he could serve his time in a psychiatric hospital rather than a prison. "He had already been harassed by other inmates in Oakalla," Bruce explained. "He felt his life was in danger, and he wanted security." Olson was hated within the prison community. He was a known stool pigeon. Now he was the lowest of the low, a pervert and a kiddy-killer.

Northorp felt a key moment in the Olson interrogation was August 20. "By the 20th, Olson knew his destiny would not be a hospital. He then jumped to the idea of gaining $100,000. Conversations with Maile and Drozda on July 30 mentioned reward money available for any unsolved homicide."

He focused on $10,000 per body. As he only had seven bodies he could disclose, he made up the shortfall of $30,000 with evidence. It would have been so easy for him to disclose other murders, if he had committed any. Significantly, he told the police about the German girl, Arnd, a victim of whom the police were unaware.

"In September 1981 I was certain Olson did not commit any murders other than the eleven he would plead guilty to the following January," Bruce stated, and he expanded on this view in a multi-page memorandum to the Serious Crime Section in October 1981. In the memo he pointed out all the contradictions he saw, leading him to conclude Olson's claims were unbelievable.

Days later, the Serious Crime Section downplayed the inconsistencies in a lengthy reply. The Section's leaning was to investigate all the other murders Olson alleged.

The pendulum had swung. The same people who had been slow to finger Olson as the lead suspect now wanted to tie him to a host of other murders.

During August and September 1981, Olson alluded to other murders he had supposedly committed. His motive was to get the last $10,000 he felt he was owed.

On August 28, Serious Crime's Proke told Northorp of a murder Olson might give the police, "a Korean girl at Golden." This appears to be a reference to Ogang Ngoc Ha, a Vietnamese girl found murdered near Golden in 1981. At the time the girl was killed, Olson was in custody on the Squamish charges.

Another Olson claim that proved false related to Suzanne Seto, a realtor murdered at Duncan, on Vancouver Island, in 1980. In November 1982, a young male, Kelly Toop, was arrested and later convicted of Seto's murder. Olson had no connection to the case.

Northorp said it was obvious Olson's claims were fabrications. In an attempt to con the police, Olson said the phantom bodies were buried six feet deep. None of his ten victims, whose bodies had been located, were buried. Northorp believed Olson claimed the bodies were buried simply to entice the police into believing his tales, as the bodies could not have been found easily.

After Olson's convictions in January 1982, a new round of confessions started. He attempted a new ploy, requesting immunity from any charges if he co-operated in solving further murders allegedly committed by him. Nothing developed, although it was clear he still had investigators interested in his mystery murders.

In November 1982, John Hall applied to the Chief Justice of B.C. to bring Olson to B.C. from the Kingston Penitentiary in an RCMP aircraft. His application was based on an affidavit by Serious Crime's Fred Maile, which stated, in part, "I have come to strongly suspect that Olson committed a number of other homicides." Olson said he was going to co-operate in the murder investigations of Suzanne Seto, Carmen Robinson (a seventeen-year-old girl missing from the Victoria area since 1973), Lee Dalum (a sixteen-year-old boy missing from Maple Ridge since 1980), and an unnamed seventeen-year-old female from Kamloops. The announcement that Kelly Toop was charged with Seto's murder was made the very day Olson was being flown to B.C. Olson did not lead the police to any bodies on this trip.

On December 4, 1982, Attorney General Allan Williams held a press conference in relation to Olson's trip. He said, "I have come to the conclusion this man is not credible. I can no longer place any credence in anything he says."

On December 23 the *Vancouver Sun* reported it had received a letter from Olson. He claimed he would be able to locate the bodies of Carmen Robinson and two unnamed persons, one from Maple Ridge and the other from Kamloops.

Olson wrote another chapter on Verna Bjerky on December 30, 1982. The *Toronto Star* reported it received a letter from Olson in which he denied killing any other persons. He claimed to be sorry for the problems he had caused everyone. This account was picked up and carried in a Vancouver paper in January 1983. The writer reported that Olson denied any implication in twelve cases. One of the names included was Verna Bjerky.

Olson simply could not be believed. Northorp had decided that fifteen months earlier. "The master manipulator was getting some sick pleasure in leading the police around on wild goose chases and getting his name in the media. He detected a willingness in some investigators to believe anything he said. That willingness went back to how quickly, in an attempt to get two other phantom victims, they had released the $10,000 on September 3, 1981, for locating Daignault's body when it had not been found."

Northorp felt Olson needed an audience with officers who were clearly skeptical of what he was claiming. He had to be told his claims were unbelievable. "My recommendation, which was not accepted by either [Superintendent] Gordon Tomalty or Larry Proke, was to keep Maile away from Olson." Northorp believed that contact was something Olson desired because he was able to manipulate the investigator. "My thinking was to deprive Olson of something he wanted and see what would ensue," Northorp explained.

Instead, it seemed to Northorp that a core group of the Serious Crime Section was on a different wavelength. He clearly recalls receiving the October 1981 memorandum authored by Maile that attempted to rationalize every inconsistency in Olson's claims. It was evident from that memo that Northorp was out of step with the Serious Crime Section. Maile continued in his role as the prime contact with Olson.

Nonetheless, although he had no proof to the contrary, Northorp stood by his opinion: "Olson is playing us for suckers."

★ ★ ★

Olson's mind games continued past 1982. In his December 1982 letter to the *Toronto Star* he denied killing any other persons except the eleven original children.

In March 1984 the *Vancouver Sun* reported he was attempting to deal with U.S. authorities in relation to several unsolved murders in six states. In August 1989 the *Globe and Mail* carried a story that claimed Olson was to reveal information on the Green River Killer. Olson alleged he knew the killer.

The 49 or so killings attributed to the so-called Green River Killer in the Seattle area commenced on July 7, 1982. The killing spree is believed to have ended in March 1984. As of 1989 it had not been established if the killings were the work of one killer.

In 1989 Olson, who had been in prison continuously since August 1981, was claiming to have knowledge of who committed the Green River murders.

"Was he suggesting the Green River Killer was with him in Kingston Penitentiary and was released on day passes from time to time?" asked Bruce. "At best, he may have suggested he knew the man responsible before any of the murders took place."

In 1996, Olson talked to the RCMP in Saskatchewan about three murders he claimed to have committed in that province. He was taken out of prison to show the locations. As usual, he produced nothing. It seemed to the police that he had never been in the areas where he claimed the bodies were located.

At his judicial review in 1997, Olson claimed to have knowledge of 143 unsolved murders, some committed by himself, some with an associate. He alleged 64 were in Canada and dozens were in the United States.

In his opening remarks he said he and a friend were responsible for the unsolved string of Green River murders. The *Vancouver Province* reported the man in charge of the Green River murders investigation scoffed at Olson's claim and said Olson would have had to be a magician, able to tunnel his way from a prison somewhere in Canada and make his way to Seattle, to have killed any of the girls.

"Nothing he has said, or will say, can be believed unless it can be substantiated by independent means," Bruce avowed. And the RCMP has said that, to date, Olson has not provided any information that can be substantiated.

The media interviewed Fred Maile at the time of Olson's judicial review. Maile said then that Olson had not committed further murders. His last visit to see Olson was in 1993. "Olson always seemed to be able to get to a phone," observed Maile. "He would phone continually about the Green River killings and others. We had to follow them down, but as time went on it was apparent he hadn't done any more. He had done eleven and he was just rubbing salt in our wounds with the other claims." When Olson suggested he was responsible for some killings in Saskatchewan, Maile warned them, "He only wants a chance to escape."

It seemed that Fred Maile was at last satisfied. Yet despite the fact that police may have suspected Olson was attempting to rattle their chains, they were in a no-win situation. They had to check

Olson's claims, no matter how outlandish his statements may have been.

Olson is, and has always been, a con artist. His claims to other murders brought the police nothing, but they brought Olson an increase in notoriety and a number of trips to different destinations. They were a ploy to relieve the monotony of prison.

In August 1997, Olson called Dr. Tony Marcus, a psychiatrist, as a character witness at his judicial review. Marcus had interviewed Olson for eleven hours in June. During the interviews Olson asked Marcus if he (Olson) had killed more people than U.S. serial killers Ted Bundy and Charles Manson.

It was clear to Bruce Northorp that Olson's perennial claims were nothing more than pathetic attempts at self-aggrandizement.

Twelve
Two Sides of Evil

Evil

Evil is a moral force regarded as the source of harm or human wickedness. For centuries, theologians, scholars, criminologists, and sociologists have attempted to determine the source of one person's wicked behaviour. In a family of four, what causes one child to progress to the nth degree of evil while the others lead normal, productive lives? Clifford Olson's sins have not only banished him from society, they even segregate him from prison's general population, where he is housed with the worst of the worst.

Olson's evil was often cloaked behind a garrulous, outgoing persona and fashionable clothing, but many people who came in contact with him were struck by his sinister aura. Kettles, Forsythe, Hunter, Maile, other RCMP, and a host of civilians later recalled their first impressions of Olson.

The only thing gold leaf about Clifford R. Olson was his business cards, which he never paid for. However, Pastor Don Carmont told the late reporter Moira Farrow, "Olson can appear to be very winning, very charming and smooth." Carmont had married the Olsons, who were regular visitors to the People's Full Gospel Chapel in Surrey. "I recognized that he might have the potential to be dishonest," the pastor added.

Olson's laywer, Robert Shantz, called his client "an affable guy, not the kind of man you felt tainted being around."

Reporter Rick Ouston, who was phoned by Olson from prison, said, "He talked fast, staccato…jumped from topic to topic. He sounded glib, slick, like a con man trying to prove he's tough and important."

Olson's habit of regularly switching cars brought him in regular contact with various rental agencies. "All talk and no substance" was the description from one agent. "Sleazy, to say the least," was another.

Most contacts with Olson were brief or superficial. One observer, however, watched Olson grow up. Jim Steenson was a cop who had already been retired for six years when the Olson horror story first made headlines.

The Other Side—Steenson and Cliffie

Olson was born at St. Paul's Hospital in Vancouver on January 1, 1940, and moved with his parents and siblings from Vancouver's east side to a quiet suburban location at Gilmore Crescent in Richmond as a youngster. One of his earliest encounters with the justice system brought him in contact with Jim Steenson, a jovial "maintainer of the right," destined to look like Santa Claus. Steenson retired from the RCMP in 1975 as a staff sergeant with twenty-seven years of service, mostly as a detective. After his retirement he directed the criminology program at Douglas College and later at Kwantlen University College.

Steenson arrived in Richmond from Alberta in the '50s. One of his first calls was a residence break, enter, and theft. "Even though I had five years of service," he reflected, "I thought the guys were pulling my leg. We just didn't have house break-ins on the Prairies."

"I remember Cliffie," Steenson said. "You bet I do. It's because of him I have the only two blemishes on my service record. I heard about Olson and his shenanigans right away when I arrived in Richmond. Nobody seemed to be able to catch him or do anything about it."

Olson used to terrorize the neighbourhood. "The neighbours were all frightened of Cliff. I couldn't believe how people let him get away with what he did. He was into everything, stealing, extorting money from little kids, shoplifting, and break-ins. You name it and he did it." Residents blamed young Olson for almost everything that happened in the neighbourhood. Most times they were right.

"He joined a boxing club," said Steenson. "That only served to help him intimidate the neighbours further." The cop decided to show the brash kid that he was not invincible. Olson became his number one project. "Olson was our thorniest problem. Even though he was into everything, I can't think of anything worthwhile he ever gained from his crimes. We had two members on CIB and we started to concentrate on him. We would frequently catch him for a break-in or some other offence. Finally, after a lot of effort, we sent him to jail.

"Olson was like Zorro. He may as well have put a big Z on his break-ins. He would bang in a door and everything would be ransacked and spread all over." As he grew older he began to break into airplanes at the Sea Island Airport. "After jail he was able to associate with a better class of criminal. He actually developed into a pretty good burglar. He was fearless, had lots of jam," explained Steenson. "From there he graduated into safe breaking and then armed robberies."

Young Clifford was proud of the notoriety gained through his escapes and other criminal escapades. "I think he escaped a total of thirteen times," Steenson recalled. "He was a bit of a Houdini. I believe he was the first guy in Canada to pick the old Peerless handcuffs with the end of a rattail comb. After that, all the crooks were carrying them to cheat the old-style cuffs. He had other stuff too. I don't remember if he actually had a professional set of lock picks, but he had devices that would open locks.

"Cliffie didn't fool me. There was never any doubt he was embarking on a lifetime of crime. Occasionally you run into a person who is bad through and through. Cliff Olson is one of those rare birds. I sent him to the penitentiary three times myself."

Olson's prison sentences steadily increased until there was nowhere left for him to go but the penitentiary. Thereafter, whenever Steenson learned that Olson was free, he would make arrangements to keep him under twenty-four-hour surveillance. "I couldn't do it alone, but Vancouver dicks like Silver Armenau, Alex Stobie, Jack Snihur, Percy Easler, and others would help out. Johnny

Alton used to set up most of my bugs. It usually never took us longer than two weeks to knock him off and put him back in jail. I think one time he may have been out twenty-nine days, but he never disappointed us. He wasn't out long."

Orderly Room

Jim Steenson has good reason to remember Olson. His two trips to Orderly Room, the RCMP internal discipline procedure, were directly attributable to Olson.

In 1964 Steenson suspected Olson for some break-ins and safe attacks. "They were typical Olson jobs. I can't remember if it was four or five, all the same night. One break-in was at Belkin Paper Box. Cliff, by this time, was the teacher and he had a kid with him. Cliff was giving him his first lesson on how to punch a safe. They took a sledgehammer and knocked off the dial. Cliff then instructed his young accomplice to take a metal rod and punch out the spindle while he went home for tea. All the way home he was reading papers from the premises, then tossing them aside as he walked. On his return to Belkin Paper he found his partner had been unsuccessful in punching the safe. He then started up an acetylene torch, which was on the premises, and instructed his partner to burn off the hinges. When this was also unsuccessful, Olson decided to show his student how to pound and peel a safe. He picked up a double-bitted axe to do the job, but beforehand they turned the safe on its side. When they did, the door fell open. On the wall there was a sign in big red letters—THIS SAFE IS UNLOCKED AND CONTAINS NO MONEY."

Olson and his protégé read and discarded more papers on the way back to the Olson residence. Steenson had only to follow the trail of documents to solve the break-ins. "We went there right away. I had been at his house so much I was treated like a family friend. I never ever had a warrant to search the Olson house. Mrs. Olson, who was a fine lady, always invited me in and allowed me to look around."

Olson and his young student were still at the house. "We searched the kid and found nothing. We were looking for marked money, three two-dollar bills and a one-dollar bill. Cliff knew the jig was up and he suddenly bolted out the back door. I chased him and knocked him down. He got up and cleared a water-filled ditch. I didn't make it and sunk to my waist in the mud. I fired a warning shot but he didn't stop."

Help was summoned from the detachment. A Vancouver Police dog and handler searched the area. Olson was arrested while hiding in a thick patch of thorny blackberry bushes. He still possessed all the marked bills. "After that Cliff somehow obtained a bank deposit bag and put his loot through the night deposit so he wouldn't get caught with marked money."

RCMP policy required Steenson to report the warning shot. Staff Sergeant Jack Friederich, the Vancouver Section NCO, investigated and asked Olson for a statement. Olson declined, saying, "My friend Jim would never shoot me." Nevertheless, Steenson was summonsed to appear in Orderly Room in red serge, sans spurs (as a sign of disgrace, the accused in RCMP Orderly Room is not allowed to wear spurs, which were earned in training), before Inspector Al Cart, where he received an official warning. "They were not interested in hearing what I had to say about it," remembered Steenson. "Thanks to Cliffie, the warning became part of my permanent service record."

Steenson described his second trip to RCMP service court, "Olson had committed a break and enter and theft at Surrey. Ray Wilson, who was on CIB with me, checked Olson and found him flush with money. Olson never worked, which meant he had stolen it. Through routine hotel checks we learned he was staying at a Richmond hotel. This was in the days before court-authorized wiretaps. Percy Easler, a Vancouver Police whiz at electronics, fired up a bug for me. We had to get the hotel to move Olson into a room where we could set up the bug easier. Ken Washington and I listened while Olson and the young crook he was teaching came in early. We heard them clunking around and went in and searched them. They had nothing on them. We finally found the money outside on the balcony. We also found a key to the Yellow Rose Motel in Surrey."

Steenson promptly telephoned the Surrey RCMP and asked them to search the motel room. Inside, they recovered Olson's large cache of stolen cigarette cartons and other loot.

"Olson learned from his mistakes," reflected Steenson. "He previously had been picked up with stolen property, so he no longer kept the stolen goods with him. Instead he stashed the loot where he could get it when he needed it.

"I talked to Bullets Johnstone [a corporal nicknamed after being shot six times responding to a bank robbery alarm in Coquitlam]. I told him we had Olson and his partner in tow. Bullets said he would send a member to pick them up. I told him Olson had a reputation for escaping. Bullets assured me not to worry; he wouldn't get away. Constable Alfie Erickson arrived alone and took custody of Olson and his accomplice. Alfie returned to the Whalley Sub/Office without incident and lodged the prisoners in the cells."

As the evening progressed, Olson, true to form, carefully watched what transpired in the police office. When he was confident all the members were on patrol and only the corporal in charge remained, he called to Pat Eastman, who had replaced Corporal Johnstone. Olson suggested that he had committed many more break-ins in Surrey and he was ready to talk about them. Eastman unlocked the cell door to interview Olson and obtain a written statement. As the cell door opened, Olson, ever the opportunist, charged out of the door past Eastman and escaped.

Steenson later received an ominous telephone call from Staff Sergeant Quigley, the Section NCO at New Westminster Sub-Division. "He politely asked me to send him a statement on this incident. Next thing I know, Eastman, Washington, and I are charged in service court. We made the long trip to Orderly Room in full dress uniform without spurs. I blew my cork before Orderly Room. I told Quigley they could charge me as the senior man, but it was not right to charge Washington as he was only acting at my direction. Things got pretty heated and finally Staff Sergeant Ernie Ruttan came in and quieted things down. Eastman was convicted for allowing a prisoner to escape. Ken Washington and I were given an official warning for turning Olson over to a single escort when he was a known criminal with a record of escape. Olson was soon arrested and sent back to the penitentiary."

By this time, Eastman had been transferred from the Greater Vancouver area. He was brought back for his Orderly Room procedure. A post-Orderly Room wake was held at the New Westminster Royal Towers Hotel. Police from around the Lower Mainland dropped in to have a drink and express their moral support for a fellow officer reduced in seniority and minus some hard-earned cash, in the form of a small fine, as a result of his encounter with Cliffie.

"I would have liked to know what Olson's IQ was," mused Steenson."In some ways, he was a near genius. He probably got some of that from his dad, who was also named Clifford. His dad had what you would call a photographic memory. He used to call bingo games in the Fraserview area of Vancouver. He could remember the number of every ball he called. I recall the old man got into trouble with the Vancouver Police over some bingo irregularities."

Olson had two younger brothers. "We never had a lick of problems with either of them," Steenson related. "He also had a younger sister, Sharon. She was always Cliffie's biggest supporter and confidant and so, to a lesser extent, was his old man. Sharon believed Cliff could do no wrong and that he was unjustly accused of all his antics."

Sharon continued to support him as Olson gravitated to more serious crimes. "When we were looking for him for kidnapping a Vancouver Safeway manager during an armed robbery, we learned Sharon was contacting him by using a neighbour's telephone. In those days we didn't have sophisticated listening devices like they do today. I had an earpiece with alligator clips to attach to the phone terminals where the line came into the house. We were concealed in the neighbour's house, ready to intercept any conversation between Sharon and Cliff. To our chagrin, Sharon came in and, before she made the call to Cliff, searched the entire house. I couldn't believe it. Of course she found us. It just goes to show the disdain Cliff and Sharon had for their neighbours. Can you imagine actually searching through the privacy of your neighbour's house? It also showed how careful Cliffie was becoming."

Olson was different from most of the young thugs Steenson chased around Richmond. "I don't remember ever hearing Cliff swear, nor do I remember him ever taking a drink. All that came later. I don't think he even drove a car in those days. He travelled a lot by cab," Steenson recalled. "He kept a notebook and was always writing stuff down." This practice would continue throughout his adult life as Darryll Kettles and others could attest.

Once when Olson was in custody, Steenson opened the notebook. The hunted had become the hunter. Olson had been busy following police cars around Richmond and charting their daily activity. "He knew our routines," said Steenson. "He recorded what time we went for coffee and meals, how many police were working, every move we made. You have to remember there were only two or three cars

Jim Steenson owes a few gray hairs to Clifford Olson. Olson, he says, had an answer for everything. He figured he could not be declared a habitual criminal if he was never out of prison long enough to have a fair chance at rehabilitation.

on duty in those days. When all the cars were on the road, there was only the supervisor and maybe the radio operator in the office.

"Olson formulated a scheme to capture the police, one at a time, and lock them in jail. He then planned to rob the Sea Island bank. Sam Ferguson, the staff sergeant in charge, was wild when he found out about Olson's plan. Shortly after, I put him back in the Pen for the third time.

"That was the last time I arrested him. The RCMP, in their wisdom, transferred me. Nobody paid much attention to Olson after that."

B.C. Penitentiary

"All this kinky sex stuff, Olson learned that in the Pen," stated Steenson. "There was never any sign of that as a kid. This homosexual stuff, he learned that in the Pen too." Steenson remembered Olson as a good-looking guy before he went to the penitentiary. "I couldn't believe how he changed after two or three trips to the Pen."

By this time Steenson was a corporal in the New Westminster CIB Section. As the designated liaison officer, he was required to spend time at the British Columbia Penitentiary. Requests for inmate interviews on behalf of police outside the Lower Fraser Valley were automatically channelled to his desk.

"If anyone was ever institutionalized it was Olson," stated Jim Steenson. "He is a product of our penal system. Whatever he became was a direct result of his experiences in our jails.

"I remember one occasion where he and two other cons planned to escape from the B.C. Pen. One morning, as the penitentiary doctor drove his car through the main gate, he commented to the guards that his steering was stiff. They made some comment but didn't check the car's undercarriage before allowing it into the Pen grounds. As he parked his vehicle he saw Olson and two other cons near his parking space. Becoming suspicious, he drove back to the main gate and asked the guards to check around the steering column. They found an Ivor Johnson revolver and forty-nine rounds of ammunition. Their accomplice on the outside had made a mistake and taped the gun and ammunition to the tie rod instead of to the steering column, making the vehicle hard to steer. Sergeant Jack White and I traced the gun to Seattle. The last we could find was that it had been in the possession of a street-level drug pusher in downtown Seattle. We couldn't determine Olson's Canadian contact that had taped the gun to the car.

"The doc was smart. Had he not gone back to the gate, he would have been knocked on the head or worse. I had been telling the guards on the gate they should install a long strip of reflective metal so they could see the undercarriage of vehicles coming through. They only had these mirrors on poles, like a dentist, but much larger.

"I would often see Cliffie at the Pen. He had worked himself into a sort of trustee. He was considered a bit of a jailhouse lawyer. He was always appealing or grieving something, mostly for himself but sometimes he hired himself out to other cons. He seemed to go anywhere he wanted. I saw him a lot around the main office. One time I tried to get into the Correspondence Officer's office. That's where they checked all the incoming and outgoing inmate mail. Since the door was locked, I knocked. The door opens and inside is Cliff Olson, all alone. As he shakes my hand he says, 'Hey Jim, how are you doing?' Locks didn't stop Cliff. I couldn't believe my eyes."

Steenson recalled another incident when Olson surreptitiously entered the penitentiary chaplain's office. Using the chaplain's typewriter he increased his sentence on the documentation of one of his many charges from six months to two years. He then filed a writ of *habeas corpus*, claiming to be unlawfully confined. This led to many trips back and forth to court, giving him opportunities to escape. Finally one of the corporals on the Court Detail carefully examined the documentation and found it had been tampered with. Document examiners subsequently found the chaplain's typewriter had been used to make the changes. "So ended Cliff's writ of *habeas corpus* caper."

Olson was always a worry for his keepers. He constantly waited for an escort to let down his guard. On one occasion during a search, pepper was found in his pockets. "Quite frankly," Steenson confided, "Olson was a pain in the ass. He was always complaining or running some scam. People hated dealing with him. You couldn't trust him, not the guards or the cons. He would rat-out on the cons. That's why he was stabbed in Prince Albert. He informed on prisoners getting drugs in a B.C. institution. They didn't get him for it until after he was in Prince Albert."

Jim Steenson never considered using Olson as an informant. He deemed Olson to be much too devious and erratic to be of any value. "I had a strict set of rules I went by for informants and Cliff would never have made it. He was too unreliable and untrustworthy," observed Steenson. "Not only that, most times he was the guy we most wanted to catch.

"One of the last times I arrested him, I told him I was going to throw the bitch at him [have him declared an habitual criminal]. In true barrack-room-lawyer fashion he replied, 'You can't bitch me, Jim. I'm never out long enough to rehabilitate myself.' Of course, he was right.

"Olson was always a show-off. To demonstrate his foolhardiness, when they closed the B.C. Penitentiary he took a friend there to show off his old cell. A guard recognized him and knew there was a Canada-wide warrant for his arrest. He called the police and they arrested Cliff and sent him back to jail. Thus, Cliffie had the dubious honour of being the last person ever arrested at the B.C. Penitentiary."

Olson did not fool the prison system. He spent most of his adult life in jail. Considering his long criminal record, he was only paroled twice. Each time it was revoked, first in April 1959 and lastly in August 1972. Obviously, he was considered a poor risk for parole.

Gary Francis Marcoux

Mission RCMP GIS Constables Cal Hood and Dave Shakespeare viewed Olson in a different light. On June 30, 1976, Hood and Shakespeare were investigating Gary Francis Marcoux regarding the disappearance of nine-year-old Jeanna Doove from Mission, B.C.

Marcoux, a known sex offender, had been released from jail on mandatory supervision. He was staying at a Mission halfway house near the trailer park where Jeanna lived with her family. Police soon discovered that he had befriended the missing girl. The investigation focused on Marcoux, and he was arrested early on July 1, Canada Day.

As they questioned Marcoux, Hood and Shakespeare became convinced he was their man. Hood still recalls the sense of urgency they felt. Even though it was summer, the nights were cool. If the child were alive she would surely be cold and suffering. She had been missing since early afternoon the previous day, so they wanted to find her soon.

Corporal Don McDermid gave Marcoux a lie detector test at the Vancouver RCMP HQ. The test was inconclusive and a second examination was scheduled for the following day. As the day wore on, Marcoux commented, "I was high last night." He claimed he had been "smoking dope" with an unnamed associate.

Hood and Shakespeare, now accompanied by Constable Art Carter, encouraged Marcoux to retrace his movements of the previous evening. He led the police from one area to another. Hours later they stopped at a remote location high on the soon-to-be-infamous Weaver Lake Road. "I remember being here" said Marcoux, pointing to a pile of gravel near the side of the road. "I remember beavers hitting their tails on the water. Do you think there are beavers here?"

"Yes, I would imagine," replied Hood as they stood in silent darkness. Eerily, as he uttered these words a beaver slapped its tail, then dove beneath the surface of the nearby water.

While Hood and Carter remained with Marcoux, Shakespeare, armed with a flashlight, descended a steep embankment. It was 1 a.m. on July 2. The three constables were distraught to discover all their efforts had been in vain. Jeanna Doove had been sexually assaulted and murdered. Marcoux was charged with the murder and returned to the B.C. Pen, where he was incarcerated in the Super Maximum Unit (SMU).

★ ★ ★

SMU housed the most dangerous and hard-to-handle convicts. Communication between inmates was difficult in SMU. They could not see or speak to one another, so communication had to be in writing. A prisoner would pass a note to the occupant of the next cell, who would pass it to his neighbour, and so on until the note reached the proper recipient. The procedure was reversed for the reply.

Fate intervened on August 20 when Clifford Olson was sent to SMU. Olson and Marcoux knew each other from Mountain Prison. Two cells, occupied by convicted killers Andy Bruce and Dwight Lucas, separated them. A message from Marcoux to Olson had to be passed by contract killer Andy Bruce to axe murderer Dwight Lucas to Olson, with the return note passing through the same hands.

Olson agreed to supply Marcoux with an alibi for the time Jeanna Doove disappeared and provided a sworn affidavit declaring he and Marcoux were together "doing marihuana" when Jeanna was abducted.

Constable Shakespeare, who knew Olson, went to the B.C. Penitentiary to question him about the truth of his affidavit. Shakespeare was angry and it was Olson who said, "Dave, take it easy, cool down. I'm working with you guys on this." Olson readily admitted the affidavit was bogus.

"I think that was Olson's plan all along," Shakespeare indicated. "He would convince Marcoux he was alibiing him, get him to confess, and then rat him out. Olson didn't need any convincing. He wanted to co-operate."

Shakespeare worked out an elaborate plan in which Olson would write notes to Marcoux seeking information regarding Jeanna's murder. Over the next several weeks, Olson, ever the opportunist, encouraged Marcoux to write out the sordid details. To top it off, he had Marcoux draw a map showing all pertinent locations.

Olson turned these damning notes over to Shakespeare—more than a hundred of them. Shakespeare and Hood were overjoyed. This new evidence was a godsend. In most of his statements to police, Marcoux did not admit guilt. When he did incriminate himself, the police feared the statements would not be admissible in court. The Marcoux–Olson notes greatly enhanced their case. Police handwriting specialists compared the writing in the notes with known samples obtained from Marcoux to verify that he had written the notes. Marcoux was convicted and sentenced to a minimum of twenty-five years. As prosecutor Robert Shantz later wrote, "Without Olson's testimony, Marcoux would have been acquitted of the murder charge."

"We treated him like royalty," said Hood. "Olson revelled in the situation and all the attention he was getting. He got nothing out of it except status and preferred treatment. He also received a letter from Robert Shantz, but that's all. We needed Olson's evidence and he provided it, no strings attached."

Olson was released on mandatory supervision between the time he obtained the incriminating notes and Marcoux's trial date. Shakespeare set up a meeting with him, but true to character, Olson failed to arrive. When Shakespeare checked into his whereabouts, he learned that Olson was driving in New Westminster without a driver's licence and was stopped in a line of cars at a police roadblock. Olson had abandoned the car, entered a nearby apartment block, and asked the occupant of a second-storey apartment overlooking the roadblock if he could use the telephone. While on the phone, he watched the scene below to see what would happen to the abandoned vehicle. The impulsive Olson looked around the apartment, saw a wallet, and pocketed it. The resident missed the wallet almost immediately and called out the window to the police below. Olson was captured and his mandatory supervision was suspended.

After being found guilty of the Jeanna Doove murder, Marcoux was sitting despondently in a holding cell, his bowed head cupped by both hands. Ironically, Olson, who had testified against him, was placed in the same holding cell. He walked over to Marcoux and said, "Gary, the best thing we can do is forget this whole fucking thing and act like it didn't happen."

Olson loves mind games. Fortunately for society, this time Gary Marcoux was his victim.

★ ★ ★

"In retrospect," declared Hood, "I think that's when it all started with Olson. He wanted to experience what Marcoux did."

Some people have gone so far as to suggest that Olson took on the personality of Gary Francis Marcoux when they were in the SMU at the B.C. Penitentiary together.

Clinical psychologist Dr. Lee Pulos disagreed. "Theoretically, the transfer of personality is a possibility but highly unlikely. It would have to be a person with a very strong personality, and even then it's very remote." Pulos said there was a term for this in psychology, *folie a deux*, meaning an identical delusion or mental disorder affecting two people living in close association.

Dr. Nicole Aube, a Vancouver registered psychologist, agreed that *folie a deux* would not happen to Olson. "This would only apply to someone with a very passive nature," she said. "He was too much in control." She classified Olson as a manipulative, unfeeling psychopath.

Olson and Maile

One aspect of this case that confounded many who watched it was the chemistry between Fred Maile and Clifford Olson. Between the confession and the trial, Maile was often seen with a smug

Clifford Olson in the field. The sight of Olson smoking his cigars and playing the bigshot had made Daryll Kettles want to vomit.

Maile had a tough role to play. He was, in essence, now Olson's bodyguard, stroking his ego and cajoling the criminal when necessary to keep Olson on side. Even after the trial, Maile appeared to be Olson's RCMP contact of choice. For whatever reason, it was Fred Maile more than any other policeman who had Olson "spilling his guts."

Maile broke Olson. It was he who asked the right question at the right time and heard the answer "No, all were local."

Much later, Maile was asked what his feelings were when he heard a serial killer mutter those four words. His response offered more on the subject than he had spoken in years.

"Shock isn't the right word," Fred said. "I was pretty tired. We had been going night and day for a long time when he came out with that. It wasn't really a feeling of elation. I would call it a feeling of comfort that we had finally got something out of all this. Yeah, it was a good feeling that he was off the street, but any elation we experienced was soon gone. We talked about it later and wondered why we didn't feel better. We all had kids, that was probably part of it. Olson had done such terrible things and he was such a bullshitter and manipulator that we couldn't even enjoy the moment.

"We knew he had done some things, but we didn't know everything and we didn't even know Arnd was missing. I also knew he was so unpredictable he could recant everything, and even if he didn't, our job was just beginning because we had to recover the bodies and put everything together for court. We had a good feeling, but the elation you would have expected just wasn't there. Olson spoiled it for most of us. He was such a creep. Our moment of happiness was short-lived because we knew what we had to deal with.

"I was emotional when I arrived home. I told my wife he had copped. When I finally got a weekend off we went to Victoria. I didn't want anyone else around me.

"We had no choice but to pay the money. I ran the whole situation about the money by my wife as an unbiased person. When she heard the situation she said we should pay the money.

"We were never allowed to feel good about this case. There always seemed to be a dark cloud hanging over us. Maybe we could have done some things differently, but with the knowledge we had and what we had to work with, we couldn't find anything we did wrong. The only recognition we ever got was when John Hall took us all to dinner.

"In the end Olson said, 'I know what you want. You want me to take you to a body.' He shut up on us right after he proposed the deal. We took him to do some more interviews, and that's when we learned the Force was going for the deal. We were to take him to McNeney's office in the Sun Building.

"There was a look of complete shock on Olson's face. He hadn't thought for one moment the deal would go ahead, and now he was boxed into a corner. On the way downtown I got the okay to take him by his parents' place. That is the coldest meeting I ever saw. We didn't stay long.

"We took him to the Sun Building. We were constantly aware he might try to escape. Arnie and Proke met with McNeney and Shantz. The lawyers wouldn't proceed until Olson talked to his wife. She came in and they talked and then the deal proceeded. We went the next day to look for bodies.

"Olson wouldn't write down stuff. It took me awhile, but I finally determined he couldn't write properly. He was a poor writer and didn't know grammar. He was embarrassed about it. He fooled people because he copied everything carefully.

"The RCMP brass wanted to know why I was doing all the writing. I didn't write anything for Olson until I confirmed I should with John Hall. He said to get as much as I could as it was all evidence. Olson dictated and I wrote down what he said. He signed it, and I witnessed his signature."

Following the interviews, Maile and other members of the Serious Crime Section had to endure the horrors of travelling with Olson to recover the bodies of his victims. To elicit his co-operation they had to mask their disgust and revulsion. Many of their colleagues could not understand this and reacted emotionally towards Maile. "I was cursed and sworn at and received threatening phone calls from RCMP members who could not understand the situation," he recalled, but Fred Maile toughed it out.

Holmes in Hot Pursuit

Author Les Holmes only came into contact with Olson once during his active years with the RCMP. It was not his finest hour.

During the 1960s, New Westminster criminal elements spoke freely of an understanding they had with the New Westminster Police. The police would not harass them, providing they committed no crimes within the New Westminster jurisdiction.

It worked fine for New Westminster, but for the Burnaby RCMP and other nearby communities the unofficial pact resulted in increased crime. To combat this situation, RCMP detectives Constable Earl "Mac" MacRae and Constable Bob Siddle developed criminal informants within the Royal City.

On one occasion, Les Holmes and his partner Bill Sparks received a call to meet Mac, who was teamed up with Constable John Middleton. One of Mac's most reliable sources had spotted the troublesome Clifford Olson drinking in the Windsor Hotel. A warrant existed for his arrest. Olson was known within the police community as an active criminal who would bolt at the first sign of police.

The RCMP contingent of Mac, Middleton, Sparks, and Holmes headed for the hotel beer parlour, which was frequented by longshoremen and street people. They had no sooner stepped through the Front Street door than Olson leapt from his chair and fled. Three RCMP pursued him, while the fourth, in an attempt to cut him off, ran across the beer parlour to a door on the north wall. Adrenalin flowing and capture uppermost in his mind, Holmes tore open the door and ran into a dead-end telephone room.

His only choice was to about face, much to the amusement of the bar's patrons. Sheepishly the constable found a more functional exit and relief from the cheering, whistling crowd. Once he caught up to the chase, Les was relieved to learn his compatriots had the elusive Olson in handcuffs.

Thirteen
Closure

Bringing closure to one police file will only serve a purpose if we learn from the experience. A disturbing article appeared in the *Vancouver Province* on February 6, 2000. It reported that seven females between the ages of seventeen and nineteen were murdered on the Yellowhead Highway between 1990 and 2000. The victims were from Prince George, Terrace, Smithers, and Quesnel.

None of the cases have been solved, and the newspaper article speculated a serial killer might be at work. Whether there is a serial killer or seven separate murderers active does not change the seriousness of the situation. A task force was to be established in 1997 to investigate the homicides, but it never materialized.

What is more telling is the comment of the RCMP media spokesperson at Prince George. "If the resources were made available, and the funds, we'd throw them into these investigations. In many cases we just don't have the manpower or the money available to take it that extra step."

The situation is worse now than in 1981. Though short of personnel in 1981, once the RCMP recognized the problem it had the resources and was quick to respond.

Since the first columns of North West Mounted Police rode onto the Canadian prairie in 1873, the Force has maintained a tradition of honourable policework. Often it has functioned in an environment of skepticism and fiscal constraint. Such is the case today.

The cost of policing in Canada is relatively low and the standards of law and order are very high. Does this mean government budgets can ignore the needs of modern policing? Budget cuts forced the RCMP in British Columbia to tie up part of its marine fleet in 1999. Cuts have affected both effectiveness and members' morale. They restrict the appointment of a co-ordinator to investigate the Yellowhead murders in 2000. What will be the final road to closure in that case?

Improvements Since Olson

Since the Olson case, advances have been made to assist investigations of serial murders.

❖ DNA or genetic fingerprinting has become commonplace. It is unlikely this would have assisted the Olson investigation, except to positively identify the remains of Sandra Wolfsteiner.

❖ In British Columbia the RCMP implemented the Violent Crime Linkage Analysis System (ViCLAS) in 1995. It was designed to compare and perhaps link sex-related murders and sexual assaults in separate jurisdictions.

❖ Inspector Kim Rossmo of the Vancouver Police developed a geographic profiling system. Rossmo based his PhD thesis on a study of known serial killers, creating a system in which data relating to geographic details of a murder are analyzed in an attempt to link various crimes and suspects. In the absence of a suspect, this system can possibly determine the area where the killer lives.

Geographic profiling might have been effective in the Johnsrude case, but Kettles was faster. Interestingly, his mental processes followed the reverse path to Rossmo's system. Darryll had a suspect and linked his identity to the victim. Les Forsythe used the same thinking to reach his conclusions in the Johnsrude and Ada Court murders.

Kettles had recognized all the information that would have been entered into ViCLAS. Not only did he know what happened in Agassiz, but he also had his suspicions about Olson's complicity in the Johnsrude murder. In addition he learned about Olson's activities at both Squamish and Richmond. This is the data that would have triggered ViCLAS.

Darryll's investigation formed a foundation to build upon. Had he not fully documented the circumstances surrounding the Sallow case, it is hard to imagine that Olson would have become a suspect for murder. The records would simply have shown that he had been arrested for impaired driving and contributing to the delinquency of a minor.

In May 1981 only two of Olson's victims had been found, one in Richmond and one in Agassiz. One had gone missing from Surrey and the other from Coquitlam. It is sheer conjecture to consider if geographic profiling would have pointed to Olson as a logical suspect without Darryll's discoveries.

When Ada Court went missing from the Burnaby/Coquitlam area and was found in Agassiz, the odds that geographic profiling would have been effective would have increased. At the time of the Johnsrude and Court cases, Olson was living in Coquitlam, whereas at the time of the Weller case, he was living in Surrey.

By July 1981, few of the bodies of Olson's victims had been found. In most instances all the police had were the locations where the missing children had last been seen. Given these circumstances, it is unlikely that either geographic profiling or ViCLAS would have been of any real benefit had they been available in 1980-81. Both Darryll and Les focused in on Olson without the benefit of a computerized system. The factors they considered would probably have brought Olson forward as a suspect in the ViCLAS system, but not any sooner.

Serial killers Ted Bundy and Peter Sutcliffe limited their victims to one sex. Olson was unusual in that his victims were both male and female. In addition, Olson attempted to lead police to believe there was more than one killer by varying the means by which he murdered. This did not have a negative impact on the investigations, but it again points out just how challenging the investigations would have remained, even with the scientific advances of the past two decades.

Fred Maile was asked about ViCLAS and Olson in 1998. He reportedly said, "I'm positive in my mind, if the system [ViCLAS] was up to date and used properly, that there could have been two or three lives, or even more, saved."

When Bruce Northorp was asked for his thoughts on Maile's comments, he saw things differently. "I don't know how he could have come to such a conclusion. Les Forsythe connected Olson to the Ada Court case by investigative ability alone. That led him to

Agassiz and he, like Darryll Kettles, concluded Olson was connected to the Johnsrude murder.

"The only other cases, other than Christine Weller, reported prior to Les's Ada Court file were Colleen Daignault—last seen on April 15 and reported missing on the 21st—and Sandra Wolfsteiner —last seen on May 19. For some days no foul play was suspected in Sandra's case. It was only in August, after the co-ordinated investigation began, that Colleen was considered a victim of foul play. As such, it's hard to believe those two would have been included in a ViCLAS system and therefore could not have expedited matters."

What might have saved some lives would have been the questioning of Olson based on Darryll's suspicions. That was not done. If alternate action had been taken after the July 15 meeting in Burnaby, four lives would likely have been saved.

"In my view," said Bruce, "ViCLAS would have done nothing. Both Darryll and Les were faster than ViCLAS could have been. If some failed to follow through appropriately on what Darryll and Les had developed, it's unlikely they would have reacted differently had the same suspect been produced by other means."

The diligence of both Darryll and Les is noteworthy. Both were investigators following up the circumstances surrounding Olson's arrests for impaired driving and sexual assualt. It would have been easy for Darryll to do nothing more than ensure Olson was charged with contributing to juvenile delinquency, then dropping it. Likewise, it would have been easy for Les to pass the sexual assault matter on to Surrey. Both officers went the full distance by delving into Olson's activities. This was the key to the solution of these crimes. Darryll's early work, reporting Olson's actions with Sallow, was critical in solving the cases, even though Darryll was not identified as the source of that information.

Good Investigations

"I feel the police, in total, did a tremendous job," Northorp concluded. "All you have to do is compare the length of time it took the police in other jurisdictions to solve their serial killings. Twenty-nine blacks, twenty-seven male and two female, ranging in age from seven to twenty-eight years, were murdered in Atlanta, Georgia, from July 1979 until May 1981. In 1981 only two of the cases were close to being cleared when Wayne Williams was indicted for the two latest murders, both of adults."

In the late 1980s the TV show *Fifth Estate* ran a special on the Atlanta killings. Williams by then had been convicted of the two murders. After the convictions, the Atlanta police blamed him for twenty-two unsolved child murders. "They simply wrote them off as 'cleared by arrest,'" observed Northorp.

Controversy was still rampant at that time as to whether or not Williams was responsible for any of the

The handling of the Wayne Williams serial murder investigation in Atlanta was much different. There the accused was found guilty of two murders, and a large number of cases were simply closed and attributed to Williams.

other twenty-two homicides. Williams still proclaimed his innocence in relation to his two convictions.

In England, Peter Sutcliffe claimed thirteen female victims in five years, from 1975 to 1980. When these cases were solved in early 1981, it was not as the result of follow-up inquiries by the investigative team. Rather, things fell into place after two vice detectives checked Sutcliffe with a prostitute.

Additionally, in both jurisdictions the victims' bodies had all been found. In the Olson case, most of the bodies had not been found, eliminating the chance of securing leads or even considering if one person was responsible.

The investigations here were not made any easier by the delay in reporting two of the victims as missing persons. Although

Christine Weller was last seen on November 19, it was not until November 25 that she was reported missing. Even then it was not by family, with whom she was living, but by a friend. Such a delay meant there was not a fresh trail to follow. Colleen Daignault was last seen on April 15, yet her absence was not reported until several days later. These are not excuses, but rather circumstances that made both cases more difficult.

"The fact that known and suspected victims were both male and female," said Northorp, "was in itself most unusual and further complicated matters. Regardless, it was May 1981 when a second murder of Olson's came to light. He was in custody just three months later, ending his reign of terror. In any investigation one can look back and say something should have been done or done differently. This case falls into that class.

"Probably a main factor was the lack of co-ordination at an earlier stage. I learned about the cases and the multiplicity of units involved by chance on July 29. The situation was corrected the next day. It should have been recognized and identified to the HQ at least after the Burnaby meeting of July 15. The need for co-ordination in what was obviously a multi-jurisdictional matter should have been apparent to Howitt and/or his immediate superiors. Perhaps senior management at Burnaby were not given a full briefing such as I was given on the 29th. The absence of key personnel on holidays may also have forestalled the identification of the problem."

The lack of co-ordination was an issue noted by others after Olson had pleaded guilty. An investigator from the coroner's office asked Northorp, "Who was in charge before you took over?" BCTV reporter Alyn Edwards asked Assistant Commissioner Wilson, "Who had overall control of that investigation during the last two weeks of July before Superintendent Northorp took it over? Did any one member of the RCMP have overall control?" Duncan Chappell, a professor of criminology at Simon Fraser University, reportedly said, "On July 30 it appears the whole investigation entered a new co-ordinated phase with a senior RCMP officer, Superintendent Bruce Northorp, assuming overall command."

"Even the RCMP's post-case analysis recognized this failing," said Northorp. "To me it was basic. The situation needed a co-ordinator."

One of the coroner's recommendations was:

RCMP senior management should review their procedures in assessing ongoing field investigations in cases of serious crimes where there is substantial likelihood that public safety is endangered. Senior management must review this type of case at the earliest possible time, with the option of assuming command where the situation is deemed to be of such a degree of severity as to warrant such control. Any change in procedure should not be done in such a way as to lessen the initiative of other levels of investigation. Assumption of control by senior management, in appropriate cases such as this, would allow such questions as public safety and the apprehension of the criminal to be looked at in a broader context. In this way priorities could be properly established for such activities as surveillance, etc.

"Surveillance was another contentious issue," commented Bruce. "Co-ordination would have resolved any problems if the HQ had been fully briefed on the issues. The manpower shortage referred to by Burnaby could have been dealt with easily. As it was, after July 23, despite the lack of briefing to the HQ, Burnaby GIS already had at least one member engaged in the case, as did Serious Crime. It doesn't seem insurmountable. Two or three other members could have been freed up to support the surveillance section. JFO were to supply the extra coverage for Special 'O', however, that never transpired. When Olson detected surveillance on him by JFO units on July 28, the officers should have realized it was a job for Special 'O' and taken up the offer for a complete team. I've little doubt that had Ed Naaykens been given the offer, it would have been accepted."

John Hall was close to the case and he was quoted as saying, "Surveillance was a tough decision for Northorp, but it turned out he was right." If some misunderstood Bruce's prudence, it only speaks to their inexperience.

A Policeman's Report Card

Bruce Northorp listed the following as the major points in the Olson investigation.

The negatives:

1. The failure to question Olson after he was put forth as a suspect by Darryll Kettles.
2. The failure in mid-July 1981 to co-ordinate the investigation.
3. Treating Olson as a source and his Surrey release on July 29, 1981.
4. Failure in mid to late July to be aware of the Surrey warrant for Olson's arrest.
5. The folly of meeting Olson when an arrest warrant existed.

The positives:

1. Les Forsythe arranging the July 15 meeting at Burnaby.
2. The decision, on August 12, to arrest Olson on Vancouver Island, then commence intensive interrogation.
3. Charging Olson with breaking and entering to intensify pressure.
4. Locating Judy Kozma's name in Olson's address book and using a charge of sexual assault to further press Olson.
5. Finding Randy Ludlow, who put Olson with Judy Kozma the last day she was known to be alive.
6. Charging Olson with the first degree murder of Judy Kozma on August 18, which ultimately resulted in a full confession.

Epilogue

Can we end the debate? Will this account bring to an end any conjecture about the RCMP investigation of the Olson murders? Most insiders have reached their own conclusions regarding the investigation; I hope now these will be more informed conclusions.

Outsiders, with limited information, no doubt have different thoughts. One "outsider" who was deeply affected by Clifford Olson, Randy Ludlow, noted the task force commenced on July 30, 1981. Twelve days later Olson was in jail. Six days after that he was charged with the murder of Judy Kozma. In Ludlow's words, "That's very fast. It's incredible."

Bringing closure to the Olson investigators and involved personnel is of paramount importance. Surely it is time to let go of any lingering shame and regret. It is time to accept the things that will forever remain the same; time to realize the only thing that can be changed is the future, through the lessons learned.

RCMP members Darryll Kettles, Les Forsythe, Arnie Nylund, Randy Schramm, Rick Boyarski, Sandy Sandhu, Ed Naaykens, Ron Paull, Norm Fuchs, Don Wilson, Cliff Kusmack, and Jim Steenson have retired and live in the Lower Mainland of British Columbia. Fred Maile is a partner in a security investigation firm. Ed Drozda works for a federal corporation. Don Brown and Brian Tuckey work for different B.C. government agencies. Larry Proke went on to head the United Nations Canadian Police Peacekeeping Contingent in Namibia. He was the Deputy Commissioner for the Pacific Region (B.C. and the Yukon) at the time he left the RCMP.

Fred Zaharia and Gordon Tomalty have retired from the RCMP and live in the Garibaldi area, while retired members Jack Randle and Bill Neill live in the Fraser Valley. Dwight Gash, Bill Howitt, Sid Slater, Dennis Tarr, and Tom Charlton have retired to the B.C. Interior.

Retired Commissioner Bob Simmonds and Deputy Commissioners Tom Venner and Henry Jensen live in Ontario.

Jim Hunter, Bob MacIntosh, Mike Lysyk, Bill Hudyma, and Dave McAree are still serving with the RCMP.

Ed Cadenhead has retired from the New Westminster Police and lives on Vancouver Island.

Don Celle retired from the B.C. Attorney General's Ministry and resides in the Greater Vancouver area. Former B.C. Attorney General Allan Williams is a city councillor in West Vancouver. James McNeney and Robert Shantz still practise law in the Lower Mainland. John Hall and Alan Filmer have been appointed judges.

Mike Chunys is living in Australia. Spud Dyer has retired and lives in Agassiz, where Gord Sciotti continues to operate Modern Tire with his family. Randy (Cook) Ludlow resides in the Greater Vancouver area. Kim Werbecky was last known to be raising a family in Alberta.

To sum up, the eleven murders were solved within three months of the Johnsrude murder. Less than five months later Olson pled guilty to all charges. Those results in that time frame represent many hours of intensive investigation by a great number of dedicated, expert police personnel, under the guidance of some highly skilled leadership. All deserve a huge thank-you; all deserve to be acknowledged; all deserve closure. To that end, I have written this book.

Appendix I

Bruce Northorp, C.M.

In December 1981 the *Vancouver Sun* reported, "Bruce Northorp has earned a reputation as one of Canada's most respected police officers." In a personnel rating, Chief Superintendent Norman Inkster, who later became the RCMP Commissioner, said that Northorp's investigative talents, his dedication to his work, and the successful results he had produced in a variety of different and complex situations had given him the well-deserved reputation of being a policeman's policeman.

He was also a parent, and the Olson case introduced him to a new and unique sense of affinity. Case studies have long depicted how traumatic circumstances can stimulate unusual reactions and abnormal bonding of very different people. As a parent and as a policeman he felt very close—closer than he ever expected—to the families of the murdered children. In 1981 Bruce received a letter from one of the family members, expressing anger and anguish at the murders and the fact that Olson would not be facing the death penalty. "My heart goes out to you and the rest of the police force. I wish to thank all of you for finding [my child]…"

Bruce wrote back within days:

> Would you please accept my sincere sympathy in the loss of your … under the most tragic circumstances.
>
> There are few who would understand the anguish and mental torture you and the other parents endured for such a long period of time. I do feel the police officers closely associated with the investigations did have such an understanding. We knew our responsibility to investigate; however, perhaps the heaviest responsibility we felt was relieving the uncertainty for all the parents in the same situation as yourself.
>
> It was due to my personal feelings and the sharing of your anguish that made my job the most difficult I have ever had to face in more than 32 years of police service. The fact that you have taken the time to write and say thank you will make this policeman's lot a little more endurable. We are deeply affected, both our families and ourselves, by the tragedies we deal with from time to time.
>
> I trust that time will heal the hurt you are feeling.

In retirement Bruce Northorp remains a keen observer of the policing community. He has maintained an archive of news items from print media, radio, and TV that covered new developments in the Olson case. Bruce made himself and his records available to the author and willingly commented on all research data uncovered. It is his hope that this undertaking will provide a source of study for policemen and criminologists and a sense of closure for all directly involved.

The Northorp Profile

After leaving high school in Vancouver, Bruce held a forest industry job and did a stint in the Army before working for a hardware wholesaler for three years in the late 1940s. A chance meeting with a member of the now-defunct B.C. Provincial Police piqued his interest.

Within weeks he applied to join that force, was accepted, and was sworn in as a constable on April Fools' Day, 1949. Occasionally along the way he was reminded of that day's significance.

His first three postings with British Columbia Provincial Police were about one year each in the East Kootenays, at Cranbrook, Trail, and Fernie. While at Trail in August 1950 he became a member of the RCMP when the men in scarlet assumed provincial duties, and in May 1952 Northorp was transferred to the Lower Mainland of B.C., where he spent the balance of his service.

May 1952—Vancouver Sub-Division – Liquor and gambling detail
November 1954—Burnaby Detachment – Uniform patrol
October 1957—Burnaby Detachment – Plainclothes duties, rising from
    constable to staff sergeant of the section for several years
September 1970—Vancouver Sub-Division – CIB co-ordinating NCO
May 1971—Promoted to sub-inspector; made OIC Richmond Detachment
June 1973—Intelligence officer for B.C., posted at Vancouver, made inspector
August 1975—OIC Internal Investigation Unit for B.C.
July 1976—Promoted to superintendent , OIC Support Services (Assistant CIB
    Officer) at Vancouver headquarters
February 1979—Documented he was not available for further promotion
December 1981—Retired

Police Training:
B.C. Police School, Canadian Police College in Regina, FBI Academy(Anti-Terrorism Course)

Commendations:
1966—*Commanding Officer's Commendation* for work on a bank robbery.
1971—Letter of recognition from J. Edgar Hoover of the FBI for boarding a
    hijacked Alaskan aircraft at Vancouver International Airport and talking a
    dangerous felon into surrendering.
1972—*RCMP Commissioner's Commendation for Bravery* for actions in the above
    incident.
1978—*Commanding Officer's Commendation* for his actions as Operations Commander at the B.C. Penitentiary during a hostage incident.

Decorations:
The Order of Canada—Canada Member (C.M.)—June 1979
War Medal
Queen's Silver Jubilee Medal
125th Anniversary of the Confederation of Canada Medal
RCMP Long Service Medal

Other:
1980—Canada's delegate to a Commission of Enquiry into unsolved murders
    in Barbados.

1984—Served on a four-person study team into murders and violence in eastern penitentiaries.

1985 to 1986—Served as a community board member of the National Parole Board.

Personal:

Born in Vancouver in 1927, he attended John Oliver High School. In 1954 he married Mabel Louisa Kerr. They have two sons (one an RCMP member) and three grandchildren.

On the occasion of Bruce Northorp's retirement, December 30, 1981, Keith Morgan of the *Vancouver Province* wrote, "Widely respected as one of Canada's top police officers... today marks the end of a career which has spanned nearly 33 years."

Appendix II

Understanding the Process of Sentencing in the Canadian Criminal Law System

In the Canadian legal system, when an accused individual stands trial and is found guilty of a crime, it is standard practice for the presiding judge to deliberate and then impose a sentence that fits the nature of the crime, and falls within the guidelines of the justice system.

If a jail sentence is imposed it is normal for the confinement to take place in the province where the case was heard when thesentence is for less than two years. Otherwise, and by definition for more serious crimes, the criminal is housed in a federal penitentiary, a measure often seen as a hardship if it takes the prisoner a further distance from friends and family.

The length of a sentence and the time when it is calculated to end are often confused, sometimes by professionals as well as laypersons. Jail time related to the sentence does not necessarily start on the date of sentencing. It is calculated based on the date of arrest if a subject has been held in custody pending his trial, and total time in jail is never expected to equal the length of the sentence.

There are two specific levels of conditional release that apply to all prisoners serving federal sentences. A convicted person may seek parole status by applying to the Parole Board after serving a minimum of one-third of the imposed sentence. If parole is granted based on a positive opinion that the individual is ready to return to society at large, then the board usually attaches conditions to the parole. Usual conditions would include avoiding association with known criminals. Specific conditions applied in some circumstances might pertain to no use of illegal drugs or liquor if they have been problems for the person in the past.

If a person is continually refused parole until he or she has served two-thirds of the sentence (as was often the case with Clifford Olson), the federal penitentiaries operate under a distinct rule. Prisoners in the past were entitled to release under mandatory supervision–now referred to as statutory release. Prevailing conditions are similar to those that apply to parolees.

It is fair to say that there are four primary conditions where a person out under mandatory supervision could get into hot water. First, a person would be in technical breach by failing to report to a parole officer, using drugs, or associating with undesirables. A second factor could be if the person was arrested for a new crime. If a person was charged with a crime and a warrant was issued for arrest, the mandatory supervision status would also be withdrawn. Finally, parole officers unable to locate their charges can unilaterally order a suspension of the statutory release.

One Parole Board publication clarifies the next step: "Once release is suspended, the individual is placed in custody and a full investigation by the Correctional Service begins. Within 14 days the suspensions must be cancelled or the case referred back to the Parole Board which can either rescind the suspension and reinstate the release, or revoke the release and order the person back to the penitentiary."

In all his time in jail, Clifford Olson only managed to gain parole status twice.

Appendix III

The Criminal Life of Clifford Robert Olson

Clifford Olson was bad news for most of his life. First apprehended in 1957, he spent most of the next 24 years in and out of custody, blessed only by the liberties of the Canadian justice system.

Olson's criminal life can be divided into two distinct periods—the years before he started to rape and sodomize teenagers, and those final dark years of freedom when he became a predator and a murderer of innocent children.

The Early Years 1957-1974

From the time he was an adolescent Clifford Olson stole the milk money. He was almost constantly in prison for thefts, frauds, break-ins, escapes, robberies, and other offences. Although Jim Steenson (see Chapter 12) recalls 13 escapes, Olson only had 6 convictions for this offence as an adult. The variance may be explained by the fact that one escape conviction was overturned on appeal. Other incidents in which Olson fled from authorities may not have resulted in charges or may have been dealt with in juvenile court and would not show up on his criminal record.

July 1957—Imprisoned for break and enter (B & E) with intent to commit a crime with a definite sentence of 9 months and an indeterminate sentence of 2 years less a day. (This would mean that he would serve it in a provincial facility. There is no indication that Olson served any of the indeterminate sentence.)

Nov. 1957—While serving his sentence in Burnaby on the above charge, Olson escaped but was soon arrested and on Nov. 13 was sentenced to an additional 3 months for the escape. On Nov. 15 he was also sentenced to 2 years for offences committed while he was at large. Olson served 21 months in jail before being released on parole in April 1959.

Feb. 1958—On appeal, the above sentence was reduced to 12 months, concurrent with sentences he was serving.

April 1959—Released on parole.

June 1959—Parole revoked. (This was no doubt due to his arrest on the charge in Surrey, described below.)

July 1959—Sentenced to 2 years less a day for Unlawfully Being in a Dwelling House. (Olson's release date is not known, but was likely after about two-thirds of the sentence was served.)

Summer 1961—Olson was convicted on a variety of charges—false pretences, possessing a firearm, theft, B & E, and escape from the Saskatchewan Penitentiary at Prince Albert. The sentences ranges from a month to a year.

July 1961—Escaped from Oakalla Prison Farm, Burnaby, where he was serving one month for a traffic violation.

Nov. 1962—Escaped from RCMP at their Whalley office after arrest for B & E and theft. Rearrested on Nov. 23 by Vancouver Police and sentenced to one year for his earlier escape and fraud and two years on the B & E charge. According to media accounts, Olson was first admitted to a federal penitentiary in 1962.

June to August 1964—Olson was convicted on 6 charges ranging from false
   pretences, B & E, possession of stolen property, and theft. The sentences
   ranged from one day to 3 years and 5 months, to be served concurrently.
April 1965—Escaped from B.C. Penitentiary guards while in custody at the
   Shaughnessy Hospital in Vancouver for treatment. He was recaptured one
   week later in Blaine, Washington, U.S.A., and sentenced to 18 months on a
   charge of escape. After his escape and before his arrest in Blaine he
   committed an armed robbery of a supermarket in Vancouver. He was
   sentenced to 9 years thereafter.
Sept. 1968—Escaped from the Saskatchewan Penitentiary at Prince Albert.
   Arrested shortly thereafter in Prince Albert and sentenced to an additional
   year. In spite of his prior record, Olson somehow made parole (for the last
   time) in August 1972.
March 1973—Recommitted as a parole violator.
1974—Sentenced to over 4 years on charges of forgery, theft, and false
   pretences. In January, Olson is placed in the B.C. Penitentiary, where he is
   known as a "skinner" and "fink." At this time he allegedly committed his
   first sexual assault—his reputed victim was a 17-year-old inmate.

The Devil Himself
Olson's first sexual assault is the most likely reason he was moved to the Super
Maximum Unit (SMU, commonly known as the Penthouse) in the B.C.
Penitentiary in New Westminster, B.C. His movements through the prison
system (a maze of bureaucracy and red tape unto itself) continue.

1976—After several months in the Agassiz Mountain Prison, opts to inform
   authorities of two fellow inmates in possession of drugs. On January 27
   another inmate learns of his "finking" and threatens his life. Olson requests
   a transfer. He eventually ends up in the Saskatchewan Penitentiary at Prince
   Albert.
Feb. 4, 1976—On arriving at Saskatchewan Penitentiary, Olson is detained in
   an integration area for a few days. At his insistence he is prematurely placed
   in with the general population. On Feb. 13, his reputation as a "skinner"
   and informer having already preceded him via the prison grapevine, Olson
   gets his wish. Within half an hour of being admitted to the convict
   environment, he is stabbed 7 times. After the stabbing he is moved to
   various prison facilities in an attempt to protect him.
July 1, 1976—Gary Marcoux, charged with murdering a young girl at Mission,
   B.C., is confined under mandatory supervision and is subsequently housed
   in the SMU awaiting trial.
Aug. 20, 1976—Olson is sent to the B.C. Penitentiary where he is housed in
   SMU with Marcoux. Over the next several months Olson, working with the
   RCMP, convinces Marcoux to talk about the Mission murder. He informs
   the authorities and later testifies against Marcoux. The prosecutor, Robert
   Shantz, will be Olson's lawyer in 1980/81.
Dec. 1976—Olson and another inmate lay an assault charge against a guard.
   Charge is subsequently dismissed.
Feb. 11, 1977—Released from B.C. Penitentiary on mandatory supervision.
Apr. 5, 1977—Mandatory supervision is suspended and Olson is returned to
   prison.
June 14, 1977—Released again on mandatory supervision.

July 11, 1977—Olson cannot be located and his mandatory supervision status is revoked (and the appropriate authority to arrest Olson is processed).

Jan. 1978—Released on mandatory supervision.

June 8, 1978—Mandatory supervision revoked.

June 14, 1978—Released on mandatory supervision.

July 11, 1978—Mandatory supervision revoked.

Aug. 3, 1978—Olson is stopped by the police in Sydney, N.S., after they receive a complaint of a man indecently assaulting a 7-year-old girl. Confronted by two police officers, Olson is asked to go to the police station. He gives his right name and cons the police by asking to go back in a hotel to tell his friends where he has gone. There he escapes cleanly. Charges laid were never proceeded with due to the expense of returning Olson to Nova Scotia, combined with the fact he was already back in prison serving a lengthy sentence. As he was never arrested on the charge, he was not fingerprinted and the incident would therefore never show up on a criminal record check by any police agency. It is interesting to note that a distinctive T-shirt was one factor leading the police to check Olson. A T-shirt was a factor in the "Kathy Sallow" case on the other coast of Canada three years later.

Aug. 31, 1978—Olson seen on a stolen bicycle in Camrose, Alberta. He is held in prison facing new charges.

Jan. 7, 1980—Released on mandatory supervision.

Feb. 10, 1980—Using the name "Les Robinson," Olson picks up a boy travelling by bus from Nanaimo to Victoria. Olson takes him to Richmond where he allegedly sexually assaults and robs the adolescent in a Richmond hotel.

May 7, 1980—Olson takes a tour of the then closed B.C. Penitentiary. A guard recognizes him, remembers there is a warrant out for his arrest, and arrests him. He is returned to prison. (The B.C. Penitentiary has since been torn down.)

June 7, 1980—Released on mandatory supervision.

June 29, 1980—Realtor Suzanne Seto is murdered at Duncan, B.C. *In 1982, while already incarcerated, Olson says he was responsible for this homicide, possibly in an attempt to receive the $100,000 reward offered in the case. A young male, Kelly Toop, was arrested and later convicted. Olson was not involved.*

Aug. 7, 1980—Marnie Jamieson murdered near Sechelt.

Aug. 16, 1980—Jamieson's body found near Sechelt. *Although he would later claim responsibility, police concluded that Olson did not murder Jamieson.*

The Murders Begin

Nov. 19, 1980—Christine Weller is last seen alive at Surrey.

Nov. 25, 1980—Christine Weller reported missing.

Dec. 25, 1980—Christine Weller found murdered in Richmond.

Jan. 2, 1981—Olson threatens youths at New Westminster and points a weapon at them. He picks up a teenage hitchhiker in the Lower Mainland and rapes and abuses her at Squamish. Also gets into an altercation with Squamish youths and points weapon at them.

Jan. 3, 1981—The teenage girl (later identified under the name Kim Werbecky) escapes from Olson by locking herself in a service station washroom and staying there until her abductor departs.

Jan. 7, 1981—Olson arrested for rape and other offences during the Squamish incident. In custody awaiting trial.

Feb. 6, 1981—Olson charged with buggery and indecent assault of male teenager at Richmond. This event was alleged to have occurred on Feb. 10/11, 1980.

Feb. 26, 1981—Oang Ngoc Ha goes missing from Banff.

Feb. 28, 1981—Body of Oang Ngoc Ha located near Golden, B.C. *In August 1981 Olson claimed he was responsible for the death of a "Korean" girl near Golden. This is the only unsolved murder near Golden, and Olson was in prison when Ha went missing from Banff. He was still in prison when her body was found. Even more than the Seto and Jamieson claims referred to earlier, this posturing by Olson seems to indicate his unreliability relative to new confessions.*

Apr. 2, 1981—Crown Counsel stays Richmond buggery and indecent assault charges.

Apr. 8, 1981—Crown Counsel stays rape and other related Squamish charges despite protests of local RCMP. Weapons charges remain. Olson released on bail.

Apr. 15, 1981—Approximately a week after his own son is born, Olson picks up Colleen Daignault and kills her at Surrey later that day or early on April 16. Olson meets and befriends Randy Ludlow about this time.

Apr. 21, 1981—Olson picks up Daryn Johnsrude at Coquitlam and kills him near Deroche B.C. Johnsrude reported missing. Olson arrested in Vancouver for impaired driving. Colleen Daignault reported missing.

May 2, 1981—Johnsrude's body found near Deroche. Verna Bjerky goes missing from the Hope area.

May 14, 1981—Police investigate alleged assault of 5-year-old girl who Olson was babysitting during a bridal shower for his wife-to-be.

May 15, 1981—Olson marries Joan Berryman.

May 19, 1981—Olson picks up Sandra Wolfsteiner and kills her near Chilliwack

May 20, 1981—Wolfsteiner reported missing by boyfriend.

May 22, 1981—Olson is in court at Squamish on weapons charges. While Crown Counsel did not feel that the alleged rape victim, Kim Werbecky, could prove a worthy witness to her own assault, when she failed to appear to support the weapons charges and face cross-examination by Olson's lawyer, a warrant was issued for her arrest. The case was put over to September 29, 1981. By that time, Olson's fate was sealed.

May 23, 1981—Olson picks up a 19-year-old girl in Surrey, on the pretext of giving her a job, feeds her booze and pills, and sexually assaults her. When Olson is arrested in August, the girl's name and phone number are found in Olson's notebook and the police contact her. As a result of her interview, John Hall lays charges of rape, buggery, and gross indecency against Olson on Aug. 18.

May 26, 1981—Kathy Sallow is picked up at Coquitlam and given booze and pills. Olson overturns vehicle near Agassiz. Charged with impaired driving and contributing to juvenile delinquency. He is released on a promise to appear.

*** *Based on first contact with Clifford Olson and other facts known to him, Corporal Darryll Kettles believes that it was Olson who killed Dayrn Johnsrude.*

May 27, 1981—Olson calls Sallow residence to establish her whereabouts and offers to bring her home from Agassiz.

June 21, 1981—Ada Court goes missing from Coquitlam. Olson kills her in the Agassiz area.

July 2, 1981—Simon Partington goes missing from Surrey. Killed by Olson at Richmond.

July 3, 1981—Olson picks up Sandra Docker and Rose Smythe at Lougheed Mall. Offers them a job starting the next Monday.

July 6, 1981—Olson meets Docker and Smythe. Later drops Smythe off at Lougheed Mall. Sexually assaults Docker in Surrey. Arrested by Burnaby RCMP. Interviewed by Corporal Les Forsythe and charged at Burnaby for impaired driving. Concurrently Surrey Detachment is investigating Docker's sexual assault complaint. At Burnaby, Forsythe suspects Olson killed local teenagers Ada Court and Daryn Johnsrude.

July 8, 1981—Corporal Forsythe and Sergeant Sid Slater of Burnaby travel to Mission to view sites where bodies had been found. Forsythe is convinced Olson killed Court and Johnsrude.

July 9, 1981—Olson, with Randy Ludlow in vehicle, picks up Judy Kozma at New Westminster. Ludlow dropped off at Lougheed Mall. Olson kills Judy Kozma near Agassiz.

July 10, 1981—Olson, wife, and son travel to U.S.

July 13, 1981—Judy Kozma reported missing to New Westminster Police Department.

July 15, 1981—Meeting organized by investigators at Burnaby to investigate crime links in different jurisdictions.

July 22, 1981—Olson returns from U.S.

July 23, 1981—Raymond King reported missing from New Westminster. Killed by Olson near Agassiz.

July 23, 1981—Burnaby contacts Superintendent Bruce Northorp at RCMP headquarters in Vancouver regarding use of Special "O" surveillance team. Terms of surveillance proposed but not acted upon by Burnaby. Detective Tarr of the Delta Police Department visits Olson at his residence on a separate matter.

July 24, 1981—Olson picks up Sigrun Arnd, a German tourist, at Coquitlam and kills her at Richmond. Burnaby investigators approach JFO office to enlist their involvement in tracking Olson.

July 25, 1981—Judy Kozma's body found near Agassiz.

July 27, 1981—Olson picks up Terri Lynn Carson at Surrey and kills her at Agassiz. JFO surveillance commences at 12:45 p.m. and Olson's vehicle is first located at 4:20 p.m. At the same time, a warrant is issued on the Docker indecent assault charge in Surrey.

July 28, 1981—Olson is under surveillance by JFO. Olson and Randy Ludlow meet with Tarr at a Burnaby restaurant. Later Olson and Ludlow pick up Ludlow's teenage friend, Ivan Jones, and the three men then pick up two female hitchhikers in Whalley. Olson is pulled over and arrested by JFO while youths are dismissed.

July 29, 1981—Olson is released at 3:20 a.m. Upset, JFO withdraws surveillance unit from case. Later that morning, at 9:30 a.m., Staff Sergeant Nylund of the RCMP Serious Crime Section advises Northorp of two murders and other missing children.

July 30, 1981—In the early morning hours, Olson takes Randy Ludlow to deserted corridor behind a strip mall, reputedly to create appearance of crime scene related to an insurance claim. Olson drugs Ludlow, takes him to his home, and sexually assaults him. Ludlow escapes and is arrested later same day.

July 30, 1981—Olson meets Tarr at White Spot Restaurant in Burnaby. These two meet the RCMP's Corporal Maile and Corporal Drozda. After their superior, Nylund, briefs Chief Superintendent Neill and Northorp at RCMP headquarters, Neill places Northorp in charge of all aspects of the Olson matter and the related child murders. (In spite of media conjecture to the contrary, the B.C. Attorney General's office had no role in the appointment of a task force.) Olson picks up Louise Chartrand near Maple Ridge and kills her near Whistler.

July 31, 1981—After Olson makes a voluntary appearance on Docker warrant (with the apparent encouragement of a Delta Police detective), this warrant was withdrawn by the court. Olson goes to Alberta with Joan and baby son before Northorp can set up renewed surveillance. Louise Chartrand reported missing.

Aug. 3, 1981—Clothing similar to that worn by Louise Chartrand is found near Whistler. Investigators determine that Olson has been changing rented vehicles frequently all summer.

Aug. 5, 1981—Raymond King's body discovered near Agassiz.

Aug. 6, 1981—Special "O" provides 24-hour surveillance once they find that Olson has returned from Alberta.

Aug. 7, 1981—Surveillance unit sees Olson eyeing a young female in the Marpole area of Vancouver. She is removed from harm's way. Later the unit observes from a distance as Olson steals money from a Burnaby residence.

Aug. 11, 1981—Still under surveillance, Olson enters two Vancouver residences and steals money.

Aug. 12, 1981—Olson travels by ferry to Victoria and commits two burglaries in a Victoria suburb. Later he picks up two young female hitchhikers near Nanaimo and drives west towards the outer coast of the island. Olson is arrested near Ucluelet for impaired driving. After police search the vehicle, they discover Judy Kozma's name in his notebook.

Aug. 18, 1981—Randy Ludlow, interviewed where he is being held in a prison hospital, confirms that Olson was with Judy Kozma the day she disappeared. During interrogation, Olson implies knowledge of murders.

Aug. 20, 1981—Olson is charged with the murder of Judy Kozma.

Aug. 24, 1981—Sigrun Arnd is reported missing by her aunt at Vernon.

Aug. 26, 1981—Louise Chartrand's body located near Whistler.

Aug. 27, 1981—Terri Lynn Carson's body and Ada Court's body are located near Agassiz. Simon Partington's body is located at Richmond.

Aug. 28, 1981—Sigrun Arnd's body is located at Richmond.

Sept. 1, 1981—Sandra Wolfsteiner's remains located near Chilliwack.

Sept. 17, 1981—Colleen Daignault's body located at Surrey.

2000—Clifford Olson is confined in a maximum security institution in Quebec. He will probably remain in prison until his death. He has not been allowed to harass his victims' families since his Section 745 hearing in 1997.

Appendix IV

Surveillance Guidelines for Special "O" Section

The following is a reconstruction from Bruce's handwritten notes. Several items are not included as they would disclose confidential techniques. This directive applied throughout the period Olson was under surveillance before August 6, when Olson was spotted. The coverage then went to PRIORITY 1 (24-hour coverage) and the area of coverage was all of B.C.

OIC Special "O" Section   81-OS-04

Re: Clifford Robert Olson

On 81-07-31 I approved surveillance on the c/n subject to commence on 81-08-0I for an indefinite period. The target is perhaps one of the most serious that has been assigned your Section and considerable thought has been given by many as to the variables that may arise.

The conditions pertaining to this target are as follows:

PRIORITY #2—Indicating both the seriousness and the fact that overtime is approved. Although overtime is approved, if in the opinion of the Serious Crime member and your Shift Supervisor overtime is not required on any given day, it should not be incurred.

AREA OF COVERAGE—Hope to Squamish, approx.—Sunshine Coast—for decision at a later date.

(Item deleted for security reasons)

CONDITIONS—Serious Crime Section will supply one rider per shift Serious Crime Section will supply one member and one unmarked car equipped with emergency equipment per shift to follow Special "O" units The responsibility for enforcement action which may be required is that of the Serious Crime member riding in the Special "O" vehicle.

EXCEPTION—The above proviso does NOT apply if any member on the surveillance has reason to believe there is immediate danger to any person who may have been picked up by Olson. Immediate danger for the purposes of this correspondence means possible loss of life, serious injury or other danger which may be indicated. If these circumstances should arise, any member should take whatever reasonable immediate action is necessary to control the problem.

Discreet surveillance is appropriate if at any time the only person(s) in his vehicle are himself and any of his relatives or known associates

- Should the target pick up any passengers, the following factors should be considered
- the person picked up is or appears to be a juvenile, a person of tender years or handicapped
- the pick up was in what is considered a prime victim area
- the time of day of a pick up is what is considered a prime time as it relates to other disappearances

- the person is in Olson's car for over 5 to 10 minutes
  (Several items deleted hereunder for security reasons)

NOTE—If several of these factors should emerge at or about the same time, the situation must be considered critical

- The general plan is to have the GIS car following check all persons who are dropped off by the target
- Variable circumstances that may arise may indicate an immediate check be made by the GIS car or time permitting a routine check by a marked local police/RCMP unit.

Please ensure that all members on this assignment read or are read this correspondence, and if any clarification from this HQ is required, please advise

(B L. Northorp) Supt

Appendix V

Trust Deed for Olson $100,000 Agreement

THIS TRUST DEED made the 26th day of August, in the year of our Lord one thousand nine hundred and eighty-one.
BETWEEN:
E (DIVISION) , DISTRICT 1, ROYAL CANADIAN MOUNTED POLICE
AND:
E. JAMES McNENEY, Barrister & Solicitor

WHEREAS the Royal Canadian Mounted Police Serious Crimes Section, Vancouver, designated Staff Sergeant Nylund by authority from the Deputy Commissioner of Operations, Henry Jensen of Ottawa, Ontario, to place the sum of $100,000.00 upon certain trusts and conditions in the hands of E. James McNeney to be disbursed under the terms and conditions hereinafter set out.

AND WHEREAS E. James McNeney has agreed to hold the said funds on the following terms and conditions and to pay those funds out for the benefit of Joan Olson and her infant son the parties hereto agree as follows:

(i) Staff Sergeant Nylund has placed the sum of $100,000.00 cash in the hands of E. James McNeney, receipt of which sum is acknowledged by the said E. James McNeney by his signature appended hereto.

(ii) Clifford Robert Olson has undertaken and agreed with Cpl. W.F. Maile, Royal Canadian Mounted Police, that he will provide to him and other officers of the Royal Canadian Mounted Police information relative to the location of the bodies of the deceased persons Louise Mary Chartrand, Colleen Daignault, Terri Lynn Carson, Ada Court, Sandra Wolfsteiner, Simon Partington, and one unidentified female.

(iii) The said Clifford Robert Olson has agreed to take members of the Royal Canadian Mounted Police to the sites where the bodies aforesaid are located in order that recovery of the said bodies may be achieved.

(iv) It shall be in order for the said E. James McNeney to release from his trust account the sum of $10,000.00 following the recovery by the police of each body referred to in the preceding paragraph upon confirmation by Staff Sergeant Nylund that the body found is the correct body; and upon Staff Sergeant Nylund being so satisfied, he will release the sum of $10,000.00 of the sum aforesaid.

(v) It shall be in order for the said E. James McNeney to release from his trust account the sum of $30,000.00 upon recovery of evidentiary article relating to the body of Kozma, namely jewelry which said article Clifford Robert Olson has agreed to point out to the Royal Canadian Mounted Police and a description of the condition of the bodies of Johnsrude, King, Weller sufficient to assist in identifying those bodies such sum of $30,000.00 to be released only upon Staff Sergeant Nylund being satisfied as to the recovery of the said item and description of condition of the bodies of Johnsrude, King, Weller so instructing E. James McNeney.

It is acknowledged by Staff Sergeant Nylund that the making of any payment or payments referred to herein are payments solely for the benefit of Joan Olson and her son aforesaid and are <u>not</u> for the benefit of Clifford Robert Olson.

If the said Clifford Robert Olson fails or refuses to provide to the police the requisite information to enable them to recover the aforesaid bodies of the aforesaid victims and to recover the aforesaid evidence then the aforesaid E. James McNeney will return to the Royal Canadian Mounted Police the sum then remaining in his trust account on the basis of disbursements being made to or for Joan Olson under the following formula:

(i) For information leading to the recovery of the body of Louise Mary Chartrand - $10,000.00.

(ii) For information leading to the recovery of the body of Colleen Daignault - $10,000.00.

(iii) For information leading to the recovery of the body of Terri Lynn Carson - $10,000.00.

(iv) For information leading to the recovery of the body of Ada Court - $10,000.00.

(v) For information leading to the recovery of the body of Sandra Wolfsteiner - $10,000.00.

(vi) For information leading to the recovery of the body of Simon Partington - $10,000.00.

(vii) For information leading to the recovery of the body of an unidentified female -$10,000.00.

(viii) For information leading to the recovery of evidence relative to the identification of the recovered body of Elizabeth Judy Kozma and descriptions of the conditions of bodies assisting in the identification of Johnsrude, King , Weller - $30,000.00.

DATED at Vancouver, British Columbia, this 26th day of August, 1981.

_____
Staff Sargeant Arnie Nylund
Royal Canadian Mounted Police
Serious Crime Section
E (Division) District 1
British Columbia

_____
E. James McNeney
Barrister & Solicitor

Appendix VI

Northorp's Briefing Notes on the Olson Case

Bruce Northorp wrote these briefing notes before he retired. He left them with his office for staff who would be answering questions on the Olson case. They became the basis for an official RCMP position paper on the subject. That document inadvertently became public. These notes did not.

For the purposes of this paper it is useful to consider the case in two basic time frames:
(a) Events prior to 81-07-30;
(b) Events from 81-07-30 forward.

The significance of 81-07-30 is that on that date at 1.50 P.M., then C/Supt. Neill, OIC CIB, decided that the supervision and co-ordination of the various missing children/homicides would be handled from District #1 HQ level.
Events prior to 81-07-30

81-04-16
Colleen Daignault, 13 years, was reported missing from the Surrey area, however at the time of the report and until early August she was considered simply as a missing person by Surrey Detachment.

81-04-21
Daryn Johnsrude, 16 years, was reported missing from Coquitlam. 81-05-02—body found at Mission, an obvious case of murder.

81-05-02
Verna Bjerky, 17 years, was reported missing from Hope/Yale area and not located as of 81-07-30.

81-05-19
Sandra Wolfsteiner, 16 years, was reported missing from Langley/Surrey area. Not located as of 81-07-30. At the early stages it was felt she was simply a missing youth and there was no suspicion of foul play.

81-06-21
Ada Court, 13 years, was reported missing from Burnaby/Coquitlam area. Not located as of 81-07-30 and although no evidence of same, foul play of an unknown nature was suspected.

81-07-02
Simon Partington, 9 years, was reported missing from Surrey. Not located as of 81-07-30 and although no evidence of same, foul play of an unknown nature was suspected.

81-07-09
Judy Kozma, 14 years, was reported missing to the New Westminster P.D., however it <u>is relevant</u> to note that this fact was <u>not circulated</u> or known to other police agencies until after her body was found in the Agassiz area on 81-07-25.

81-07-23
Raymond King, 15 years, was reported missing to the New Westminster P.D. Not located as of 81-07-30 and although no evidence of same, foul play of an unknown nature was suspected.

81-07-27
Terri Lynn Carson, 15 years, was reported missing from the Surrey area, however at the time of the report and for some weeks thereafter, she was considered simply as a missing person by Surrey Detachment.

2. For the purpose of reading ease, it is useful to consider the police position or "state of mind" about 81-07-06. At that time, one missing person had been found murdered (Johnsrude). Additionally, there were four missing persons, three female and one male, who did not fit the runaway pattern, (Bjerky, Wolfsteiner, Court and Partington). Despite the difference in sex and areas the five subjects had disappeared from, police investigators were suspicious that the occurrences were related.

3. Burnaby RCMP investigators were doing the follow-up in relation to the disappearance of Ada Court and during their investigations in early July developed Clifford Robert Olson as a suspect. It was primarily our Burnaby investigators that were suspicious the occurrences were related and to this end set up a meeting of investigators from Lower Mainland police agencies at Burnaby on 81-07-15. At this meeting the information which had been developed on Olson was discussed and the five cases mentioned in para. 3.

4. The following is not intended as criticism, however it must be mentioned to alert the person(s) who may be making a response to the media in this case. New Westminster Police Dept., investigators were at the meeting of 81-07-15, however they did not raise the name Kozma. It may be the NWPD investigators attending the meeting were not aware of the Kozma case.

5. The meeting resolved that Olson should be considered a suspect in the matters in question and the RCMP Serious Crime Section would complete a profile on Olson and Burnaby would request Olson be placed under surveillance. It should be mentioned at this time that investigations at a later stage failed to locate Olson. It was learned later that Olson left this area on 81-07-10 for a holiday in the U.S.A. and returned on either 81-07-20 or 21.

6. Surveillance was placed on Olson by a combined team of JFO/VIIU investigators on both 81-07-27 and 28. This surveillance required a "check" of Olson during the late P.M./early A.M. of 81-07-28/29 as he had picked up two young females.

7. On the morning of 81-07-29, the Serious Crime Section of the RCMP advised the Acting CIB Officer of the developments at that time, which were advanced from those outlined in para. 2. Other factors raised were:
(1) Kozma's body found in Agassiz on 81-07-25;
(2) King missing from New Westminster on 81-07-23;
(3) Olson may have information pertaining to "bodies" and had been acting as an informant for a Delta police member.

At this time it was obvious there was a multi-unit/police department interest in Olson and the matters in question. Co-ordination/control of the matters was essential. On 81-07-30 the OIC CIB directed that insofar as the RCMP was concerned, the investigation would be directed from the RCMP Headquarters in Vancouver. Supt. B.L. Northorp was named as the officer to be in charge, overall.

Events on and following 81-07-30
8. On 81-07-30 at 1350 hrs., the decision referred to in para 7 was made. Pursuant to this decision it was essential the District HQ be briefed and to this end, Supt. Northorp attended a "brain-storming" meeting of investigators set for the morning of 81-07-31. This meeting included investigators from all RCMP Detachments/Sections having case responsibilities plus the New Westminster P.D. investigators. Also present were

investigators from RCMP Detachments/Police Departments which had no cases under investigation. The meeting lasted from 0950 hrs. to 1100 hrs.

9. The seven cases in question (5 in para. 2 and 2 in para. 7) were reviewed. Other matters covered were planned surveillance of Olson, possible proceedings against him as a Dangerous Sexual Offender, plus a media response, as they were aware of the meeting being held. Supt. Northorp advised the group that his presence at the meeting and involvement in the cases reflected the serious view District HQ held and that support was available from any resource as far as the District HQ was concerned.

10. It is opportune at this stage to make an observation pertaining to "surveillance". Generally, surveillance is engaged in in an attempt to develop intelligence, crime patterns, etc. In some instances it is used in an attempt to apprehend a subject during the commission of a crime. In certain cases such as possible armed robbery, there is always the danger of loss of life or serious injury if the crime were allowed to occur. Certainly in the case of Olson, where he was suspected of murder, it was not intended to keep him under surveillance and take a chance of his committing a murder under "police eyes:. That would have been unthinkable. The situation we had to face was, no surveillance or some surveillance. The first option would have been an abdication of duty. The option was to place Olson under surveillance with safeguards in place that would protect any of his possible pickups. These safeguards were drawn up at 1600 hrs. on 81-07-31 by Supt. Northorp. The surveillance would commence as soon as Olson could be located.

11. For the purposes of continuity it should be mentioned that on 81-07-30 Louise Chartrand, 17 years, was reported missing from Maple Ridge and although her name was not raised at the meeting of 81-07-31, as days went by concern developed that she had met with foul play.

12. On or about 81-07-31 it was apparent that a meeting of senior police managers of RCMP Detachments having a case responsibility was required and this was arranged for and held during the morning of 81-08-05. D/ Chief Cadenhead of the NWPD attended the meeting which was chaired by Supt. Northorp.

13. Significant decisions were made:

(1) Missing persons—all new complaints of this nature be monitored to ensure potential homicide victims were identified immediately.

(2) Missing persons—all outstanding missing persons files back to 81-01-01 be reviewed to ensure the proper assessments have been made.

(3) Special patrols—agreed that special patrols be implemented at prime times in prime areas in an attempt to develop suspects.

(4) Hitchhikers—to be checked and cautioned.

(5) Complaints—all copies of sex-related offences or suspects be forwarded to   Serious Crime Section.

(6) Computers—use of computers for case management/suspect correlation was agreed upon.

(7) Other police departments/RCMP Detachments—agreed they would be advised of our strategies so they could complement them where applicable.

14. As a direct result of the meeting of 81-08-05, Surrey Detachment identified Colleen Daignault mentioned in para. 1, as a possible victim. Later, Surrey Detachment identified Terri Lyn Carson, also mentioned in para. 1, as another possible victim. Both girls were surfaced as the result of the review of an old file or close examination of a new report.

15. It would now be opportune to report that Olson left the Vancouver area on 81-07-31 and did not return until 81-08-06. His whereabouts during his absence were not known at that time.

16. As soon as Olson returned to this area he was observed. According to plan he was placed under 24-hour surveillance, which was authorized to proceed anywhere in British Columbia. The guidelines to ensure the safety of any possible "pickups" were clearly enunciated for the benefit of all members engaged on the surveillance.

17. From 81-08-06 until 81-08-12, and suffice to state for the purposes of this report, Olson was observed in a variety of situations; he attempted to pick up a young girl, watched others including a female member engaged on surveillance. He was also observed entering some premises under unusual circumstances and checks immediately thereafter revealed he had committed offences of Break & Enter and in one case Theft.

18. On 81-08-12 Olson went to Vancouver Island (Victoria area) where he picked up two female hitchhikers and proceeded north to the Port Alberni area and thence towards Ucluelet. At this point the surveillance team felt the two young women were in jeopardy and moved in. Suffice to state Olson was at that moment arrested and charged with impaired driving.

19. A search of Olson's rental vehicle located an address book which proved to be his and in it the name of Judy Kozma was written. It appeared to be in handwriting other than that of Olson and it was suspected to be Kozma's handwriting. A decision was made in the early morning of 81-08-13 that the address book would be retained and Olson questioned in relation to Kozma's murder at an appropriate time in the next day or two.

20. On 81-08-18 a statement was taken from one Randy Julian Cook which placed both Cook and Olson with Kozma for a considerable period of time on the day that Kozma disappeared. As far as Cook was concerned, he was dropped off by Olson while Kozma was still with Olson. At this time it appeared there were grounds to charge Olson with the murder of Kozma. The matter was discussed with Mr. John Hall who had been provided as ad hoc counsel by the Ministry of the Attorney General and he concurred. Consequently a charge of first degree murder was laid against Olson on 81-08-20 and he was advised of this on 81-08-18.

21. It is important to note at this time that Olson was identified as a suspect by standard but outstanding police work at an early stage (81-07-06). He was investigated by standard police procedures and also arrested and charged with one count of murder by these same procedures. The charge laid was at best circumstantial and at most it was felt by all concerned that a conviction of <u>second</u> degree murder <u>might</u> be obtained.

22. It should be recorded now that Olson is a very "street-wise" criminal in that he has spent most of his adult life in prison and has faced a multitude of charges. Olson was a witness in a "child-murder" case in 1976 as he co-operated with the Crown in giving evidence against a fellow inmate. By experience Olson is most aware of strategies the police employ.

23. After Olson's arrest on 81-08-12 he was moved to the Lower Mainland where a variety of undercover RCMP members were placed in the cells. Essentially, no evidence was gained, however at this time the investigative body were of the opinion that Olson was responsible for some of the murders/ disappearances mentioned herein. It was noteworthy that while Olson was absent form this area from 81-07-31 until 81-08-06 and under surveillance thereafter there had not been any further disappearances of young

children in this area. This was a radical change from the <u>known</u> pattern of late July, i.e., July 23rd, 27th and 30th.

24 About 81-08-18 Olson began to make remarks, some made under "warned" conditions and some "unwarned", indicating he was responsible for the murders of King, Johnsrude, Kozma and Christine Weller, who was found murdered in Richmond on 80-12-25. Chartrand, Court, Partington, Carson, Daignault and one unidentified, at that time, female from West Germany. This girl was subsequently identified as Sigrun Arnd, who probably was last alive on 81-07-24. It is sheer conjecture at this time to know if any of the statements made by Olson to our investigators would have been admitted in evidence.

25. A recapitulation of the situation on 81-08-18 is that Olson was in custody charged with other offences and a strong suspect in the death of Kozma. The bodies of Weller, King, Kozma and Johnsrude had been located. There was absolutely no indication where the bodies of the other victims might be.

26. On 81-08-18 Olson began to talk of a "deal" relating to the location of other bodies for some consideration in his eventual incarceration. When he eventually came to a realization that this was impossible he began to speak of a "deal for money". The brief details were as follows:

81-08-18
Initial "deal" offered by Olson was that he be guaranteed that after conviction he would serve his sentence in a mental "hospital" and not in a Federal penitentiary. He stated this would have to be in writing. In return, he would supply "evidence" concerning the four homicides where the bodies had already been recovered and lead us to the bodies of the other seven (7) victims. He first wished to discuss this matter with his wife and then his lawyer on 81-08-19. It should be noted that during his discussions, he stated that this deal would "cost us".

81-08-19
Olson spoke to his lawyer by telephone and then said that he would be meeting with his lawyer on 81-08-20 after which an agreement would be finalized.

81-08-20
Olson stated that "we" cannot ensure that he goes to a hospital; the Court decides that. He then proposed a $100,000.00 deal "and you'll get statements with bodies. I'll give you all the evidence, the things only the killer would know". Initially he stated, "I'll give you a freebie—a body and a statement" to show his good faith. After he was finished, $10,000.00 would be handed over by one of our members to his wife. When he confirmed this through conversation with his wife he would then go to the next body. Olson then spoke to his lawyer. He then insisted on an agreement being drawn up, a copy of which would be delivered to his lawyer prior to any action being taken. Later this same date Olson talked of completing a deal without his lawyer, that is, strictly between the Police, himself and his wife. Olson then hand wrote an "Undertaking and agreement between the RCMP and Clifford Robert Olson", including a list of the eleven victims, to be finalized the following day.

81-08-21
Olson appeared in Court and was remanded for 30-day psychiatric examination and escorted to Colony Farm. Olson was told the RCMP needed time to finalize.

81-08-24
Olson advised that the deal would go ahead; still no lawyer involved

81-08-25

Olson now insisted that his lawyer handle the matter and the lawyer would be drawing up the necessary agreement.

27. On 81-08-24 a decision had to be made as to whether or not the RCMP should attempt to further the investigations in the manner proposed by Olson. The same date Supt. Northorp recommended to the Headquarters of the RCMP that $100,000.00 be expended, if necessary, to secure evidence. The considerations at that time insofar as the RCMP at Vancouver were concerned were:

(1) The cases were without precedent in Canadian history. One victim had a nail driven in his head for no apparent reason, as it was not the cause of death. During July alone there were five known murders/disappearances: July 2nd, 9th, 23rd, 27th, 30th and according to Olson a sixth, now known as Arnd. In effect, there had been a <u>maniac</u> on the loose.

(2) The first consideration was that Olson may enter into some agreement whereby any money handed over could be recovered by an actual seizure. Essentially a sophisticated "flash roll" of money was the concept. Concurrently it was realized that Olson's lawyer might become involved and a seizure not possible, however later recovery by civil action was a step that would be taken. In essence, the plan was to effect the recovery of bodies (in fact, evidence) using $100,000.00 cash as the "carrot". It was also realized that depending on circumstances all or some of the monies could be lost or not recovered.

(3) The prime consideration in recommending to $100,000.00 "plan" was to locate bodies which would be solid evidence necessary to prove that Olson was indeed responsible for the matters in question.

(4) Secondary considerations beyond the reason in sub-para. (3) above were:
(i) The peace of mind the parents would have if or when the bodies were located.
(ii) The peace of mind to the community, knowing that the menace had been removed. It appeared from a police perspective many parents in the Lower Mainland were in a state bordering on terror or panic.

(5) There was a real possibility that Olson would attempt a "money deal" with the media for bodies (based on Olson's remarks) and there was a suspicion he might directly or indirectly "sell" bodies to the parents in question.

(6) The proposal outlined in sub-para. (2) above had the full support of the Ministry of Attorney General.

(7) The whole proposition hinged on the fact it was the position of the authorities to recover any money which might be released.

28. The proposition to spend the monies, if necessary, on the basis of the recommendation from Supt. Northorp was APPROVED on 81-08-25 at RCMP Headquarters by Deputy Commr. (Ops.), H. Jensen.

29. As suspected, after the approval to expend money, if necessary, Olson's lawyers did get involved and the so-called "trust deed" was drawn up. Considerations after the recommendations of 81-08-24 in the minds of the police authorities were:

(1) Olson's lawyers had become involved and it could not be suggested Olson's rights were not protected.

(2) If Olson had approached the police for relocation expenses for his wife to ensure her safety as the "consideration" it would likely have been agreed to (approved).

(3) When the "trust deed" was drawn up the police position was that it <u>must</u> show the monies were <u>not</u> for the benefit of Olson.

30. The foregoing is not intended to cover in depth the investigations in question. It is simply intended to give the reader(s) of same the major developments, chronologically, that show:

(1) the known victims,

(2) when the police "suspected" or identified the problem,

(3) Olson identified as a suspect at an early date,

(4) investigative steps taken leading to the arrest of Olson on 81-08-12,

(5) investigative steps taken after 81-08-12 leading up to the agreement which resulted in the later recovery of bodies/evidence.

Glossary

AG - attorney general
APB – all-points bulletin
ARU – Alouette River Unit
B.C. – British Columbia
B.C. Pen – British Columbia Penitentiary
BCTV – British Columbia Television
CBC – Canadian Broadcasting Corporation
CIB – Criminal Investigation Branch
CIS – Crime Index Section
CLEU – Co-ordinated Law Enforcement Unit
CO – commanding officer
CPIC – Canadian Police Information Centre
Delta PD – Delta Police Department
DIA – Department of Indian Affairs
DCI – director of criminal investigations
Dick – detective
GIS – General Investigation Section
HQ – headquarters
i/c – in charge
JFO – Joint Forces Organization
NCO – non-commissioned officer
OC - officer commanding
OIC – officer in charge
RCMP – Royal Canadian Mounted Police
SMU – Super Maximum Unit
Special "I" – technical section
Special "O" – surveillance unit
ViCLAS – Violent Crime Linkage Analysis System
VIIU – Vancouver Integrated Intelligence Unit
VPD – Vancouver Police Department
WiSViS – Witness Suspect Viewing System

Index

Photo Credits

All photos and *Vancouver Sun* and *Province* news clippings and articles reproduced in this book have been provided by the author Les Holmes and Bruce Northorp. The cartoon on page 153 is provided courtesy of Les Peterson and the *Vancouver Sun*.